ANEAN SEA

EGYPT

R. Nile

A

RED SEA

CHAD

SUDAN

White Nile

Blue Nile

L. Tana

Gulf of Aden

FRENCH
SOMALILAND

SOMALI

ETHIOPIA

AFRICAN REPUBLIC

R. Shibelli

REPUBLIC OF THE CONGO

L. Albert

UGANDA

L. Kioga

L. Rudolf

R. Zaire (Congo)

L. Edward

KENYA

R. Juba

INDIAN OCEAN

A HISTORY OF
AFRICAN EXPLORATION

DAVID MOUNTFIELD

Had I known all the hunger, hardship, toil and time
required, I might have preferred a strait-waistcoat
to undertaking the task; but having taken it in
hand, I could not bear to be beaten by it.

Livingstone, 1870
(in a private letter quoted by Tim Jeal)

I can die, but I will not go back.

Stanley, 1876
(in a private letter quoted by Richard Hall)

We let the streams run on, and do not enquire
whence they rise or whither they flow.

Casembe to Livingstone, 1868
(quoted by Stanley in his *Autobiography*)

*Opposite: Members of the Richardson expedition to the Sudan. Clockwise from
top left, Richardson, Overweg, Vogel, Barth; with a map and scenes
of Egyptian ruins, Murzuk castle, Lake Chad (with animals) and
Ghat. This was the attractive frontispiece of August Petermann's
account of the expedition (1855).*

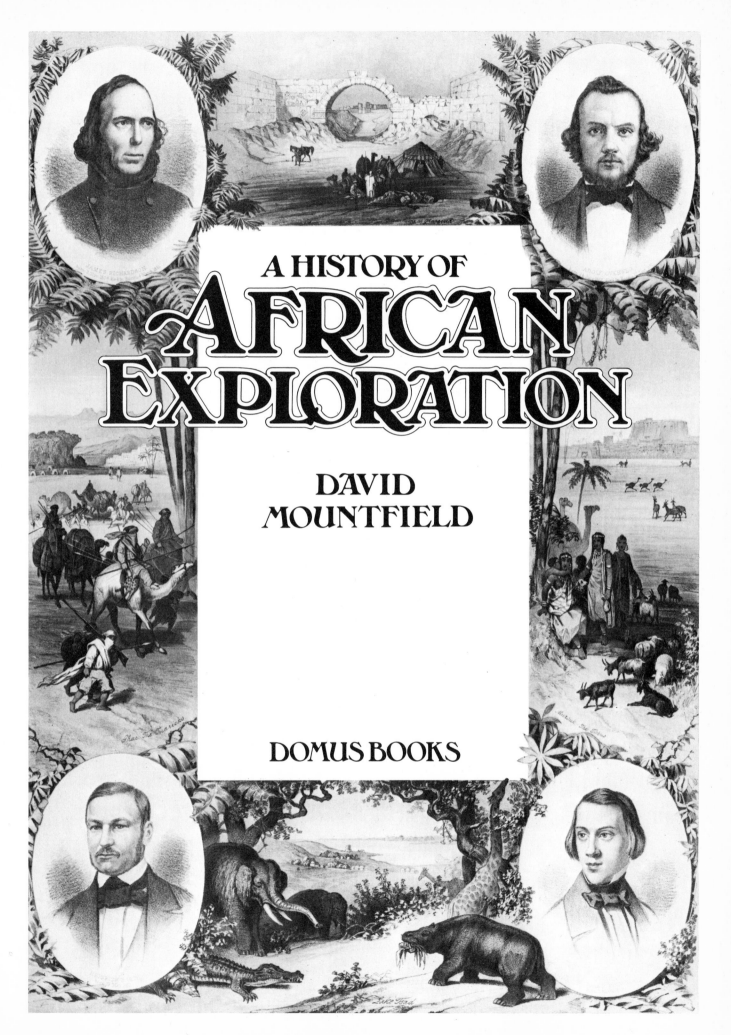

A HISTORY OF AFRICAN EXPLORATION

DAVID MOUNTFIELD

DOMUS BOOKS

Proper Names

The spelling of names of people and places in
this book generally follows the form most familiar to
English-speaking people or the form used by the
explorer quoted, although this often results in
inconsistency and sometimes in plain error.

Author's Acknowledgments

Grateful acknowledgment is due to many
people who have helped with text and illustrations,
especially to Robin Hallett, who very kindly
read the MS, and to Gervase Mathew and John
Blashford Snell who read parts of the MS and
generously lent photographs. Also to the staff
of the Royal Geographical Society, the London
Library, the British Museum Map Room, Richmond
Public Library, and all the agencies and
institutions listed in the illustrations credits; to
Pamela Baker, Hazel Harrison, Margaret Taylor,
the Earl of Elgin, Roderick Grant, Michael
Stapleton (most helpful of editors) and, not least,
a great many writers, especially those listed in the
Note on Books.

Originally published in Great Britain by
The Hamlyn Publishing Group Limited
Feltham, Middlesex

© Copyright 1976 The Hamlyn Publishing Group Limited

First published in the United States in 1976 by
Domus Books
400 Anthony Trail
Northbrook
Illinois 60062

ISBN 0–89196–003–1

Library of Congress Catalog Card Number 76–7331

Printed in Great Britain by
Jarrold & Sons Limited, Norwich

Contents

Introduction

Until quite recent times, the history of Africa meant little more to Europeans than the history of European activity in Africa. It began with the Portuguese voyages in the 15th century and flipped rapidly through the years up to the establishment of European colonial rule at the end of the 19th century.

The almost total neglect of the Africans themselves until comparatively recent times arose partly from racist assumptions of European superiority and partly from the apparent absence of historical evidence other than a few accounts by non-African travellers. Little was known, and what was known seemed hardly worth knowing. Some of the most enlightened persons, real friends of Africa, were interested only in changing things, seeing nothing in African society that was worth preserving and assuming that the all-too-evident horrors of poverty, disease, and the slave trade were endemic and universal. Of course there were exceptions, but most Europeans in the 19th century saw in Africa south of the Sahara a perfect example of life in a Hobbesian state of nature – nasty, brutish, and short.

Nowadays we know better. Archaeology, language studies, the assembly of oral traditions, and the discovery of unsuspected Arabic written records have given us an *African* history at last. The structure is far from complete, in some parts the foundations have scarcely been laid, and the plan is complex, with many winding corridors and hidden doorways, sharp corners and blank walls. But it is standing proudly, and although it will never be finished to the last chimney tile, it will grow much larger yet.

Anyone returning to the study of African history today after neglecting it for the past ten or twelve years would be astonished and exhilarated (or possibly depressed) by the vast amount of work that has been published in the interval. Besides the thousand and one detailed studies by linguists and anthropologists, new histories of Africa have been pouring off the presses like the Nile in flood. African scholars are now playing a large and increasing part in writing the history of their continent, although it is still the case that most of the more general works are written by people of European descent. This is perhaps not important. Current historians of Africa are more enlightened than most (not all) Africanists of two or three generations ago; in fact, sometimes, the vicarious guilt that most whites feel when considering the history of Europe's relations with Africa seems to tempt them, by way of compensation, into too favourable a view of certain aspects of 'pre-European' African society. The exciting revelations of the medieval empires of the western Sudan have led to some rosy reconstructions. After reading one or two modern accounts of the old kingdom of Mali, one begins to think that the Holy Roman Empire was a tuppenny-ha'penny organization by comparison. And there is still a tendency to judge Africa by European standards, for example in treating manifestations of political power and material advancement as the signs of a happy, healthy society, a view that may turn out no less mistaken than the romantic view of pastoral, tribal, 'stagnant' society as some kind of Rousseauesque garden of Eden.

These reservations apart, it is both satisfying and exciting that African history is no longer just a part of European history. Although the exploration of Africa by Europeans is still important, it is much less so than it was a century ago. In the Penguin *Short History of Africa*, the great period of European exploration in the 19th century is covered in about five pages.

The exploration of Africa is inevitably associated with imperialism and therefore affects many Europeans with guilty misgivings. Whether they were aware of it or not (on the whole they were not), the European explorers were the forerunners of imperialism. They prepared the way for the division of the continent into colonies of the European powers, and whatever the advantages and disadvantages of colonial rule, citizens of African states today can hardly be expected to regard the recent domination of their societies by whites as wholly unexceptionable, especially when some of the nastiest aspects of white rule are still evident in neighbouring states.

* * *

The cradle of European civilization, as everyone knows, was the Mediterranean basin; indeed, it was not only the cradle but the nursery, the study, and the kitchen garden as well. Not until the Atlantic sea routes were opened at the end of the 15th century did the centre shift towards the northern cities. But the Mediterranean is not only a European sea; it laps the shores of three continents, and until late medieval times there was more intercourse, not always friendly, between the various shores of the Mediterranean than between the Mediterranean and the regions to the north-west.

Still, the coastal region of North Africa has always been closely linked with the European world. Evidence of racial links are apparent in the light skins of Berber peoples, and enduring marks of the Roman occupation can be seen from Morocco to Egypt. Every crash course in the history of western civilization begins, not in Europe, but in North Africa, with Ancient Egypt, although it is only in recent times that the civilization of Egypt has come to be seen as an 'African' civilization no less than a 'Mediterranean' one.

In spite of the close connection throughout history between North Africa and Europe, the continent beyond the narrow coastal belt in the north remained for centuries almost entirely unknown to Europeans. Not until the 15th century did Portuguese sailors establish its outline, and not until the 19th century was the interior of tropical Africa deeply penetrated. In a few places – in the extreme south and up some of the rivers – Europeans had settled as colonists or traders. But for thousands of miles, Europeans had not advanced much farther from the coast than they could have thrown a stone – or fired a shot. Not much more than one hundred years ago, Africa was for most Europeans still the 'Dark Continent', in the sense that they knew nothing whatever about it.

The term 'Dark Continent' implied not only European ignorance but also an assumption that African society was culturally primitive. This superficial impression was not altogether correct. While Africa, like other continents, would have seemed 'backward' to any inhabitant of Europe from about the 14th century onwards, in a longer historical view Africa was comparatively advanced. The discoveries of L.S.B. Leakey and others in East Africa suggest that this was the region, or anyway one of the regions, where man originated. In the late Middle Ages, roughly the northern third of Africa belonged to the world of Islam, a more highly developed culture than that of Christian Europe, and a series of large, centralized states had risen, flourished, and declined in the western Sudan.

With the use of iron and the development of settled agriculture over two thousand years ago occurred the expansion of Negro peoples from the forest fringes of West Africa. They adapted more readily to the settled life of the farmer than did the hunting-and-gathering ancestors of the Bushmen and the Pygmies. The 2,000-year-old Nok culture of northern Nigeria, with its modelled clay figures, is the best-known of early, village-dwelling, agricultural communities in the savanna region south of the Sahara.

Very broadly, it appears that Negro peoples spread eastward across the savanna belt, mingling with 'Hamitic' peoples whose ancestors probably came from south-west Asia, and into most of the southern half of the continent, where their descendants are called Bantu (a term, however, of linguistic significance only).

In spite of the apparent lack of communications, African societies south of the Sahara, from Senegal in the west to Somalia in the east and Rhodesia in the south, shared some superficially similar characteristics, although it must be said that every new study illustrates the great variety of African societies. Politically, many societies tended to be small and relatively unstable, but some kingdoms lasted for centuries and, by conquest or other means, extended over very large areas, so that it is not inappropriate to speak of 'empires'. Cattle and other animals were kept; millet and other cereals grown. Trade in gold and ivory with Arabia was carried on by kingdoms far from the east coast, for instance by the rulers of Monomatapa, and there was regular commerce between the western Sudan and the Maghreb.

Whatever the original sources of the 'Sudanic' African kingdoms, it is now clear that powerful states existed in the interior of the continent a thousand and more years ago, and that the old notion of an Africa shaped entirely by exterior influences spreading inwards from the coasts is very misleading.

How was it that Europe remained ignorant of these large and important African societies until the 19th century? A number of fairly well-known reasons are generally put forward.

It is said that navigators venturing ever farther from European ports found the coasts of Africa uninviting. South of Morocco, the desert stretches down to the sea, and the surf pounds a barren shore, with no major river mouth until the Senegal is reached. A similar desert coastline extends the length of Angola and almost down to the Cape, while in West Africa the coast is low and lined with uninviting mangrove swamps. There are few peninsulas, bays, or offshore islands to provide shelter for ships. Nevertheless, the coast is obviously not universally inaccessible; business was conducted at numerous anchorages in West Africa.

The generally straight, uninterrupted shoreline contributes to the comparative shortness of the African coast. The ratio of coastline to area is low compared with other continents, and internal distances are immense – up to 5,000 miles from north to south and 4,500 from east to west. Sheer distance was not the least of the factors inhibiting travel in the interior.

The rivers, which in other continents provided the main highways from the coast inland, are said to have offered little assistance to early visitors to Africa. For a start, there are few of them, because much of the continent is extremely dry. Some rivers are very short, and some have no outlet to the sea. Most are subject to dramatic seasonal changes in volume: a miserable trickle in the dry season is transformed into a raging torrent during the rains; both discourage navigation. The great rivers like the Nile, Niger, and Zambezi tend to form muddy deltas at their mouths, with sandbars and shallows barring entry to all except the smallest boats; only the Zaire has a deep-water estuary. Many rivers are interrupted by steep cataracts and falls quite close to the coast. Some lose themselves in almost impenetrable swamps, like the Sudd on the Upper Nile. Some run through sheer-sided gulleys carved in the rock, or broaden out into shallow, unbridgeable pools.

However, rivers such as the Senegal, Gambia, and Zambezi did provide avenues inland and, beyond the coastal belt, the great rivers are often navigable for long stretches, at least by canoes and shallow-draught boats. They provided both the avenues and the objectives of European exploration in the 19th century.

The puzzles offered by the great rivers exercised geographers for centuries: the search for the source of the Nile is one of the great themes of Western man's investigation of his environment; the early European exploration of West Africa was largely concerned with the course of the Niger; Livingstone's greatest journey roughly followed the course of the Zambezi along most of its length; and the vast but elusive Zaire called forth the most elaborate, the most tenacious, of all European expeditions.

Africa consists basically of one enormous plateau, much modified by erosion and earth movements, which stretches from the Atlas Mountains in the north to the Cape ranges in the south. In most places, the plateau closely approaches the coast (the average distance of the edge from the sea is hardly more than twenty miles), where it falls away sharply, forcing rivers to descend in sharp steps to the sea. As Dr Livingstone put it, Africa 'resembles a wideawake hat with the crown a little depressed' (Speke said 'a dish turned upside down'). 'So long as African rivers remain in what we may call the brim, they present no obstruction, but no sooner do they emerge from the higher lands than their utility is much impaired by cataracts.' Changes of altitude in the interior, though on the whole much slighter than in other continents, are similarly inclined to occur as abrupt cliffs. Earth movements in the distant past produced the faults and rifts that present still more formidable barriers to travel, especially in East Africa.

The equator runs almost exactly through the middle of Africa, and therefore a very large proportion of the continent (about 9 million square miles out of a total of 11·7 million) lies within the tropics. Excessive heat and enervating humidity in the tropical lowlands, and the diseases associated with these conditions (malaria and yellow fever, sleeping sickness, dysentery, bilharzia and others) discouraged Europeans from penetrating the interior and cut short the careers of many who did. The phrase 'white man's grave' was no myth invented by old West Africa hands to dramatize their own survival. The mortality rate – as high as 50 per cent in the first year – among the missionaries, slave-trade factors and early colonial officials in West Africa was not an encouraging object for contemplation by their successors.

The aridity or semi-aridity of large areas of Africa helped to isolate the different regions and made travel difficult and dangerous. The separation of the Maghreb from the rest of Africa, though less complete than once was thought, was the inevitable result of thousands of square miles of inhospitable desert lying beyond the Atlas mountains to the south. There was always traffic across the Sahara: before the days of the camel it was crossed by ox and cart, and less than 10,000 years ago the Sahara, or most of it, was not desert at all (traces of easier times may be seen in the long-dry wadis and in the rock pictures of the now scarcely inhabited highlands). Farther east, the Nile provided a passage to the interior, and it has become clear in recent years that the influence of Egypt, as manifest, for example, in the institution of divine kingship, passing through Kush and Darfur and filtering

The great African grasslands, which supported numberless herds of game. Livingstone at the junction of the Kafue and the Zambezi in 1856 saw 'more large game on [the plain] than anywhere else I had seen in Africa. Hundreds of buffalo and zebras grazed on the open spaces, and there stood lordly elephants feeding majestically, nothing moving apparently but the proboscis. I wished that I had been able to take a photograph of a scene, so seldom beheld, and which is destined, as guns increase, to pass away from earth'.

8

south and west into the Sudan, eventually penetrated the forests of the Zaire basin and the Ethiopian desert, and reached into southern Africa.

Parts of the Sahara confirm the popular idea of a vast sandy plain dotted with oases, though the sandy parts are not flat, consisting of shifting hills ('dunes' fails to convey their size), and altogether they make up only a relatively small area, hardly more than 10 per cent, mainly in the north. The truly desolate regions of the central Sahara, where fierce winds blow and rain never falls, are stony expanses with, here and there, raised rocky plateaus; but less than a quarter of the total area of the Sahara supports no vegetation whatsoever.

There are also mountain ranges. Europeans tend to think of the Tibesti Highlands, if they think of them at all, as nothing more than a large outcrop of rocks; in fact, the total area is about one-third that of the Alps, and the peaks are nearly as high as the peaks of the Rockies.

The desert begins to merge into the savanna on the latitude, very roughly, of Timbuktu (obviously a straight line cannot be drawn; moreover, the desert seems to be slowly moving its frontier farther south). Vegetation is sparse at first, growing thicker towards the south until, at some indefinable point, the savanna belt is reached. Here the land is generally flat, with varied vegetation and tough, twisted trees; the horizon is occasionally broken by granite hills and sandstone ridges. Fringes of forest cling to river banks, and begin to appear more thickly as the tropical rain forest draws nearer. The savanna belt (the Sudan) stretches right across Africa, until it comes to an abrupt stop at the massive cliffs that rise to the Ethiopian plateau. Beyond, semi-desert conditions prevail in the Horn of Africa.

South of the Sudan lies the rain forest, pushed back in places by human cultivators and interrupted in parts of West Africa where the savanna extends to the coast. Elsewhere, the rain-forest belt is over two hundred miles wide, the upper foliage so thick that sunlight never penetrates to the ground. The greatest area of rain forest is the basin of the Zaire, where the dense tropical vegetation reaches eastward to the Great Rift Valley. A narrow strip of grassland connects the northern savanna with the great plains of south-central Africa, which eventually peter out in the fringes of the Kalahari and Namib deserts. There the Bushmen, retreating before the advancing Bantu, found a refuge. In the south, beyond the high veldt of the Transvaal, lie serried hills and depressions and, beyond the mountains, the 'Mediterranean' environment of the Cape, a pleasant place for European settlement.

Although some 40 per cent of Africa is classed as desert or semi-desert and almost as much again is troubled periodically by drought, statistically Africa is not short of rain. Kano in northern Nigeria, a city that might be supposed to be on the edge of the desert, in fact has more rain than many towns in England. The trouble is that the rain is strictly seasonal and, worse than that, its annual volume and time of arrival are unpredictable, so that farmers have to gamble on the right time to sow their seed. This aspect of the climate has had profound effects on African history, for instance in holding down population and in encouraging mobility. It also caused difficulties for explorers.

That well-named pest, the tse-tse fly, with its 'nasty little jet-styled wings', hindered travel in the interior by virtually

Europeans crossing a river in West Africa. From Dupuis, Journal of a Residence in Ashantee, *1824.*

excluding draught animals from the forested zones. There were no roads in tropical Africa, and the only way of moving about was on foot along narrow forest paths. Over a large area, the wheel was unknown, and goods depended on human transport.

However, explorers seldom travel on wheels, and some of the other reasons advanced to explain the long delay in Europe's exploration of Africa appear, on closer inspection, only a little more convincing than the absence of wheels. The physical conditions – unattractive coasts, unnavigable rivers, unpleasant climate – are hardly sufficient by themselves to explain the apparent failure of Europeans to press into the interior, even if allowance is made for the exaggerated reputation of these features. There were more substantial reasons, which had nothing to do with physical geography.

For Renaissance Europe, Africa's most alluring charm was her gold. 'I speak of Africa and golden joys', ranted Pistol, voicing a popular image, and gold was certainly one of the motives for the Portuguese voyages in the 15th century. But in this case as in others, the promise was not fulfilled by the event – at least, not immediately. The South African mines were eventually to bring forth wealth to satisfy the most grasping Renaissance merchant, but they were not dis-

Virgin Strand: Colonel John Blashford Snell strides ashore on Monkey Island in the Zaire River. Surrounded by ferocious rapids, the island was probably unvisited by man until the powerboats of the Zaire River Expedition reached it in 1974–75.

covered until much later. The gold mines of west and south-east Africa proved, for European exploiters, rather disappointing. (The Portuguese in the early days imported substantial quantities from the Gold Coast, although even that alluring name was born of hope as much as experience.) But Africa provided other products – ivory, feathers, pepper and, above all, slaves. For much of the period covered in this book, the slave trade dominated Europe's connections with Africa, and the slave trade was conducted almost exclusively on the coast. Europeans were not impelled inland because they could make themselves rich on Africa's most valuable product almost without leaving their ships.

Still, it was not just that Europeans did not *need* to travel inland. They were not permitted. With some exceptions, African rulers, in West Africa particularly, did not encourage incursions by the white man, and until political rivalries in late 19th-century Europe sent military expeditions into Africa, the African rulers were perfectly capable of keeping unwanted visitors out. In 1758 the British Board of Trade, commenting on a suggestion that gold-bearing land should be bought in Guinea, stated that 'The British Interest, both in Possession and Commerce, depends chiefly, if not entirely, on the good Will and Friendship of the Natives, who do not allow us even those Possessions, limited as they are to the bare spots on which our Forts and Factories are situated, without the Payment of an annual Quitrent . . .' They would certainly not allow the British to buy up their gold mines.

*   *   *

The 'classic' period of African exploration, from Bruce and Mungo Park to Livingstone and Stanley makes a reasonably coherent subject: most of the chief explorers were British or in British employment, and although many expeditions were government-sponsored, the patronage of the African Association and its successor, the Royal Geographical Society, provides a continuous thread. The names of the great explorers are well-known, and certain incidents, such as Stanley's meeting with Livingstone at Ujiji, have almost passed into folklore.

No one needs to be persuaded that the pursuit of knowledge, geographical or any other kind, is a worthy occupation. On the other hand, no one supposes that the explorers of Africa were motivated solely by altruistic, scientific considerations, although these often played a large part. Any discussion of the objects of the African explorers must be left to individual consideration, but it is worth asking, more generally, whether these men deserved the fame that most, though not all, achieved.

For explorers, priority was a matter of vast importance. There was little glory in being the *second* man to cross the African continent. Everyone has heard of David Livingstone; few of Verney Lovett Cameron. True, posterity sometimes changes things: Captain Scott is better known than Amundsen although Amundsen beat him to the South Pole. Nevertheless, Scott was almost literally destroyed by the knowledge that he had lost the race.

In the polar regions, especially the Antarctic, there was little argument over priority. It was usually obvious who had first explored any particular region. Africa is an entirely different case – a vast continent, inhabited in nearly all parts, with – in the north – a culture that in the Middle Ages had

been in advance of Europe. Nothing in Africa could be 'discovered' except in the sense that it was new to the discoverers – the Europeans. And most of the places discovered by the European explorers had received alien visitors before. The cities on the upper Niger, unknown to Europe until the early 19th century, had been visited regularly by North African merchants for centuries. On Burton's and Speke's expedition to Lake Tanganyika they were following a route known to many Arab slave-traders.

In many cases, moreover, the places discovered by the great men of Victorian Britain had even been visited by Europeans, or at least by traders of part European descent. Every step taken by James Bruce in Ethiopia had been taken by Portuguese or Spanish missionaries before him. Most of Livingstone's journeys in central and east Africa took him through regions known to earlier Portuguese travellers. In fact, Judith Listowel remarks that, with the insignificant exception of Lake Bangweulu, Livingstone ('a modest explorer') made no true discoveries at all!

It may turn out, though it seems less and less likely, that Columbus was preceded as discoverer of America by some Welsh hero, Bristol fisherman, or one of the other trans-Atlantic candidates that are enthusiastically promoted from time to time. The well-known argument over Columbus, while providing occupation and entertainment for many, has no real importance because, in the first place, Columbus was ignorant of and thus in no way assisted by his predecessors (though this too has been disputed, some arguing that Columbus visited Iceland and took a course or two from the heirs of Eric the Red), and in the second place, because the hypothetical earlier visitors had no effect on history: their visits were merely isolated episodes, signifying nothing.

Similarly, the fame of the European – especially British – explorers of Africa in large part relies on the events that followed their journeys. In 1800, very few Europeans knew much or cared anything about Africa beyond their concern for or against the slave trade. In 1900, almost the entire continent had been taken under European control. Without entering the argument over the hows and whys of the colonization of Africa, it is clear that public interest in and knowledge of the African interior was largely created by the tales of the explorers in the 19th century. It is hard to imagine the 'scramble' for African colonies without the previous exploration (not that the explorers described in this book were the conscious agents of imperialism). In a sense, the modern history of Uganda begins with the arrival of John Hanning Speke in 1862. Similarly, British involvement in what is now Malawi can be dated from the presence there of David Livingstone at about the same time.

The question of the extent to which the explorers were assisted by their less famous predecessors is more arguable. Nearly all of them might have had some idea of what they were going into. There was a very good history of Ethiopia available in Europe before Bruce went there, and he had read it; while at one time there had been more or less continual contact between Ethiopia and Europe. The discoveries of the Portuguese in Africa have been generally underrated, but largely because the Portuguese authorities were so secretive. Documents lying hidden in the Lisbon archives naturally could not help later explorers.

However, by the time the British (in particular) began 'ripping Africa open' in Speke's unattractive phrase, the

A Masai woman with her baby. The African has, for better or for worse, learned to live with his environment but the effect on the pioneers of exploration in Africa was often devastating. The mother and baby shown here do not seem unduly distressed by the flies but those universal pests could cause trachoma – and blindness.

Portuguese had been settled in Angola and Mozambique for 300 years. Livingstone was assisted by his conversations with Portuguese traders and officials on both sides of the continent, but probably that assistance was less than some recent writers have suggested, and certainly it does not make his own travels less remarkable. Indeed, Livingstone himself felt that the activities of slave-traders operating from the Portuguese settlements in Angola and on the Zambezi had made travel more difficult.

Of far greater assistance were native Africans. The early 19th-century explorers of the Sahara and the Sudan usually travelled with Arab caravans, and they could not have survived for long without them. Early expeditions in South Africa were accompanied by Hottentots, usually half-castes, who acted as interpreters and, sometimes, guides. Virtually all explorers in central Africa were dependent on local guides, and the servicing of European expeditions to East Africa became a notable minor industry in Zanzibar during the last third of the century. Some Africans travelled farther than their European masters, and their names deserve to be better remembered. Most people have heard of Susi and Chuma, the loyal lieutenants of Livingstone (they later travelled with other explorers). Few remember Muhammad El-Gatroni in the Sudan or the remarkable Sidi Bombay in East Africa. These men were more than loyal servants carrying out the orders of their employers. Both El-Gatroni and Bombay undertook long trips on their own in the course of the expeditions they accompanied. Mungo Park's guide followed his entire route a few years after him. Susi and his party brought Livingstone's body from Lake Bangweulu to Nyanyembe in five months – a speed that would have astonished their late master.

There is something faintly incongruous about the whole notion of African exploration as it was seen by the European explorers and their admiring public. The Fulani sultan, Muhammad Bello, who was well-informed about British conquests in Muslim lands, would have been startled at the idea that his own considerable dominion had been 'discovered' by Hugh Clapperton. Less sophisticated African

Rocky pillars on the Tassili Plateau, where rock paintings suggest substantial habitation in early times.

Suk tribesmen of north-west Kenya collecting water from a well in a dry river bed.

Below: Modern explorers advancing through swamps. Gervase Mathew and John Moffat leading the way on the Songo Mnara expedition, 1950.

rulers may have had a more limited outlook, but they saw the arrival of the explorers merely as an opportunity to acquire guns and other useful objects that would augment their power in the world where they lived and where their fathers and grandfathers had lived before them. The assertions of the explorers that they had come to 'discover' them, if they were comprehended, seemed of little significance.

The European explorers, guided by Africans, relying on African interpreters, and in some cases moving through long-established African societies, might have provoked the Red Queen's response to Alice's statement that she had lost her way: '"I don't know what you mean by *your* way," said the Queen: "all the ways about here belong to *me* . . ."'

Still, none of this seriously detracts from the remarkable achievements of the explorers. The perils that confronted them were real enough. Disease was the worst, at least until the effectiveness of quinine against malarial fever was painfully learned, and any European travelling in West Africa before the middle of the 19th century had a very short expectation of life. The soldiers who accompanied Mungo Park on his second expedition, although the poor wretches probably did not realize their danger, had little hope of coming back alive. And malaria was only one of half a dozen serious endemic diseases in tropical Africa. Though comparatively few of the great explorers, almost by definition, died of disease in Africa, many suffered ruined health, and only a small number lived to be old men. But what is so remarkable about them is not that they risked death, but that they kept on going in spite of the intense physical discomforts of illness and the mental depression that often

follows fever. Livingstone, so feeble he could not sit on an ox, is again the outstanding example, but many more performed feats of comparable endurance. Speke, at Lake Tanganyika, was weak from fever, half-blind with trachoma and half-deaf with an abscess in the ear, but a few weeks later he was ready to undertake his notable diversion from the route home on which he discovered Lake Victoria.

Perhaps more deadly was the hostility of local inhabitants. Early travellers in the Sahara had to run the gauntlet of nomadic tribes who preyed on passing caravans. Religious hatred was even more frightening in parts of Muslim Africa, and appears to have been the chief reason for the death of Gordon Laing, among others. The hostility of Arab traders in slaves and ivory was partly religious and partly economic, but could be equally dangerous. In many areas disturbances caused by slaving raids, war, famine, or other causes, created difficulties and compelled diversions.

On the other hand, it should be said that a pleasant welcome and a helping hand were frequently extended to European explorers, and the friendliness of many early contacts between black and white is one of the most attractive aspects of the story.

One of the more popular perils as far as the readers of African travel stories were concerned was wild animals. For that reason, perhaps, there were many tales of exciting confrontations with rhinoceros, buffalo, and elephant. Mungo Park's invaluable Isaaco fought a tremendous drawn battle with a crocodile, Livingstone was badly mauled by a lion, and the early big-game hunters in southern Africa survived many a narrow shave in the bush. Some animals, of course, can be hostile, though if treated with reasonable caution, comparatively few (as General Woundwort was always telling his lapine subordinates in *Watership Down*) are really dangerous. On the whole, the explorers were a far graver peril to the animals than the animals were to them. Insects were a worse nuisance (though it was not known that malaria is transmitted by mosquitoes).

By our standards, African explorers had very little idea of how to equip themselves for a long journey in unknown tropical country. A British tweed sporting suit, fine for the grouse moors, hardly seems suitable garb for struggling through thick forests or marching across sun-baked plains. The list of equipment for Colonel John Blashford Snell's Zaire expedition of 1974 bears only a slight resemblance to that of H.M. Stanley's expedition one hundred years earlier,

well-known men while ignoring those of explorers only a little less remarkable. There are one or two exceptions: for example, Heinrich Barth, though he made no sensational geographical discoveries, receives more space than in most earlier general accounts. Many authorities would now agree, however, that Barth was one of the greatest of early explorers in the Sudan.

The decision to bring the story to an end with Stanley's conquest of the Zaire in 1874–77 also requires explanation, for not only does it leave Stanley cut off in mid-career, it excludes altogether such remarkable explorers as Savorgnan de Brazza, Joseph Thomson, and Hermann von Wissmann. However, for reasons of space already mentioned, it is necessary to reject rigorously all matters not immediately concerned with actual exploration, which means ignoring not only African history (except for brief comments to place the explorers in context) but also European politics, especially European colonial involvements; after 1877, imperialism raises its large and hairy head.

Mangrove roots, a formidable barrier to the exploration of many lakes and rivers.

'A Frightful Incident' – but one, thus dubiously depicted, that made travellers' tales the more titillating.

and still less to that of Speke and Grant in their expedition to discover the source of the Nile (printed in Appendix I). The mind boggles at iron beds, though Grant observes that they came in very handy. Contemplating such a list one is again conscious of the Looking-Glass World and the outfit of the White Knight, whose amiable character indeed bears a faint resemblance to that of Grant (though not to that of Speke).

*   *   *

Finally, a word should be said about the scope of this book. To attempt to describe so vast a subject as African exploration in one rather brief volume may be presumptuous. Some hard compromises have to be made and comfort sought in the hope that people may perhaps be stimulated to read more substantial books, including the stories of the explorers themselves, which are almost without exception gripping and mostly available in accessible and, in the case of mammoth accounts, abridged editions. The compromises consist chiefly in ignoring the exploits of the less notable explorers, especially in the crowded 19th century, and concentrating on famous journeys concerned with outstanding geographical problems, such as the courses of the great African rivers. Unfortunately, this approach inevitably perpetuates long-standing injustices in emphasizing the exploits of a few comparatively

Explorers before 1874 were of many types: humanitarians like Livingstone, sportsmen like Baker, adventurers like Stanley, and intellectuals like Burton, though the categories are not mutually exclusive. Up to that time, political interests were either absent or muted. Thereafter, they intruded and, in many cases, became the dominant motive behind exploring expeditions. Thus Stanley, having completed Livingstone's geographical work, became an agent in the Congo for King Leopold of the Belgians, while De Brazza laid the basis for the future French Congo; Von Wissmann stimulated German interest in both sides of the continent, and Karl Peters helped create the German protectorate of East Africa. The imminent European takeover was signalled by the international conference, ostensibly concerned merely with exploration and trade, that met in Brussels in 1876.

Of course, exploration did not cease; nor has it ceased yet, though modern expeditions are different from those before 1875 and even more different from those of the colonial era, being mainly concerned with advanced scientific research. Still, Colonel Blashford Snell has just arrived back from the Zaire with stirring tales of huge trees disappearing in whirlpools as well as encouraging new discoveries that might lead to the eventual eradication of 'river-blindness' in West Africa. Nothing could make exploration more worthwhile.

Ancient Travellers

The strongest motive for the exploration of unknown lands has always been trade. Curiosity, religious zeal, lust for conquest, a spirit of adventure – all these at times outweighed commercial interest, and often a number of different motives combined to send an expedition into the bush. But trade was the most common, and trade was surely the first.

The ancient Egyptians ventured south through Nubia and south-west to Darfur more than two thousand years before the birth of Christ. They reached Darfur by the old 'Forty Days Road', which leaves the Nile near Aswan, and brought back ebony, ivory, and frankincense, as well as a 'dancing dwarf'. Their caravan consisted of 300 donkeys, a third of the animals carrying water.

The later behaviour of the Egyptians set a pattern that was to become all too familiar in the next four thousand years or so. Commercial enterprise was followed by military conquest, as Egypt enforced her dominion on the middle Nile. Egyptian influence, if not armies, was to spread much farther.

Eventually the tide turned; the wave of conquest was reversed, as Kush expanded from the south. By the time Herodotus appeared on the scene in the middle of the 5th century BC, the Kushites had established their capital at Meroë, north of the present Khartoum. Much more will be learned of these interesting and accomplished people when their curious form of writing is more thoroughly understood.

Herodotus himself, to his regret, never journeyed farther south than Aswan, but with his indefatigable curiosity and shrewd discernment he put together an account of conditions farther south which, wherever it can be compared with other evidence, proves fairly reliable.

As Herodotus described it, North Africa had a strip of fertile land along the coast with, beyond it, a zone inhabited by wild animals (extinguished since Herodotus' time), 'huge snakes, lions, elephants, bears, asps, and horned asses', to say nothing of 'men with dogs' heads and men with no heads but eyes in their chests' (but, Herodotus adds, 'I would not swear to it – I merely repeat what the Libyans told me'). Past the zone of wild animals lay the desert, 'a thirsty land, exceedingly dry', but coming to an end somewhere far in the south. Herodotus repeated a story he heard in Cyrene of an expedition that had set out from one of the little oasis settlements of the northern desert fringe towards the south-west. After a long journey through the desert, the five men in the party came to a country of fields and trees where, as they were helping themselves to some fruit, they were ambushed by a number of 'dwarfs'. It is a natural assumption that such early reports of 'dwarfs' refer to pygmies, but it is highly unlikely that these people were pygmies, whose presence in the Sudan is not confirmed by other evidence. They may have been merely an unusually short, Negro people.

The interlopers were taken to a town, where all the inhabitants resembled their captors in appearance and spoke a language that the Libyans (this was the classical name for North Africans, roughly equivalent to Berbers) did not understand. The town stood on the bank of 'a swift and violent river, flowing from west to east'. They were released unharmed and made their way home, where their account of their adventures was no doubt heard with much interest.

The identity of the river on which the 'dwarfs' town' stood raises an intriguing geographical problem. Herodotus' informants thought that so large a river, flowing in the direction described, must be the upper Nile, and he agreed with them. Of course, it was not the Nile, but it may well have been the Niger. The Libyans had probably seen the lower Nile, yet they were deeply impressed by the size of the unknown river beyond the desert. There is no really suitable alternative, and if the river was the Niger, then the town may have been an early version of Timbuktu.

While it may be an exaggeration to speak of 'regular' journeys across the desert in the first millennium BC, the expedition described by Herodotus was clearly not unique. Evidence of Saharan journeys is to be found in the rock pictures of the Sahara, which show horse-drawn carts crossing the desert, although, on long journeys, oxen were the probable means of transportation. Oxen could still be seen in the Sahara quite recently. Although they are slower than camels, their ability to go without water is not greatly inferior.

Herodotus also mentions Carthaginian dealings with African peoples beyond the Maghreb.

The Carthaginians, like the Portuguese later, preferred to conceal their activities from the curiosity of others, and their commercial operations in Africa were probably more extensive than modern knowledge of them suggests. One important trade road ran roughly south into the desert from the Gulf of Sirte, into the country of the people called Garamantes, in the Fezzan. Up this road came precious stones (carbuncles), probably gold, slaves, and perhaps such products as ivory. While the story of the man who crossed the desert three times on a waterless diet of barley grains is, like the barley, hard to swallow, it seems likely that Carthaginian traders did cross the Sahara.

The Carthaginian empire, though hardly an empire in the sense of a solid territorial block, stretched beyond the Pillars of Hercules and down the Atlantic coast of Morocco. On this coast the Carthaginians obtained gold through the curious and compelling practice of the 'silent trade', first described by Herodotus but still current in recent times.

On arriving at their destination, the Carthaginians unloaded the goods they had brought to trade on the beach, arranging them in an attractive display. Then, re-embarking in their ships, they drew out to sea, and raised a smoke signal. Alerted by the smoke, shadowy figures appeared from the interior. They inspected the goods laid out on the beach and placed a quantity of gold beside them before withdrawing quietly from the scene. Now the Carthaginians again approached. If they considered the gold a fair exchange, they took it and sailed away. If not, they boarded their ships once more, leaving the gold and their own goods untouched on the beach, and waited patiently for their partners to return and add more gold. This ghostly bargaining might continue for some time before the Carthaginians manifested satisfaction by taking the gold left for them.

Rock paintings in the Sahara (the largest figure is about three feet high), probably the work of a Negro people before they were driven south by the increasing aridity of the region. The great German explorer, Heinrich Barth, was one of the first Europeans to take an interest in such art forms.

During the transaction, says Herodotus, perfect honesty prevailed on both sides. The Carthaginians would not touch the gold until it amounted to what they considered fair value, while their desert partners would not touch the Carthaginian goods until the gold had been removed. As a method of doing business, it had drawbacks, yet there is something very attractive about that ancient scene on a remote and desert shore.

The Carthaginians occasionally ventured farther, prompted, no doubt, by the desire to locate the source of the gold. Their most famous expedition, which probably took place soon after Herodotus' time, was the voyage of Hanno to West Africa. Unfortunately, what survives of the accounts of this voyage is complex and contradictory, so that the aims, incidents, and extent of the expedition remain matters of argument.

It was a large expedition – one account, highly doubtful, mentions 30,000 men – and Hanno, its leader, was one of the chief men of the state. After passing the Pillars of Hercules, the Carthaginians sailed south along the coast, founding a number of trading posts at places where they landed. Reaching the desert coast south of the mountains, they established another trading colony on an island, possibly Arguin, in the north-west corner of the modern state of Mauretania, where the Portuguese were to make their first West African base. Next they came to a river, full of hippopotamuses and crocodiles, probably the Senegal, and after returning briefly to their island colony, resumed their voyage to the south. They saw a great fire that touched the sky, while all the land below it was in flames.

One rather unlikely explanation of this astonishing sight is that they had reached the vicinity of Mount Cameroun, a 13,000-foot volcano, which is still active today. But it is now thought that Hanno could hardly have gone so far (and if he did, that he could not have returned). If the whole story is not dismissed, perhaps the sky-touching fire was an eruption of Mount Kakulima, a much more modest volcano in Sierra Leone.

Three days later, the story goes, the Carthaginians came to a gulf, where there was an island inhabited by hairy savages (apes?), most of them apparently female. Three females were captured, but they resisted so fiercely that they were killed. Their skins went back to Carthage. However, the latter part of the story of Hanno's voyage, at least, is now regarded as probably fiction.

No doubt other Carthaginians besides Hanno ventured along the West African coast, but archaeology has not produced firm evidence of Carthaginian influence in West Africa, and attempts to interpret (for example) the arts of Benin and Ife as Mediterranean-influenced are not widely accepted.

There is a well-known legend that long before Hanno, probably about 600 BC, the Phoenicians sailed all the way around Africa, from east to west. It depends upon a statement of Herodotus, who says that the voyage was accomplished within three years and included two rather lengthy stops for sowing, growing, and reaping crops. Herodotus' statement is tantalizingly brief, and there is no other evidence that such a voyage took place. Although it is not perhaps outside the bounds of possibility, and ingenious constructions have been built upon Herodotus' words, it is hard to accept the truth of the story on so slight a basis.

*   *   *

When the Romans at last destroyed the rule of Carthage, they found themselves in a position familiar to later imperial powers, forced to defend, and extend, a territorial empire which was already an encumbrance. They were no more interested in exploration than the Carthaginians – so far as Africa was concerned, rather less in fact – and the few interesting journeys they did make were, with one exception, primarily military in character.

A general named Balbus led an expedition into the Fezzan at the end of the 1st century BC with the purpose of subduing the Garamantes – no less formidable a people than they had been in Carthaginian times. The expedition took the Garamantes by surprise and succeeded in capturing their main oasis-centres of Garama and Cydamus (Ghadames). A mountain where precious stones were produced was captured, and a river was reached which has been tentatively identified as the Niger, but it seems unlikely that Balbus's soldiers travelled so far. The Romans never again successfully invaded the country of the Garamantes, who were not to be caught napping twice and checked any future attacks by the simple expedient of filling in the wells along the road at the first hint of Roman invasion.

A century later, the Romans and the Garamantes had resolved their differences, for they co-operated in at least two joint expeditions against the 'Ethiopians' (the name applied by classical writers to all black-skinned peoples in Africa), presumably with the object of taking slaves. This was a common occupation among the Garamantes: their raids against the 'Ethiopians' were recorded by Herodotus.

After a journey of four months from Leptis Magna (near Tripoli), the allies came to 'the country of the Ethiopians, where the rhinoceros lives'. The name of this country, according to the near-contemporary Alexandrian geographer Ptolemy, who borrowed the story from an earlier writer, was Agisymba. The name is one more instance of what may be regarded, depending on individual outlook, as frustrating ignorance or fascinating possibility. Candidates for identification with Agisymba include Tibesti, Aïr, and even Adamawa, some three hundred miles south of Lake Chad! Tibesti seems the most likely, being a fairly obvious objective for a power expanding from the Fezzan, and inhabited by a Negro people. There are no rhinoceros in Tibesti now, but 2,000 years ago there may have been plenty.

Until contrary evidence turns up, it is safe to assume that Tibesti was the farthest south the Romans reached, though they had knowledge – or theories anyway – about more distant country which they did not visit.

Ptolemy represents the peak of Western geographical knowledge until the Renaissance; in fact, some of his more misleading notions were still going strong in the 19th century. Many of the places named by Ptolemy – towns, tribes and physical features such as rivers and mountains – have only been identified in very recent times. Some have not been conclusively identified yet, and some probably never will be because Ptolemy's information was not in every case accurate. To generalize, Ptolemy tended to enlarge everything he knew about (a natural enough tendency), and thus, for example, extended the Sahara some way south of the equator. But the extent of his knowledge was remarkable, and on the whole it was sound. In many areas, 18th-century Europeans knew far less.

* * *

While Europeans 2,000 years after Herodotus readily believed stories that Herodotus himself (not, according to his contemporaries, the least gullible of travellers) would have scoffed at, their ignorance was not universal. During Europe's Middle Ages a large part of Africa was brought within the bounds of Islam, and a succession of cultured, perceptive travellers, usually described too sweepingly as Arabs but at any rate writing in Arabic, recorded their experiences in north, west and east Africa.

The surviving Arab accounts, on which much of the history of the Sudan in the Middle Ages is based, are not all first-hand, being the work of scholars as well as travellers. One of the earliest, Al-Masudi, who died in AD 956, travelled very widely through the world of Islam, but did not (apparently) visit the Sudan, which had hardly been penetrated by Islam at that time. His near-contemporary, Ibn-Hauqal, on the other hand, visited the kingdom of Ghana and saw the Niger which, like earlier and later travellers, he believed to be the upper Nile. Given the direction of the river, it was an easy assumption to make, and Ibn-Hauqal, unlike later and weightier writers, at least got the direction of flow correct.

When Ibn-Hauqal visited the Sudan, he was unfavourably impressed by the people, not yet Muslims. As one who loved wisdom, skill, piety, justice, and stable government, he remarked, he would not exalt the African blacks by giving an account of their countries. Very annoying of him. Neverthe-

Roman ruins in Tunisia. The remains of the Capitol of the city of Dougga.

less, it is largely to Ibn-Hauqal that knowledge of 10th-century Ghana is due. He was naturally interested in the western Saharan trade in gold, and visited the northern desert city of Sijilmasa, from which the Tuareg controlled the trade routes. The gold actually came from beyond Ghana, from the mysterious, half-legendary land of Wangara (probably Bambuk), lying roughly between the upper Senegal and the upper Niger and reached by a route that, says Ibn-Hauqal, was 'dangerous and difficult'. The gold was exchanged for salt, always a very precious commodity in West Africa.

A more systematic account of North Africa and the Sudan appeared in the works of Al-Bakri, who, however, never left his native Spain. He died about one hundred years after the death of Ibn-Hauqal, and about five years before the birth of Al-Idrisi, the most influential of Arab geographers.

Al-Idrisi, like Al-Bakri, came from a prominent family

*A camel caravan in the desert, from a German book published in 1710.
Camels came to North Africa towards the end of the Roman period,
and one effect was to strengthen pastoral and predatory nomads, and
discourage settled agriculture.*

Tuareg slavers after a successful raid on a village.

settled for many generations in Spain. His grandfather was Emir of Malaga, but subsequently the family got into trouble with the new Almoravid dynasty and was exiled to North Africa, where Al-Idrisi was born in 1100. He travelled widely as a young man, and his knowledge of the world brought him to the attention of the Norman king of Sicily, Roger II, who hired him as his librarian. Thus Al-Idrisi's great work – a detailed description of the known world – was known as the *Book of Roger* (1154).

The section of the *Book of Roger* devoted to the Sudan described eight major states, some of which are today nothing but names, though archaeology may yet give them greater substance. Far the greatest of them was the kingdom of Ghana, under its dynasty of Mande rulers. It was a wealthy kingdom, a fact attributed to its access to the gold mines, and its king had fitted to his throne a chunk of gold that weighed thirty pounds. Even the dogs that guarded the royal palace wore gold collars.

Like Al-Idrisi, Ibn-Khaldun, born over two hundred years later, came from a family that had left Spain after the Almoravid invasion and settled in North Africa. He was a civil servant of the type that became familiar in Europe during the Renaissance. That is, he was a political operator of talent, ambition, and cunning. He held a large number of posts throughout North Africa, his machinations usually ensuring that he did not keep his position long. But while he was ambitious, he was not dishonest, and was credited with improving the administration of justice in Egypt when he was cadi in Cairo. He was also a man of immense learning, and the author of the outstanding history of Islam in Spain and Africa.

A widely travelled man who, at the age of sixty-eight, had himself let down by a rope over the walls of the city of Damascus in order (partly) to fulfil his ambition to meet the Tatar leader Tamerlane, confident that his reputation would secure him a safe-conduct back to Egypt (it did), Ibn-Khaldun never seems to have travelled in Africa beyond the Maghreb. Though he moved about a good deal in the course of his long and active career, he did not have the itchy feet of the true explorer.

One who emphatically did was his near contemporary, born in 1304, the greatest of all the Muslim travellers in medieval Africa (and the only one whose works can be read in a good, modern, comprehensive, English translation), the incomparable Abu Abdullah Muhammad Ibn-Batuta.

Ibn-Batuta, like many of his predecessors, was a Moor, born to a prosperous family in Tangier. He left home at the age of twenty-one to perform the *haj* (pilgrimage) to Mecca, and thus began the travels that took him, as his scribe wrote at the end of Ibn-Batuta's memoirs, across 'the whole body of Islam' in the course of thirty years, and made him the kind of international figure usually associated with the age of jet-borne statesmen. Travelling in West Africa, Ibn-Batuta on one occasion made the pleasing discovery that his host was the brother of a man he had stayed with in China.

He went first to Alexandria, picking up two wives on the way, then to Cairo, the greatest city in the world outside China, to Palestine and Syria, to the holy cities of Arabia, to Persia, Mosul, back to Mecca where he stayed three years, down the Red Sea and along the East African coast, visiting the great commercial centres of Kilwa and Mombasa, among others. After further travels in the Middle East, often through little-known regions, he crossed the Black Sea and continued north in hope of reaching the Arctic and witnessing the short summer night, but the farthest point he reached was about 55° North, in Siberia. He visited Constantinople in the entourage of a Greek princess, revisited the court of Uzbeg Khan on the Volga, crossed the Hindu Kush and entered India. At Delhi he found his reputation had preceded him, and he remained there for eight years in the government's service. In 1342, partly perhaps to escape his considerable debts (Ibn-Batuta was always a big spender), he joined a Chinese embassy returning home. After a narrow escape from shipwreck, he returned to India and, shunning Delhi, took part in a war in Goa, visited the Maldive Islands, which he liked and where – cause or effect? – he acquired four wives (it is uncertain what happened to Ibn-Batuta's numerous womenfolk). Next he went to Sri Lanka and, after various deviations, to Bengal, whence he sailed via Java to China and achieved his ambition to see Peking. He made his way back across the Syrian desert to Damascus, where he learned of his father's death fifteen years earlier. Making another side-trip to the holy cities (his fourth) on the way home, he finally returned to Morocco in November, 1349. He was, he said, glad to be home.

It is a characteristic of many great travellers that they react with obviously sincere relief and satisfaction when they arrive home after a long absence in strange countries and yet, in no time at all, they are eager to be off again. Robert E. Peary earnestly swore to his long-suffering wife that he had done with the Arctic for ever after each of his last four expeditions but, within weeks, he was planning a new journey towards the pole.

So Ibn-Batuta was soon off again, this time to Spain, where the Moors were under heavy pressure from Alfonso XI of Castile, and on his return from there, he visited, this time with some reluctance, the last great region of Islam that he had not seen – the Sudan.

One reason for Ibn-Batuta's reluctance to visit the Sudan was his prejudice against blacks (Negroes). It was a common attitude among northern Muslims, shared by Ibn-Hauqal among others, and manifested much later by European admirers of the Arabs such as Sir Richard Burton. Like all forms of racial prejudice, it was chiefly founded on ignorance, and it is noticeable how all but the most bigoted, after closer experience of African society, came to adopt more favourable opinions. Even Burton did to some extent.

When Ibn-Batuta visited the western Sudan in 1352, the kingdom of Ghana, impressively described by Ibn-Hauqal and others, had long since disappeared. Its place had been taken by the kingdom of Mali which, unlike Ghana, was under Muslim rule. Its capital was Niani (also called Mali) and it stretched from the coast south of the Senegal, eastward to the vicinity of the modern town of Niamey on the Niger, an immense area although, by 1352, it was already on the verge of decline. Its greatest moment, at least as far as the rest of the world was concerned, had occurred in the reign of Mansa Musa (1307–32), who had set out on the *haj* in 1324 with a host of courtiers (8,000 according to one account) and so much gold that his lavish expenditure in Cairo astonished the world and seriously depressed the price of gold in Egypt for several years.

Ibn-Batuta travelled south on the road from Sijilmasa and journeyed for two months before he reached the outlying town of Walata in the kingdom of Mali. He was still not reconciled to his journey, and he was not impressed by the hospitality at Walata. He was reluctant to accept an invitation to the house of a prominent citizen and his worst suspicions were confirmed when he was served pounded millet in a bowl with a little milk and honey. On inquiry, he learned that this was all the guests might expect. He was disgusted by such poor fare, and felt tempted to return at once to Morocco.

In the end, he decided to go on to Niani and, as the country was so peaceful (a fact that aroused enthusiastic admiration in an experienced traveller like Ibn-Batuta), he was able to travel with one or two companions only, buying food at the villages he passed through with beads, salt, and herbs. The Niger (like his predecessors, Ibn-Batuta thought it was the Nile) was crossed and Niani safely reached. There were many Moroccan merchants in the city, and when Ibn-Batuta fell ill he was able to call on an Egyptian doctor.

The king's court was impressive but, in Ibn-Batuta's eyes, somewhat barbaric. There was much evidence of power and wealth, but Ibn-Batuta disapproved of the ritual of abasement – dressing in rags and throwing dust over one's head – adopted by anyone approaching the king. He was shocked by the gift of a female servant – for eating purposes – to some visitors from Wangara.

Nevertheless, Ibn-Batuta soon came to see that the society of Mali had many admirable aspects. He was particularly impressed by the absence of crime and the general horror of injustice. 'Neither traveller nor inhabitant has anything to fear from robbers or men of violence. They do not confiscate the property of any white man who dies in their country, even if it be uncounted wealth, [but] give it into the charge of some trustworthy person among the whites, until the rightful heir takes possession of it.' He praised too the dutiful religious observance of the people of Niani, and the careful religious upbringing of their children.

Even the faults of this society, as indicted by Ibn-Batuta, do not seem too serious. It is not surprising that they were prepared to eat forms of meat that the more fastidious, urban-bred Berber would not touch. Nor would an infidel be so upset by women and girls going about naked, a custom on which Ibn-Batuta dwelt with heavy disapproval.

Ibn-Batuta seems to have overcome his objections to the dreadful sight of all those naked women quite effectively, for he stayed in Niani for nearly nine months.

On the journey home, he visited several of the chief cities of the western Sudan, but did not remain in any of them for very long and so had less to say about them. In Timbuktu he looked at the tomb of the Moorish (Spanish) architect and poet As-Saheli, who had been brought there by Mansa Musa

Details from the Catalan map of Charles V of France 1375, with the figures of Mansa Musa (bottom right) and a Berber nomad (Tuareg). The map shows a greater knowledge of north and west Africa than Europe generally possessed: Sijilmasa and Taghaza are among the places marked.

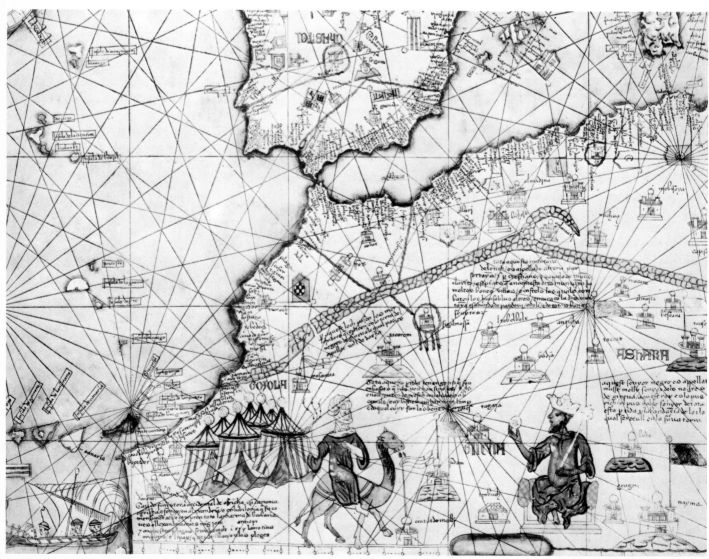

to add the distinction of bricks to the mud-built city. Canoeing along the Niger, Ibn-Batuta acquired at one of the villages a young slave-boy who remained with him for many years, and at the Songhai town of Gao he lingered for a week or two, observing that it was one of the finest towns he had seen in the Sudan. At the prosperous trading centre of Takkeda, on the main caravan road to Cairo, he remarked on the luxurious life of the inhabitants, living on the profits of Egyptian fabrics and locally mined copper (all trace of Takkeda seems to have disappeared).

From Takkeda, Ibn-Batuta made the long journey across the Sahara, travelling with a large caravan via Aïr and Tuat and arriving at Fez in the summer of 1354. His travels were over at last although, fortunately, he had many years of life yet, in which he dictated his account of probably the most extensive travels undertaken by any individual known to history up to that time.

*   *   *

By the time that Ibn-Khaldun and Ibn-Batuta had passed from the scene, the most brilliant period of Islamic culture was drawing to a close. In Spain, the Christians were marching south; the last Moorish kingdom disappeared before the end of the 15th century. The Europeans were soon to appear in Africa, but before the Portuguese make their entrance, there is another influential Moorish traveller to consider, the man best known by his adopted name of Leo Africanus (Leo the African), otherwise Al-Hasan Ibn-Muhammad Al-Wazzan.

Leo was born, probably in Granada, at about the time it fell to the Christians (1492), but he grew up in Fez. As a young man he travelled widely in Africa and the Middle East and he had already sketched a draft of his great *History and Description of Africa* when he was captured by Christian pirates in the Mediterranean in about 1518. Impressed by his bearing, his captors sent him to Rome as a present for the Pope. Leo X was a Medici and a fairly typical Renaissance pope – strong on culture, weak on piety. In the learned young Moor he had a treasure as great as a Leonardo or a Michelangelo, and he appreciated the fact, giving the young man his freedom and having him baptized a Christian with his own names, Giovanni Leone, or Johannes Leo. In later life, Leo Africanus apparently returned to Islam (he died in Tunis about 1552), but he was possibly not greatly exercised by changes in faith or culture. He remarked, 'When I hear Africans attacked, I say I come from Granada. When Granada is criticized, I say I am an African.'

The manuscript of Leo's work was completed some years after the death of the Pope (1523) and published in 1550. An English translation appeared in 1600. The works of Ibn-Khaldun and Ibn-Batuta were not then known in Europe, and the best account of the African interior available was that of Al-Idrisi. Leo's colourful description of the Sudan became the chief source of knowledge for over two hundred years.

Leo set out to write a description of Africa, not a personal account of his travels like Ibn-Batuta, and it is sometimes difficult to follow his movements. He seems to have reached the Sudan by the main western trade route, from Sijilmasa to Timbuktu. He travelled in the service of the sultan of Fez, who had appointed his uncle as leader of a mission to the Songhai king.

The Songhai kingdom was the last and greatest of the Sudanic Negro empires, and Leo visited it when it was near its peak, during the reign of Askia the Great (1492–1528). It stretched from the Gambia in the west to the kingdom of Bornu in the east, including the Hausa states (northern Nigeria) and the Tuareg centre of Aïr, and with a northern arm reaching far up into the desert to the vicinity of Taghaza, though the authority of the Songhai ruler was somewhat remote in these outlying areas.

Taghaza lay outside Songhai control when Leo reached it in (probably) 1513. Its importance was due to its deposits of

The strange-looking world map of Al-Idrisi, early 12th century. The Nile appears at top right; the Mediterranean, not surprisingly, is the largest sea in the world. Al-Idrisi, though superior to contemporary European cartographers, was less accurate than Ptolemy. Map-making was not a strong point of Arab geography.

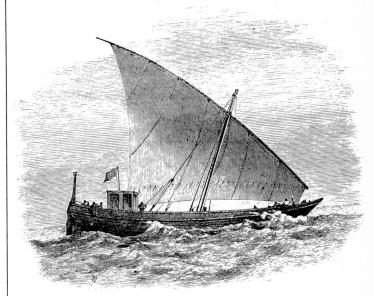

Arab slave ship, from a 19th-century drawing.

salt, a product of enormous value in the Sudan, and at this time not obtainable anywhere else, except from the distant sea. Taghaza had plenty of salt but, according to Leo's description, it had practically nothing else. The houses in Ibn-Batuta's time, even the mosque, were built of salt; water from the wells was distinctly salty. No one lived permanently in Taghaza, for there was no food except what was brought in by caravans from the north or south. If the caravans failed to arrive, the salt miners, who were Negro slaves of the local Tuareg tribe, simply died and were in due course replaced. Leo was glad to get away from the place after three days.

Soon afterward, he entered the borders of the Songhai empire, whose people were (still are, some West African travellers would say) a great deal friendlier than the nomadic desert people. Leo's objective was the city of Timbuktu. Although Gao was the capital of the Songhai kingdom, Timbuktu was the next most important town and a great centre of trade and learning. When Leo arrived, the king was in residence there (unless, as some say, the 'king' of Timbuktu that Leo mentions was merely its govenor).

Timbuktu – the El Dorado of Africa. Although Timbuktu, unlike El Dorado, did exist, the real Timbuktu bore no resemblance to the popular European image. The name was known in Europe in the Middle Ages, although its location remained a mystery until the end of the 18th century. It was known that gold came from Timbuktu, and gold was responsible for the romantic legend. The river bottoms glistened with it, and the roofs of the houses were said to be tiled with the stuff (this was a very popular architectural illusion: gold roofs were also anticipated in China, the East Indies, and South America). There *was* gold in Timbuktu, and there were other nuggets of truth in the European legend. Timbuktu was believed to be a great seat of scholarship, and it did have its scholars and libraries, although not the great universities, nor the uncorrupted classical texts preserved through the centuries in a desert Utopia, that European travellers hoped to find.

The legend died hard. When the African Association became interested in Timbuktu in the 1780s, it engaged two Moors who happened to be living in London and who asserted that they had visited the fabulous city. Agreeably (and for a fee), they did their best to fulfil European expectations with stories of immense treasure, erotic delights, and fabulous luxury. The king was surrounded by hundreds of

A Chinese flask dating from about AD 1300, found in Tanzania and now in the National Museum, Dar-es-Salaam.

exquisite female slaves, the court packed with musicians, acrobats, and dancers. One of these men agreed to lead an expedition to Timbuktu, but when the time came to be off, he was nowhere to be found.

In the preceding 200 years, virtually the only account of Timbuktu available to Europeans was that of Leo Africanus, and it would seem that Leo must have been responsible for the popular misconception. But, curiously enough, Leo's account of the city, if read in its entirety, provides little foundation for the legend.

In Timbuktu Leo saw no houses roofed with gold; he says they were thatched. There are no towers and monuments in Leo's account, only the mosque built by As-Saheli ('a most stately temple') and one 'princely palace'. There was indeed much singing and dancing in the streets, and the citizens kept many slaves, but no one could reasonably construct a great marble city out of Leo's description. On the contrary, he remarked on the danger of fire, and mentioned that almost half the town was burned in the space of five hours while he was living there.

Nevertheless, Leo's picture of Timbuktu is, on the whole, highly attractive. The people were 'gentle and cheerful', and 'exceedingly rich'. There were many 'doctors, judges, priests, and other learned men', who were subsidized by the state like modern scholars, and many 'manuscripts or written books brought out of Barbary, which are sold for more money than any other goods'. Corn, cattle, milk, and butter were

The riverside at Gao, ancient capital of the Songhai empire on the Niger. Bundles of firewood – a scarce commodity – are for sale.

Above: Remains of the Great Mosque at Kilwa. There was probably an Arab settlement hereabouts in pre-Muslim times; but Kilwa became a powerful, stone-built city in the late 12th century, when it captured the Sofala gold trade. Ibn-Batuta, visiting Kilwa in 1331, called it 'one of the most beautiful and well-constructed towns in the world'.

Below: Gondar, the capital of Ethiopia in the days when 'the kingdom of Prester John' had a powerful hold on the imagination of explorers. The Portuguese were the first Europeans on the scene, and these remnants of Portuguese-Ethiopian architecture are striking testimony to their influence.

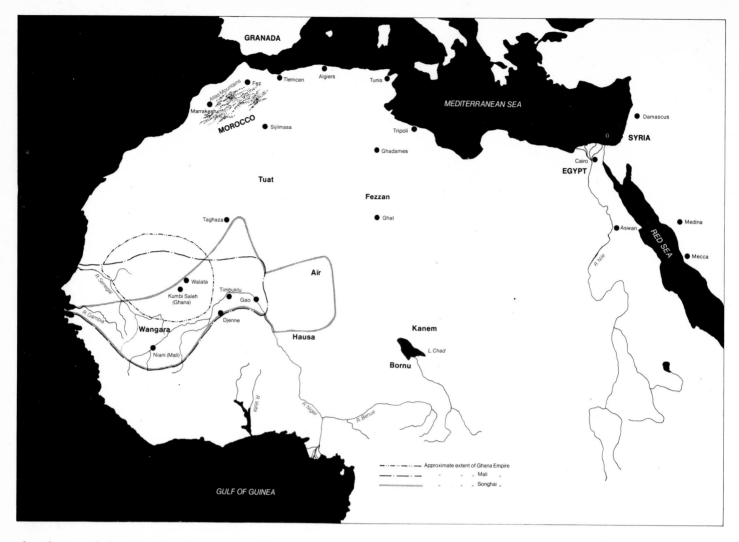

GRANADA

MEDITERRANEAN SEA

Fez
Tlemcen
Algiers
Tunis
Atlas Mountains
Marrakesh
MOROCCO
Sijilmasa
Tripoli
Ghadames
Damascus
SYRIA
Cairo
EGYPT
Tuat
Fezzan
Ghat
Aswan
Medina
R. Nile
RED SEA
Mecca
Taghaza
Air
R. Senegal
Walata
Timbuktu
Kumbi Saleh
(Ghana)
Gao
R. Gambia
Djenne
Wangara
Hausa
Kanem
L. Chad
Niani (Mali)
Bornu
R. Volta
R. Niger
R. Benue

GULF OF GUINEA

Approximate extent of Ghana Empire
"   "   "   Mali   "
"   "   "   Songhai "

abundant, and there were many merchants' and craftsmens' shops, especially linen and cotton weavers'. European goods, imported via Morocco, could also be bought. As it happened, Leo visited Timbuktu when it was at the height of its prosperity. By the time his book was read in England, it was out of date, for in 1591 Timbuktu was captured by the invading Moroccan forces that destroyed Songhai, and it fell into a long decline.

Leo's description of the 'magnificent and well-furnished' court at Timbuktu provided a little encouragement for romantics. Some of the royal sceptres weighed 1,300 pounds, and they were solid gold. The king had an army of 3,000 cavalry and a much larger number of infantry, armed with bows and poisoned arrows. Curiously, when the king went to war, surrounded by his horsemen, he himself rode a camel. Ibn-Batuta had been compelled to ride a camel in the Sudan because he could not afford a horse, and Leo himself goes on to say that horses were scarce, the best being imported from Morocco, and that the king paid a very good price for the best horses available.

On leaving Timbuktu, Leo apparently sailed up the Niger to Niani, the old capital of Mali, its power now much reduced and its king a Songhai vassal. Leo found it still reasonably prosperous, and commented once more on the friendliness and hospitality of the people, who in this region 'excel all other Negroes in wit, civility and industry'.

Returning east, he visited Gao: mean houses, a royal harem, rich merchants, a lively slave market, horses fetching five times their price in Europe, and salt, as usual, very expensive.

He passed through the Hausa states which, recently conquered, were suffering oppression, and the vigorous kingdom of Bornu, which was never incorporated in the Songhai empire.

Leo was a highly intelligent, relatively unbiased observer, especially good on economic matters. In general, his account is very accurate – his description of certain farming methods is still relevant to some parts of West Africa, and his own mercantile interests gave him a sharp understanding of Sudanic trade, his account of which is especially impressive. But as a geographer, Leo was less than perfect. He was not interested in maps, and his work would be even more fascinating if it were possible to follow his movements more exactly. A number of errors in 17th and 18th-century maps (for instance, belief in the existence of a huge lake in the middle of the Niger valley) can be traced to Leo, though they were due to misinterpretation of his data rather than his own mistakes. Yet Leo did make one large, inexplicable, and influential blunder.

Leo travelled along the River Niger for a considerable distance. The river, he wrote, 'flows westward into the ocean', and from Timbuktu to Niani, 'we navigated it with the current'. It is interesting that he emphasises this point. No question here of inadvertently writing 'west' for 'east', a mistake that easily occurs in writing travel books.

Many early writers, from Herodotus onwards, had stated that the Niger in the Sudan flows to the east. This is, of course, correct, though it led to the incorrect assumption that the Niger flowed into the Nile. But Al-Idrisi, writing in the 12th

A waterfall in the Sneeuberg Mountains, Cape Province, South Africa. From Samuel Daniell, African Scenery and Animals, *1805.*

A peaceful scene, as a Boer family of trekkers stops by a stream for the night under a skilfully improvised tent. In the course of their north-easterly migration, the Boers entered regions unknown to Europeans.

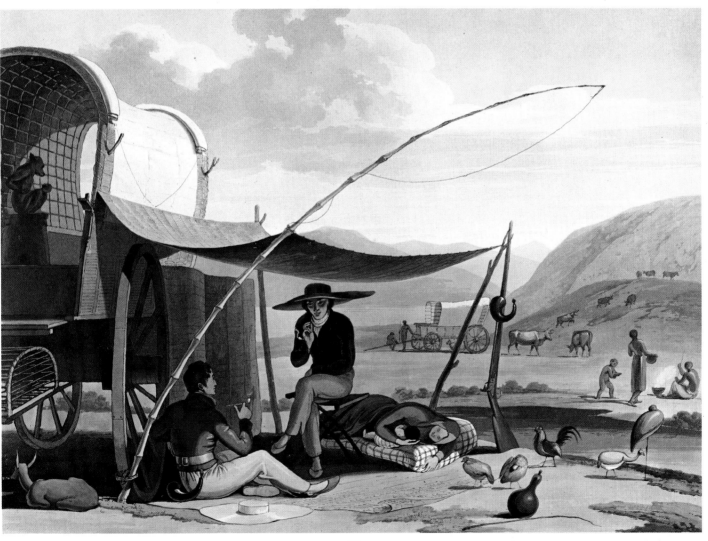

The Tissisat Falls. When Bruce visited the falls after the rains, the flow was much greater and presented 'the most magnificent sight that I ever beheld . . . that ages, added to the greatest length of human life, would not efface or erradicate from my memory; it struck me with a kind of stupor, and a total oblivion of where I was, and of every other sublunary concern'.

A precarious route up to the Ethiopian plateau. Such means of access were subject to flooding, and easy to defend. Ethiopia preserved a Christian kingdom in the midst of Islam: 'encompassed by the enemies of their religion,' said Gibbon, who was almost an exact contemporary of James Bruce, 'the Ethiopians slept for near a thousand years, forgetful of the world by whom they were forgotten'.

Loading salt at a mine in the Sahara, about 300 miles north of Lake Chad. A rare necessity in the Sudan – but common in the Sahara – salt was the principal item in trade between Berber and Negro peoples long before the Phoenicians began their mysterious voyages.

28

century, had turned the river around, making it flow westward towards the Atlantic. He had not, of course, visited the region, and possibly identified the Niger with the Senegal (the upper reaches of two tributaries of the Niger and the Senegal are less than twenty miles apart at one point). But Al-Idrisi was the most modern, most reliable authority known in Rome at the time that Leo was writing. Leo seemed to be merely confirming a known fact.

Leo has aroused scepticism in some readers, who have accused him of, at the least, exaggerating the extent of his travels, and his resounding error over the Niger gives them some reason for doubt. It has also been suggested that Leo was bullied into error by Italian scholars who refused to believe that the respected Al-Idrisi could be wrong on such a point. Another possible explanation is that Leo suffered a kind of visual transposition, seeing in his mind's eye an image of the river flowing west and, with his comparative lack of interest in physical geography, failing to realize that the mental image was reversed. Many people have experience a similar phenomenon, recollecting (for example) a visit to New York and 'seeing' the United Nations building standing quite plainly beside the Hudson instead of the East River.

The reason for Leo's error remains a nagging puzzle. But whatever the cause, the Niger continued to flow westward in most people's minds and maps until that day in 1796 when Mungo Park stood on the bank and looked at the great object of his mission, 'as broad as the Thames at Westminster, and flowing slowly *to the eastward'*.

* * *

If North and West Africa were, relatively, accessible from Europe, East Africa (from Somalia to Mozambique) was much closer to Asia. The behaviour of the trade winds in the Indian Ocean facilitated contact between East Africa on the one hand and India, Persia, and Arabia on the other, the direction of the winds being approximately north-east in the winter and south-west in the summer so that Asian traders could sail with the wind in both directions. Zanzibar is only 1,700 miles from Aden, 2,200 from Muscat, and 2,500 from Bombay – no more than the length of the Mediterranean from Gibraltar to Palestine – and contacts were made at an early date. Certainly there were Asian traders in East Africa long before the first surviving written description of the country. Arab traders from Oman, Persians from the Persian Gulf, possibly Assyrians and Jews were other early visitors to East Africa.

The earliest known account by a visitor to East Africa is in the form of a guide for seamen and merchants, the *Periplus Maris Erythraei* (i.e. 'Voyage Around the Indian Ocean'). It was written about AD 100 by a man who is variously identified as a Greek merchant or 'possibly . . . a rather illiterate supercargo . . . a representative for some firm at Berenice on the Red Sea' (Gervase Mathew). He described the towns of the Red Sea and the Indian Ocean as far south as Mombasa or Zanzibar. Unfortunately, many of the places he mentions have not been identified, and the racial identity of the inhabitants of the East African coast nearly two thousand years ago remains a matter of argument. It is usually assumed that the Bantu expansion had not reached the area at so early a date.

The picture that emerges from the *Periplus* is of a number of small, settled communities or 'markets' involved in well-established and varied commerce with India, Roman North Africa (via the Red Sea ports), Arabia, and the Persian Gulf. The chief African exports are ivory, rhinoceros horn, tortoiseshell, and slaves. The inhabitants are men 'of piratical habits, very great in stature, and under different chiefs in each place'. The beginnings of that mingling of Arab and African which gave rise to the Swahili language and people may be apparent in the 'Arab captains and agents, who are familiar with the natives and intermarry with them', gaining their friendship by bringing wheat and wine and, in some places, iron. It is not clear whether the Arabs had already established some kind of suzerainty over the region.

The Arabs 'know the whole coast', says the author of the *Periplus*, and it was presumably from them that he learned how, south of Tanganyika, 'the unexplored ocean curves around towards the west and, running along by the regions to the south of Ethiopia and Libya and Africa, it mingles with the western sea (i.e. the Atlantic)'.

Greater detail is to be found in Ptolemy, whose *Geography* probably reflects the knowledge of East Africa in the Mediterranean in the 4th or 5th century (Ptolemy himself lived in the 2nd century, but his work was revised by later hands). The coastal trading settlements, from Somalia to Kenya, had increased in number and size since the *Periplus*. Farther south, the greatest place (described as a 'metropolis') is Rhapta. This was also the most southerly town visited by the author of the *Periplus*, who described it as 'the very last market of the continent . . . in which there is ivory in great quantity and tortoiseshell'. Rhapta has not yet been rediscovered. It lay some distance up a river, and has been tentatively placed somewhere in the delta of the Rufiji. Its importance stemmed from its control of trade with the interior, like Sofala at a later period, and it probably governed a fairly large area round about.

South of Rhapta, the ocean was no longer quite unknown. Ptolemy says that by sailing south-east a ship may reach a cape, which is now identified with Cape Delgado, the northernmost promontory of Mozambique. The people of this region are cannibals – 'man-eating Ethiopians'. In the far south lay an undiscovered continent, *terra australis*, which linked southern Africa with India and turned the Indian Ocean into a vast lake. On this point, of course, Ptolemy was wrong and the author of the *Periplus* was right.

Of greater interest is what Ptolemy has to say about the interior of north-east Africa, which was to be one of the most inaccessible of all regions for European explorers. Beyond the narrow coastal plain, which is less than thirty miles wide at Mombasa, there lies what Professor Coupland called 'one of the most formidable barriers imaginable to the movement of man and the transport of his goods – a stretch of rising ground, over 100 miles in breadth, waterless for the most part and clothed with a dense jungle of thorn-trees and thorn-bushes', a region worse than any sandy desert. None of the rivers offers a useful route through this thorny wasteland, as most of them are navigable only for a very short distance from the coast. It is unlikely that traders from the Red Sea ports ever penetrated this wilderness, yet someone had described to Ptolemy (or his editors) the outstanding physical features that eluded the sight of Europeans until the middle of the 19th century. Inland from Rhapta, says Ptolemy, there is a great snow-covered mountain. If Rhapta is to be placed as far south as the Rufiji, this is not a particularly accurate map reference for that mighty protuberance on the face of Africa, Mount Kilimanjaro. But it can hardly be anything else. The reported presence of permanent snow within a few miles of the equator was to arouse the scornful jeers of sceptics many centuries later.

Ptolemy was responsible for another famous legend that was not far removed from fact, concerning the sources of the Nile. According to Ptolemy, the upper Nile divided into two streams, which flowed from two large lakes south of the equator.

Most of Ptolemy's geography, even in regions that he ought to have known fairly well (like the eastern Mediterranean) was rather crude, and baffled many generations of cartographers. Certainly his version of East Africa cannot be described as anything more than an approximate sketch. Nevertheless, his theory about the sources of the Nile was closer to the truth than most of the notions advanced by later students of this endlessly fascinating problem until the true situation was fully revealed in the 19th century.

Ptolemy's knowledge of the sources of the Nile was based partly on information percolating through to Egypt from the south, partly on information from the Red Sea and East African ports, and partly on what he knew of Roman explorations in the preceding two centuries.

Under the Emperor Nero (54–68), an attempt was made to discover the origins of Egypt's great artery, one of the earliest examples of an expedition concerned primarily with geographical exploration although, admittedly, it was connected with planned military operations against Axum.

Following the river south, the Roman explorers came to 'immense marshes, the outcome of which neither the inhabitants knew nor can anyone hope to know, in such a way are the plants entangled with the waters, not to be struggled through on foot or in a boat'. They saw 'two rocks, from which a great river came falling', but admittedly they were not certain that this was what it appeared to be – the source of the Nile. The two rocks are puzzling but, judging from the remarks about the *sudd*, that area of the Nile where the river degenerates into a watery expanse of decaying vegetation, it can be assumed that a point was reached not far below the junction of the Sobat, a region that was not visited again by Europeans before the 19th century.

The map that showed snowy mountains and lacustrine sources of the Nile was based on information from the east coast rather than the Nile valley. An early Greek traveller was stranded at Rhapta by a storm, and brought back news (and a map) of the 'Mountains of the Moon'. It is unlikely that he had been there himself; no doubt his informant was an Arab, who in turn may have questioned people living farther inland.

After Ptolemy, little is heard of East Africa until the age of Islam and the appearance of the great Arab geographers of the Middle Ages. The coastal culture had become predominantly Arab, but the settlements, by this time stone-built towns, usually located on islands off the shore, still remained independent of each other although, at various times, one or other of the towns rose to achieve some degree of control over its neighbours. At the time of the Portuguese arrival, Kilwa was still enjoying what had been a long period of superiority.

Ibn-Batuta visited Kilwa in 1331, describing it as 'one of the most beautiful and best-constructed towns'. He was impressed by other places on the coast as well. Mombasa, where he spent only one night, was a large town, Mogadishu 'an exceedingly large city' where the people were both pious and polite to strangers, two qualities that Ibn-Batuta rated highly. It was the custom, he said, for arriving traders to be met by the local merchants who invited them to stay in their homes. He himself was greeted as he stepped ashore by the cadi and a group of his pupils. He lodged at 'the students' house' as guest of the sheikh. He was well entertained there, dining on meat, fish or fowl, with a great plate of rice and vegetables, plantains boiled in milk, pickled lemons and peppers, and fruit. It sounds delicious, but as the bloated traveller reported with faint desperation, 'One of these people eats as much as several of us. It is their custom. They are extremely fat.'

Ibn-Batuta moved among the Arab elite who, from his account and other evidence, enjoyed a life of considerable luxury. He did not venture beyond the coast, and neither did the Arabs. Contact seems to have been limited to trade and warfare. At Kilwa, Ibn-Batuta reported frequent fighting with the mainland: 'The inhabitants of Kilwa are addicted to the *jihad*, for they occupy a country adjoining that of the infidel Zenj' (or Zanj, from a Persian word meaning black; hence Zanzibar – 'Black Coast').

Among other visitors, some of whom settled on the coast and contributed to the development of the Swahili culture, were Indian and Persian traders. From a greater distance came the Chinese.

Two visits by the Chinese to Mogadishu are recorded in the early 15th century. They were probably the first, although the Chinese were certainly capable of sailing to East Africa a thousand years earlier. Al-Masudi records Chinese ships trading in Oman in the 10th century. However, the only evidence of the presence of Chinese traders in Zenj before 1400 consists of numerous artefacts, including Sung porcelain, which undoubtedly arrived by some indirect route, probably via Indian merchants.

The Chinese did know something about East Africa at a very early date. The Emperor Ping – not an invention of W.S. Gilbert, he was reigning when Jesus Christ was born – received a rhinoceros among other imperial tributes. There were many Negro slaves in Canton in the 12th century, and such products as ivory, tortoiseshell, and perhaps gold, were known to come from Zenj. But China's knowledge, like East Africa's porcelain, was probably derived at secondhand, perhaps through India or Indonesia.

The Chinese decision to establish direct contact with East Africa early in the 15th century seems to have had political rather than economic motives, being part of an imperialistic effort to boost the prestige of the Ming dynasty. The fleets were led by a famous Muslim admiral, Chang Ho, the 'Three-Jewel Eunuch', but sadly, the Chinese records of the voyages of 1417 and 1431 are sparse and unreliable, probably as a result of the clamp-down on foreign voyaging that occurred later in the 15th century. Other Chinese accounts of East Africa do not add much to the description of Arab writers.

When the Chinese visited Zenj, the Islamic culture was reaching its peak. There were nearly forty towns along the coast between the Red Sea and Mozambique, and many of them were built in stone. Kilwa has been called by one historian of Africa 'a true Venice of the south'. But, far away, a new race was preparing to intrude upon the prosperity of the Swahili society, 'like an unseasonable monsoon for which the inhabitants were wholly unprepared' (Kenneth Ingham).

Portuguese Century

In the 1440s a construction programme was nearing completion at Sagres on the south-western tip of Portugal near Cape St Vincent. The 'Prince's Town' (*Villa do Infante*) was gathered around a palace, a church, a naval arsenal, and an observatory – one of the first in Europe, looking out over the Atlantic. For many years, until his death in 1460, the governor of the Algarve and progenitor of Prince's Town lived in the palace there, organising the great maritime effort that, within one hundred years, was to span the world with the ships and trading posts of a nation that numbered no more than one and a half million people. This was Prince Henry, third son of King John I (and, incidentally, a grandson of John of Gaunt), Governor of the Order of Christ, known to posterity by a humbler surname of which he would not have been ashamed, 'the Navigator'.

At the beginning of the 15th century, the Portuguese, who drove the Moors from Portugal more than two centuries earlier than the Spaniards succeeded in driving them from Spain, were poised to carry the struggle into enemy territory. They invaded North Africa and, to everyone's surprise, captured Ceuta in 1415. Still more surprising, they managed to hold the place against determined counter-attack. Later campaigns against the North African Muslims, though they resulted in additional Portuguese bases, were less successful: the attempt on Tangier in 1437 ended in disaster and left Prince Henry's younger brother a prisoner in a Moroccan dungeon for the rest of his life. Nevertheless, at Ceuta the Portuguese had a foothold on the African continent, the first European foothold since the Romans had withdrawn. It was the first step in the European conquest that was to be completed, in a frantic burst of annexation, more than four and a half centuries later.

Prince Henry took a prominent part in all these events: the capture of Ceuta in which he and his elder brother won their spurs (the campaign was partly designed for just that purpose), the successful defence of the city three years later, and the unsuccessful attack on Tangier. Henry the Navigator was not the stoop-backed recluse, poring over charts and globes, that he is sometimes made to appear. He was campaigning vigorously in Morocco at an age that in modern Britain would have entitled him to the Old Age Pension.

The Portuguese descent on Africa promoted by Prince Henry thus began as a continuation of the medieval Christian crusades against Islam. It is customary nowadays for historians to emphasise economic motives in history, and certainly the crusading zeal of the Portuguese, like that of the Spanish *conquistadores* in America, was mingled with commercial motives – particularly the search for gold, which was in such short supply that Portugal had abandoned gold coinage in 1383, and later for spices and slaves. Religious and commercial motives are not easily disentangled in the 14th century and, in any case, economic warfare was not the least effective method of attacking Islam. It seems probable that the Portuguese knew about the trans-Saharan gold trade before they captured Ceuta, though how large a part their knowledge played in provoking the attack is a matter of dispute.

A third connected motive in the Portuguese drive to the east was the desire to establish contact with the Christian kingdom of Prester John and thus outflank Islam in the south. The cogent legend of the great priest-king, who reigned in gorgeous splendour attended by ecclesiastical princes, his dining table made of emeralds and his roofs (inevitably) of gold, originated in remote tales concerning the kingdom of Ethiopia, where a primitive Coptic Church still survived – a mountainous island of Christianity preserved from the surrounding sea of Islam. Ethiopian monks had occasionally appeared in Jerusalem and one had reached Lisbon in 1452, but the Portuguese had only the haziest idea of the location of Prester John's kingdom. They knew it was 'in the east', but that was all. It was confused with other legends of lost Christians. When an irritated North African merchant in Calicut asked one of Vasco da Gama's men what the devil he expected to find in India, the reply was 'Christians and spices'.

When Vasco da Gama reached India in 1499, only sixty-four years had passed since the first Portuguese ships had rounded Cape Bojador, which lies about one hundred and fifty miles beyond the present frontier of Morocco. The rapidity of the advance down the West African coast, around the Cape of Good Hope, and across the Indian Ocean shows that the Portuguese possessed all the necessary equipment for long voyages in the 15th century. It was not difficult to sail down the north-west coast of Africa. Getting back was the problem: wind and current made it necessary to head out into the Atlantic to catch the trade winds on the return voyage, but no navigator willingly sailed out of sight of land. Otherwise, the obstacles the Portuguese had to overcome were largely psychological – the fear of the 'Green Sea of Darkness' (the Atlantic), the belief that Europeans could not survive in tropical latitudes or, more reasonably, that if they did they would be turned into Negroes. When these fears were dissolved by experience, progress was rapid.

The Portuguese ships that sailed from Europe to India were the highly successful result of a marriage between the tough, tubby, square-rigged ship of traditional European design and the sleeker, lateen-rigged vessel used by the Arabs in the Red Sea and the Mediterranean. The offspring was a three- (sometimes four) masted ship, the foremast and often the mainmast square-rigged, the mizen lateen-rigged; it embodied the best qualities of each parent in speed and manoeuvrability. The early vessels were lateen-rigged caravels, not much over 100 tons, but by the time of da Gama's voyage, larger vessels of the new type were also employed (Columbus's ships are usually called caravels, but the description fits only his two smaller vessels).

The Portuguese ships possessed another asset that, while it made no contribution to sailing capacity, proved a very weighty advantage in any conflict with towns or ships in the Indian Ocean: superior gunnery. Arab or Indian traders had no answer to a Portuguese broadside.

The navigational instruments of the 15th and 16th centuries, though they seem extraordinarily primitive now, were adequate for the task at hand. Most important was the compass, derived, like so much else, from the Arabs, and by them probably from the Chinese. The astrolabe, for taking bearings on a star, was difficult to use at sea, and by the end of the 15th century was largely replaced by the quadrant.

As for maps, those that existed were virtually useless for practical navigation and, obviously, no charts existed of waters that no ship had sailed. But the Portuguese were quick to translate the results of exploring voyages into 'portolan' charts for the convenience of the next expedition. The early navigators never, if they could help it, sailed out of sight of land; accurate calculation of position at sea was therefore not so important. Latitude could be measured by the stars, though problems arose south of the

Prince Henry 'the Navigator'. He was 'cast in the particular heroic mold so respected by the Portuguese [and] if we are to believe the historians of his time, devout, humourless, austere [with] an extraordinary capacity for patient hopeful planning' (James Duffy). Detail from a painting by Nuño Gonçalves at Lisbon.

equator, where the Pole Star was invisible. The publication by the Portuguese-Jewish astronomer, Abraham Zacuto, of tables giving the degree of the sun's declination in both hemispheres made the calculation of latitude from the sun a practical proposition before the end of the century. Longitude, on the other hand, could never be measured accurately until the invention of the chronometer in the 18th century; but this seldom proved a really serious problem even on trans-Atlantic voyages, and for sailors following the African coast it was but a minor handicap. Navigators in the 15th century, and indeed much later, relied also on nautical know-how – the colour of the water, the character of the drifting flotsam, the behaviour of the weather, and dozens of other indications significant to experienced sailors.

Vasco da Gama's voyage to India, in some ways a more remarkable feat than the first voyage of Columbus, showed how far the Portuguese had improved their methods of navigation in the course of the 15th century, chiefly by making the most intelligent use of their own experience, in the tradition founded by Prince Henry. Da Gama abandoned the cautious coast-following of his predecessors in order to make the best of winds and current, and sailed out of sight of land for a much greater distance than his predecessors (including Columbus). Yet he made his landfall north of the Cape of Good Hope with reasonable accuracy.

* * *

According to the Portuguese chronicler of Guinea voyages, there were fifteen unsuccessful attempts to pass Cape Bojador before Gil Eannes at last rounded it, and he managed it only after Prince Henry had stiffened his backbone by scoffing at the alleged dangers: 'Even if these things that are reported had any authority, however small, I would not blame you, but you tell me only the opinions of . . . mariners . . . from the Flanders trade, or from other ports that are very commonly sailed to, who know nothing of compass or chart.' With this princely scorn in his ears, Gil Eannes plucked up courage, set course for the south, and left the bogey cape behind him. He brought back wild flowers as evidence of his arrival on the unknown coast to the south.

Thereafter, progress was more rapid. In 1441, Antão Gonçalves brought back the first captives, taken after a deliberate Portuguese night attack on a peaceful nomads' encampment. One of those taken was a man of some authority who was later returned home by Gonçalves for a ransom (which in fact was not paid). Gonçalves was also the first of Henry's captains to bring gold from the West African coast, only a little gold dust, but enough to encourage future voyages. From this time, if not earlier, others besides the servants of Prince Henry made journeys to Guinea.

A six-ship expedition in 1444 captured 235 people in the neighbourhood of Arguin, the island south of Cape Branco which became the first Portuguese trading station. It is often said that the early Portuguese slaves were well-treated, at least by comparison with later times and other places. Perhaps they were, but the chronicler's account of this first large European slave sale describes cruelties that were later to become sickeningly familiar.

'[The captives], placed all together in that field, were a marvellous sight, for amongst them were some white enough, fair to look upon and well-proportioned, others were less white like mulattoes; others were as black as Ethiops, and so ugly . . . as almost to appear the images of a lower hemisphere. But what heart could be so hard as not to be pierced with piteous feeling to see that company? For some kept their heads low and their faces bathed in tears, looking one upon another; others stood groaning very grievously, looking up to

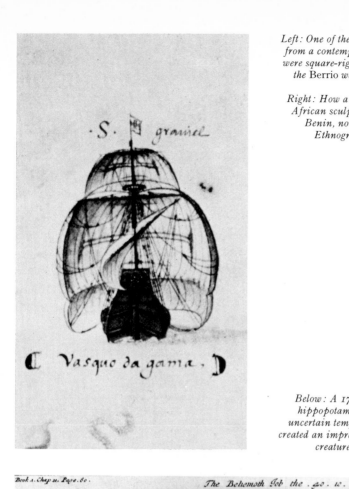

Left: One of the ships of Vasco da Gama, from a contemporary manuscript. They were square-rigged ships (naos), though the Berrio *was classed as a caravel.*

Right: How a Portuguese looked to an African sculptor. Bronze relief from Benin, now in the Museum of Ethnography, Leningrad.

Below: A 17th-century view of the hippopotamus, whose great bulk, uncertain temper and lack of caution created an impression of a more fearsome creature than it really is.

the height of heaven, fixing their eyes upon it, crying out loudly, as if asking help of the Father of Nature; others struck their faces with the palms of their hands, throwing themselves at full length upon the ground; others made their lamentation in the manner of a dirge, after the custom of their country. And though we could not understand the words of their language, the sound of it right well accorded with the measure of their sadness. But to increase their sufferings still more, there now arrived those who had charge of the division of the captives and who began to separate them one from another in order to make an equal partition . . . and then it was needful to part fathers from sons, husbands from wives, brothers from brothers. No respect was shown either to friends or relations, but each fell where his lot took him.

'And who could finish that partition without very great toil, for as often as they had placed them in one part, the sons, seeing their fathers in another, rose with great energy and rushed over to them; the mothers clasped their children in their arms, and threw themselves flat on the ground with them, receiving blows with little pity for their own flesh, if only they might not be torn from them.'

Thus from the very beginning, Europe's relations with Africa became associated with the beastly business of the slave trade. It is but small compensation that, from the beginning too, there were men like the chronicler Gomes Eannes de Zurara who witnessed the sufferings of the Africans with sympathy and recorded the brutalities of his compatriots in feeling words; or that the trade in slaves was an old one, conducted by Arabs and Africans before the Europeans arrived, and in a manner that, whatever may be said about the benevolence of slavery as an institution in Islam, was sometimes hardly less brutal (casualties in slave caravans across the Sahara may have been as high as on the Atlantic passage).

Slave-trading was not one of Prince Henry's objects, though it resulted in the 'saving of souls' ('they turned Christians with very little ado', says Zurara, a trifle naïvely) and in profit. Later, he forbade his captains to seize captives; but others, less idealistic, were quick to recognize the commercial possibilities in slave raids.

There were friendly contacts too. In the year after the first large slave sale, a man named João Fernandes elected to live for a time with the people on the coast near Arguin, his motive being, apparently, plain curiosity.

Fernandes stayed with a family one of whose members had been to Portugal, and he was well looked-after. He dressed in a burnous like his hosts, and wandered about over a considerable area with the nomads, who never stayed in one spot longer than eight days because of the sparse grazing. Milk was the chief food, and wheat a desirable luxury. Those who lived near the sea ate mainly fish, raw or dried. Besides their sheep, the people owned horses and dogs, but selling captured Negroes to North African Moors was their major source of profit. In their journeys they were guided by the stars, like navigators at sea, or by the flight-paths of birds. Fernandes

John II, the patient and determined planner of Portuguese expansion.

was an intelligent observer: among his remarks on wildlife, he noted the presence of the swallows that left Portugal in the autumn, and the storks passing by overhead to winter in the Sudan.

When Gonçalves's caravel came for him, Fernandes was fit and sun-tanned. Seven months amid sun and sand, and a diet at times exclusively of milk, had apparently done him no harm at all.

By 1448 the Portuguese caravels had sailed well south of the Senegal and made contact with Negro peoples of the Sudan – sometimes friendly, more often hostile; marked by violence, sometimes justified, more often not. The Portuguese came to be wary of poisoned arrows. Their progress was not remarkable when compared with the large number of voyages made, but most of them were concerned exclusively with trade or raiding for slaves. Only a handful of Prince Henry's best captains pressed on with the main task (though possibly not yet recognized as such) of exploring the coast for a route to the east.

For strategic reasons, the Portuguese were secretive about their voyages to the south. Pioneers they were, but they were not without rivals. Castilian ships were also sailing to Guinea in the 15th century, though when Columbus returned from his westward voyage in 1493, announcing his discovery of a passage to the Far East, the Spaniards began to lose interest in the south-eastern sea route to Asia.

Portuguese reticence may be the reason why the fullest account of West Africa from any 15th-century explorer is the work of a man who, though he sailed under Prince Henry's patronage, was by birth a Venetian.

Alvise de Ca'da Mosto, anglicized as Cadamosto, made two voyages to West Africa in 1455–56. After visiting Madeira and the Canaries, he sailed to Cape Branco and took on water at Arguin. He reported at length on the people and customs of the interior, with special emphasis on trade. Though he did not venture far inland himself, he was extremely well-informed, describing (for instance) the salt-gold trade and the entrepôt at Taghaza in accurate detail, with a particularly interesting picture of the exchange of salt for gold at the southern end of the trade route, where business was conducted through the convention of the 'silent trade' almost exactly as described by Herodotus nearly two thousand years earlier in Morocco. In some respects, Cadamosto knew more than European traders in Guinea in the 18th century.

From Cape Branco, Cadamosto sailed south to the Senegal, where by this time the Portuguese had a trade agreement with the inhabitants. The river, says Cadamosto, was called the Niger by the ancients, and shares a common source with the Nile. His confusion of Nile, Niger and Senegal was a common one at the time.

Some fifty miles south of the Senegal, Cadamosto visited a Negro king called Budomel, known to the Portuguese as an honest trader, at whose capital, some twenty-five miles from the coast, Cadamosto stayed for a month.

Since the decline of the empire of Mali, the region of

Senegambia had broken up into tiny, more or less independent states. Budomel's little kingdom was nothing more than a group of villages with houses built of reeds. Nevertheless, the king had 200 attendants, he was surrounded by elaborate formalities, and he received the utmost respect from his subjects. As Cadamosto remarked, if God himself should come to earth, he could hardly expect greater reverence.

The king was a Muslim, but less fanatical than the Berbers of the north or, for that matter, the Christians in their religion. When Cadamosto brashly insisted that the Muslim religion was false and the Catholic true and holy, the king merely laughed and said that Christianity must certainly be a good religion since God had so favoured Christians with riches and knowledge. And yet, he added, Islam was a good religion too, and the Negroes had a better chance of salvation, for God had given such advantages to the Christians that they were enjoying Paradise in this world, so few to the Negroes that they could surely anticipate Paradise in the next.

Cadamosto was the first white man seen in these parts. The people wonderingly licked their thumbs and rubbed his skin, to see if its curious and unhealthy colour was painted on. No less astonishing were the guns of the caravel, which made such a terrifying noise. It was easy to believe the white man's claim that 100 men might be killed by a blast of his ship's guns. Surely, they said, this was the work of the devil.

The bagpipes, on the other hand, once seen to be not the living animal they were first taken for, must have been made by God, because they gave forth such sweet and diverse sounds.

After his interesting stay at Budomel's court, Cadamosto joined company with two more Portuguese caravels that had arrived at his anchorage, and sailed south in search of the Gambia. They sailed three or four miles up the river, but met with a hostile reception from the inhabitants. Having beaten off an attack without much difficulty, they succeeded in opening negotiations and learned that Christians, though known by reputation only, had a very bad name on the Gambia. They were suspected of cannibalism – an accusation that was bandied about very freely in the age of discovery and was often as erroneous when applied to Africans or American Indians as it was when applied to Europeans.

The captains were eager to sail farther up the river, but the sailors wanted to go home, and in such arguments in those days the sailors usually had the last word. Having observed from the mouth of the Gambia a constellation which seems to have been the Southern Cross (barely visible north of the tropics), they sailed home to Portugal.

Cadamosto made a second voyage the following year (1456). His ship was blown off course by a storm and led him to the fortunate discovery of the Cape Verde Islands (though his claim was disputed, in his own time and since). Thence he sailed again to the Gambia, where this time his reception was more favourable. He made contact with a chief living some sixty miles up river, and exchanged his European goods for slaves, gold (though not much), cottons, and animals such as baboons and civet cats. Cadamosto described some familiar African flora and fauna that were to exercise the pens of many later explorers – baobab trees, elephants, and a 'horse-fish': 'It is amphibious, and its body is as large as that of a cow, with very short legs and cloven feet; the head is the shape of a horse's with two big tusks like those of the wild boar . . . It comes out of the water and walks like other quadrupeds.'

After leaving the Gambia and its hippopotamuses, Cadamosto sailed farther south to the Bissago archipelago and the wide estuary of the Geba. His interpreters were unable to understand the language spoken there, and Cadamosto, whose chief interest was trade, not discovery, returned home. He appears to have remained in Portugal for some years before going back to his native Venice, where he died about 1477.

Cadamosto was followed up the Gambia by Diogo Gomes, a member of Prince Henry's household, who went farther up the river to the large town of Setuke, about 150 miles from the coast as the crow flies (much more as the Gambia twists and turns). There he found evidence of a substantial trade in gold. He was to repeat mouth-watering stories of the riches of Timbuktu and other great cities of the Sudan (exaggerated no doubt, either by Gomes himself – an instinctive diplomat – or by his informants). While making inquiries about the political situation, he was told that the land north and south of the river was ruled by two kings who had recently been at war with each other. When Gomes repeated this to his master, Prince Henry told him he had already heard about it from a merchant in Oran – an impressive illustration of Henry's intelligence network.

Gomes seems to have been better qualified than most of his contemporaries to establish friendly relations with the people of Guinea. Although he made no significant advances in exploration he was one of the most capable of Henry's lieutenants.

The Prince himself, having 'passed all his life in purest chastity', died in 1460, but though there were few geographically important voyages in the years immediately after his death, other voices urged Portuguese expansion in Guinea. (Indeed, Prince Henry's responsibility for Portugal's south-eastern impulse has probably been exaggerated.) The caravels still advanced.

In 1462 Pedro de Cintra reached the coast of what is now Liberia. Between 1469 and 1474 ships sent by the Lisbon merchant, Fernando Gomes, reached the Gold Coast (Ghana), soon the site of the castle of Elmina ('the mine'), then Benin, and Cameroun, where the coast disappointingly turned south again, baulking hopes of a quick passage to the Indies. The equator was crossed by Lopo Gonçalves, and Ruy de Sequeria discovered Cape Catherine (Gabon).

* * *

The most dramatic Portuguese advances came under King John II (1481–95), who was as determined as Prince Henry, more impatient, and rather less scrupulous. A tough policy was needed, as the Guinea trade (the term Guinea was applied to the whole West African littoral) was suffering encroachments by Spaniards, Flemings, and English. Supported by the series of papal bulls that confirmed a Portuguese monopoly of non-Christian lands between Morocco and the Indies, John was determined to exclude all interlopers, while, at his direction, Diogo Cão and Bartolemeu Dias set out on their voyages to the south.

Diogo Cão sailed in 1482 with the expressed purpose of carrying exploration farther. He passed Cape Catherine, until then the farthest point reached by the Portuguese, and discovered the Zaire (Congo) river, where he erected a massive stone column (*padrão*) transported from Portugal for such a purpose. On the banks of the river he found a flourishing Negro society. The people were friendly, and goods were exchanged. Four Portuguese remained to pay respects at the court of the ruler, the Manicongo, while Cão sailed on to the south. He erected a second column on a promontory of southern Angola and returned to the Zaire, where as his countrymen were still absent, he took four hostages. Back in Portugal, an enthusiastic King John raised him to the dignity of the nobility.

Portugal's connection with the Kongo kingdom was, as Professor Duffy says, 'a unique experience in Portuguese African history, and one which has captured the imagination of panegyrist and critic alike'. In a brief summary it makes miserable reading, however. Early developments were promising: an alliance between equals for mutual benefit, with Portuguese evangelism unmarred by violence or slave raids. For the Portuguese, the Kongo kingdom represented a step towards Prester John; for the Africans, the Portuguese alliance brought the benefits that Renaissance Europe could offer without the usual attendant disadvantages. For a time all went well.

The Manicongo's heir, who succeeded his father as Afonso I in 1506, was as 'European' as the Portuguese, as Christian as

King John but, inevitably, this background divorced him from his people, and as the Portuguese, their interests having by this time shifted to the south and east, failed to provide the support promised, Afonso's dream of a 'European' African kingdom faded. The lack of good men from Portugal opened the way for the slave traders based on São Tomé; the missionaries themselves often succumbed to the temptations of the slave trade. Sporadic efforts were made by the Portuguese government and by the Jesuits to retrieve the situation, but any improvement was slight and short-lived. Afonso's pathetic appeals to Lisbon ('We beg Your Highness not to leave us unprotected or allow the Christian work done in our kingdom to be lost, for we alone can do no more') went unheeded. The death of Afonso, sad and despairing, after a reign of nearly forty years, caused a bloody civil war and began a period of strife and invasion by hostile neighbours. The Manicongo's throne was preserved, largely by Portuguese troops, but the dream had died long since.

Diogo Cão, who started it all, of course knew nothing of these hopes and disappointments. Although a Portuguese chronicler says he got back safely to Portugal, other sources say he died on his second voyage, at his farthest point south, Cape Cross, about eighty miles north of Walvis Bay. (Eric Axelson recently investigated a grave thought to be that of Cão, but the body he unearthed turned out to be, puzzlingly, a sealion.) Though less well-known than his successors, Cão deserves to stand with Dias and da Gama as the third great maritime explorer of Africa's southern shore.

The famous voyage of Bartolomeu Dias in 1487–88 was

Africa in Martellus' world map, about 1489, showing the fruit of early Portuguese voyages along the western coast and the hypothetical courses of the Nile and the Niger. The Sahara Desert, which barely exists here, continued to be underestimated for 500 years: some of the early 19th-century explorers discovered, to their discomfort, that the distance across it from north to south was greater than they had anticipated.

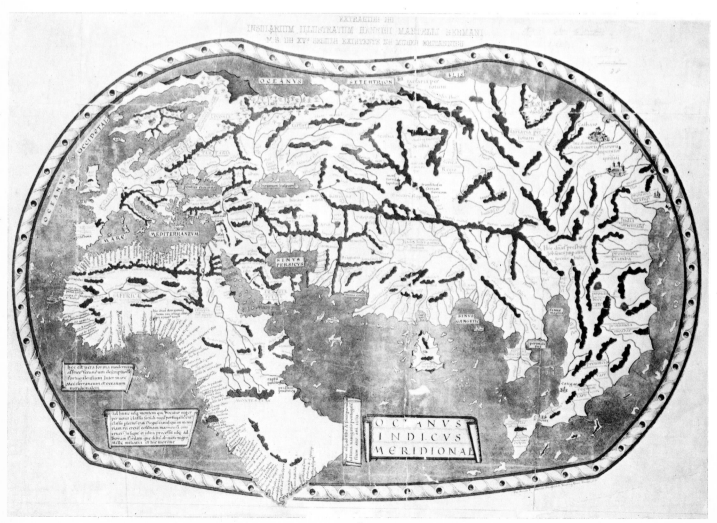

one half of a double project aimed at discovering Prester John and the route to India. While Dias followed in the wake of Diogo Cão and the earlier maritime explorers, Pero da Covilham was sent overland via Rhodes, Cairo, and Aden to India, which he reached in 1488. On his return, Covilham made a diversion down the coast of East Africa, apparently as far as Sofala, which he was probably the first European to visit. Covilham, it was said, knew 'all spoken languages of Christians, Moors, and Gentiles'. He was one of the most enterprising explorers of that most enterprising time, and it is a shame that so little is known of him.

At Cairo, on his way back to Portugal, Covilham met an emissary from King John with new instructions to seek out Prester John, whose kingdom was by this time accurately located in Ethiopia. The emissary returned to Lisbon bearing Covilham's report on commercial affairs in the Indian Ocean and on the ease of travel between East Africa and India. It is not quite certain that the report ever reached its destination: Vasco da Gama was to show ignorance of some matters that Covilham would presumably have explained, although other incidents of his voyage suggest that he knew more about the Indian Ocean than might have been expected if he had lacked the benefit of Covilham's experience.

When Covilham received his new instructions in Cairo, he had been away from Portugal for about four years. He had knocked about a bit in his time – he had once been a secret agent – and had lived in Spain and North Africa. But after four years of difficult and dangerous travelling – he had been given up for dead on at least one occasion – he must have been eager, at the age of forty-five or thereabouts, to go home and receive his well-earned reward for a mission successfully accomplished. But no, said the King, go to Prester John, and off this indomitable Portuguese squire went. Poor man, he little knew how often in the years ahead he would long for Portugal and home.

On his way to Ethiopia, the adventurous Covilham made another hazardous diversion – to Mecca, in the guise of a Muslim pilgrim (anticipating Richard Burton by 360 years). He also visited Medina before, in 1493, he finally arrived in Ethiopia. He remained there until his death more than thirty years later.

Covilham was welcomed ecstatically by the King, the 'Prester John' of European legend. Estates were bestowed upon him, an aristocratic wife provided; everything that could reasonably be done for him in that curious kingdom, with its disconcerting mixture of barbarous brutality and simple piety, was done. There was only one snag. The King would not hear of him leaving.

Some people have found it hard to believe that so capable a person as Pero da Covilham was unable, in thirty years, to give the Ethiopians the slip. Was he really so eager to escape a country where he was held in higher respect than in his own? When a Portuguese expedition from India reached Ethiopia in 1520, Covilham greeted them, it is said, with tears of joy. But he annoyed Da Lima, the leader of the expedition, by disappearing to his estates when he was most needed as an interpreter. Covilham was not the only European who found it harder to get out of Ethiopia than to get in, but perhaps he came to realize that he had no strong desire to go home.

An Italian named Pietro Rombulo had spent many years in Ethiopia during the first half of the 15th century, though his account is known only at second hand, and there had been

Elmina in the early 17th century. The first Portuguese fort on the Guinea coast, it was later captured by the Dutch, and this is not the original building. It passed into British hands along with other Dutch possessions in 1872, an event which helped to provoke the Ashanti War of the following year, described by Henry M. Stanley for readers of the New York Herald.

other Italian visitors later. But it was the Portuguese rather than the Italians who enjoyed the greatest influence in the country in the 16th century. Within ten years of the Da Lima mission from India, Ethiopia was attacked by Ahmad Gran and his ferocious army from the hostile Muslim states in the south-east. An appeal for help was answered by the Portuguese, who in 1541 sent a small expedition commanded by Vasco da Gama's younger son, which eventually repelled Gran's Somali warriors. For nearly one hundred years thereafter, the Portuguese received favourable treatment, until they were driven out of Ethiopia in the anti-Jesuit reaction of the 1630s; which followed the conversion (1625) of an Ethiopian emperor to Roman Catholicism.

While Covilham's part in King John's double expedition proved to be a lifetime's work, the part of Bartolomeu Dias was speedily completed.

With two caravels and a supply ship, Dias sailed from Lisbon in August 1487. Like earlier mariners, he followed the coast, reaching Walvis Bay towards the end of the year and leaving his supply ship somewhere on that coast, probably Baía dos Tigres. Then he headed southward out of sight of land, perhaps driven by a storm, or perhaps because he was

One of the old castles at Gondar, the Ethiopian capital, with (in the foreground) the ruins of a bridge built by the Portuguese.

tired of tacking against the prevailing wind. The weather was cold enough to cause serious discomfort, although it was midsummer in the southern hemisphere. After several days, Dias turned east, heading back towards the coast. He sailed for several days, but no breakers appeared, and he guessed that he had passed the end of the continent. So he turned due north, and eventually struck the coast, no longer running north to south, but east to west. The caravels put in to Mossel Bay, where the Portuguese admired the condition of the Hottentots' humped-backed cattle. After friendly barter, some kind of misunderstanding occurred, and the Portuguese left hurriedly after killing one Hottentot herdsman. Dias followed the coast as far as the cape east of Algoa Bay, where the coastline turns towards the north-east. Supplies were low by this time, the store ship was far behind, and the sailors expressed the opinion that they had gone far enough. They agreed to continue for two days more, during which they reached the Great Fish River, or perhaps the Keiskama. But that was the limit.

Clearly, they had passed the southern cape, though they had not seen it. Dias put about and began to follow the coast back towards the west, until at last the long-sought cape came into view. A cherished tradition says that Dias named it 'Cape of Storms', as a rueful reminder of the rough weather encountered on the outward voyage, and that King John, thinking of Prester John and oriental trade, renamed it Cape of Good Hope. But it is more likely that Dias himself struck the optimistic note from the first.

There is an impressive inevitability, a sense of determined purpose, about the steady progress of the Portuguese towards the East. On closer inspection, such appearances of historical

Perils of military manoeuvres in Ethiopia: six hundred knights falling off a cliff on a dark night. From the original edition of Ludolf's History of Ethiopia, *published 1681.*

symmetry tend to disintegrate, the broad lines being obscured by numerous diversions; yet history, after all, largely consists of making patterns from apparent chaos, and from the perspective of five centuries it is legitimate to distinguish purposes, motives, driving forces, which were less evident at the time. By the end of 1492 (assuming that Covilham's report on the Indian Ocean was known), the jigsaw puzzle was complete – all but the last piece. It remained for Vasco da Gama to fit that last piece into place.

John II died in 1495 and was succeeded by Manuel 'the Fortunate', but the choice of Da Gama, rather than the experienced Dias, to lead the first trading expedition to India had been made earlier. On this voyage, navigational ability

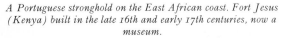

A Portuguese stronghold on the East African coast. Fort Jesus (Kenya) built in the late 16th and early 17th centuries, now a museum.

was less important than ambassadorial prestige and strong leadership. These the high-tempered Da Gama could supply.

The scene on the banks of the Tagus as Vasco da Gama's four ships prepared for departure in July 1497, and many of the later events of the voyage, are probably best known through the picture of them in the greatest work of Portugal's greatest poet, the *Lusiads* of Camõens, written sixty years later. Voices are heard in the work of the poet that are silent in the pages of official chroniclers. We hear, for instance, that some people opposed the idea of Portuguese expansion to Africa and India. There is more important work to do here in Portugal, says the old man in Canto IV, why go dashing off to the other side of the world when so much needs to be done at home? The argument has not grown less familiar through the centuries. Nor has it lost its force.

In less than three weeks, Da Gama's robust little fleet reached the Cape Verde Islands. Thereafter, his course differed from that followed (as far as we know) by all previous Portuguese captains. He swung away from the coast, sailing south through the Atlantic in a great arc that took him nearer Brazil than Africa, finally turning east to strike the coast a short way north of St Helena Bay, less than one hundred miles from the Cape. Da Gama thus established the route that all sailing ships have followed since. So bold a manoeuvre, taking the ships out of sight of land for ninety-six days, has suggested to some historians that Da Gama must have had knowledge of some unrecorded voyage that had revealed the new route since Dias rounded the Cape. But without any evidence of such a voyage, it seems more just to give the credit for discovering it to Da Gama himself. Possibly Dias, who sailed with the fleet as far as the Cape Verde Islands, had suggested it as a way of avoiding the storms he had encountered.

On Christmas Day, the ships were off an unknown coast, which Da Gama named Natal. A few weeks later they entered the region of Muslim culture on the East African coast.

Vasco da Gama. His expedition was not a voyage of exploration nor even a commercial venture so much as a heavily-armed scouting expedition. Although he was appointed to the command ahead of Dias, he was in fact the third choice – after his father, who died, and his elder brother, who refused. Engraving, from a portrait in the Lisbon Museum.

familiar ring.

The Portuguese were astonished to find in East Africa an advanced society where the people wore fine linen and cotton, with silk borders embroidered in gold. At Mozambique, the Sultan came aboard and was presented with 'many fine articles'. But he was unimpressed by the Portuguese gifts. 'He was so proud that he treated all we gave him with contempt, and asked for scarlet cloth, of which we had none.' At Malindi, the Sultan wore 'a robe of damask trimmed with green satin, and a rich *touca*. He was seated on two cushioned chairs of bronze, beneath a round sunshade of crimson satin attached to a pole'. All this was very different from the simple pastoral society of the Hottentots, whom the Portuguese had encountered in South Africa a few weeks earlier.

Mombasa, wrote Duarte Barbosa, who first saw the place a year or two after Da Gama's visit, 'is a very fair place, with lofty stone and mortar houses, well aligned in streets after the fashion of Kilwa. The wood is well fitted with excellent joiner's work. The men are in colour either tawny, black, or white, and their women go bravely attired with many fine garments of silk and gold in abundance. This is a place of great traffic, and has a good harbour, in which are always moored craft of many kinds and also great ships . . . Here are found many very fine sheep, cows, and other cattle in great plenty, and many fowls, all exceedingly fat. There is much millet and rice, sweet and bitter oranges, lemons, pomegranates, Indian figs, vegetables of divers kinds, and much sweet water'. Clearly, the more fortunate citizens still lived as well as they did when Ibn-Batuta visited these parts.

In another respect, times had not changed. The men of Mombasa were 'often at war and seldom at peace with those of the mainland [Mombasa, like most of the Swahili cities, was on an island], but they carry on trade with them, bringing great store of honey, wax, and ivory'.

On 24 April, the Portuguese left Malindi and set out across the Indian Ocean. Less than four weeks later they anchored off the great entrepôt of Calicut. In reaching India, Vasco da Gama had achieved his object, but he had sailed a long way from Africa and thus out of the pages of this book.

Once the route had been established, many Portuguese ships follows in Da Gama's wake. As a result of their activities in East Africa, the Swahili cities rapidly fell under Portuguese rule. In less than ten years, every one of them lost its independence; their inability to co-operate against a common danger led to their downfall. The Portuguese, however, failed to turn the commercial prosperity of the Swahili cities to

On his first voyage, the chief cities visited by da Gama were Mozambique, Mombasa, and Malindi. He missed Kilwa, which was probably still the greatest; his Swahili pilot, taken on at Mozambique, guided him past the city, perhaps deliberately, for the Portuguese were unwelcome visitors everywhere except Malindi, whose sheikh was willing to be friendly even with Christians if they were the enemies of Mombasa. But 'those who knew the truth [about the Europeans]', says the near-contemporary Kilwa Chronicle, 'confirmed that they were corrupt and dishonest men who had come to spy out the land in order to seize it'. It all has a

The imposing outline of Table Mountain, north of the Cape peninsula, became a familiar sight to East Indiamen stopping in Table Bay (where the Dutch colonists landed in 1652) to take on fresh supplies.

their own benefit. Trade declined, and the fine stone buildings crumbled under bombardment, poverty and neglect. Some towns eventually disappeared completely. The supply of gold from the Monomatapa kingdom in the interior, which had once flowed freely through Sofala, dried up almost completely – to the irritation and bewilderment of the conquerors. The Arab merchants retreated northward, while the Portuguese bullied and sweltered and died of fever. Several attempts were made in the 16th century to open up the interior in hope of locating the origins of the gold, but without great success. What the Portuguese had destroyed, they were never able to rebuild. Late in the 16th century, the southerly cities were ravaged by the ferocious Zumba, while the Turks raided the north. The Portuguese hung on doggedly. Not until 1729 did they finally forfeit the remnants of their authority north of the Rovuma (the northern frontier of Mozambique), but in most respects their East African empire was a failure from the start.

*   *   *

In pursuit of the gold that constantly eluded them, the Portuguese undertook a number of expeditions into the interior. One of the most enterprising of early travellers in Africa, a man of shady background named Antonio Fernandes, reached the Monomatapa kingdom in the first decade of the 16th century, and saw some of the mines with his own eyes. Acting on his advice, the Portuguese tried to establish a route inland along the Zambezi, building a settlement at Sena and, later, another at Tete. From there they managed to wield some influence at the Monomatapa court, but it was short-lived, and an attempt to gain control of the kingdom by force ended in the death of the leader of the expedition along with most of his men.

Looking at their maps, the Portuguese could hardly fail to observe that Angola and Mozambique lay roughly opposite each other and, as their maps underestimated the width of the continent, a trans-continental link seemed both desirable and practicable. Among the many unduly optimistic theories about African geography that floated about at various times, there was one in the 16th century that placed a lake in the centre of the southern part of the continent supplying the rivers of the east and west coasts. Efforts were made to seek out this route, but none of them led to any reported new discoveries. The dream of the trans-continental link remained but, so far as we know, it was not the cause of any great journeys of exploration until the beginning of the second age of discovery towards the end of the 18th century.

Nevertheless, the whole Portuguese achievement in the 15th and 16th centuries is impressive. They had virtually sailed around the continent, delineating thousands of miles of coast that no European had visited before. Africa at last assumed its (more or less) true outline on the map; no comparable advance in learning its geography was to be made until the 19th century.

The conception of this first great period of African exploration as an exclusively coastal enterprise conducted by the Portuguese needs qualification in two respects. The Portuguese, although they seldom ventured far inland, did make some appreciable progress in certain areas. Ethiopia is one obvious example. The Congo is another, although penetration here was much slighter. There were Portuguese missionaries at Benin before 1500, and in the western Sudan the Portuguese travelled farther than is usually supposed. They maintained a trading station for some time at Wadan, tenuously linked with their base on Arguin Island. A Portuguese expedition may have reached Timbuktu in the mid-16th century, although only one member of it got back safely to Arguin. Altogether, the Portuguese have received less than their fair share of credit for exploring the African interior, in this period and later.

On the other hand, it would be wrong to suppose that all exploration of Africa, by sea or land, was carried out in this early period by the Portuguese exclusively. The driving national purpose of Portugal gives prominence to Portuguese pioneers, while others, pursuing humbler aims, tend to get overlooked. In many parts of Africa, the Portuguese were preceded by other Europeans, particularly Italian merchants. When Da Lima's expedition reached Ethiopia in 1520, Covilham was not the only European they found. There was quite a little colony at the Ethiopian court, most of them men who had escaped from Muslim slavery.

There are some very odd stories told of isolated visits to the Sudan by early European travellers. The legend of Anselm d'Ysalguier is an example. A Frenchman from Toulouse, he possibly served in the Norman expedition to the Canaries in 1402, and he was captured in North Africa and sold into slavery. At any rate, when he reappeared in Toulouse more than ten years later he was married to a black African princess and attended by three eunuchs and three female slaves. He had apparently made this advantageous match while living in the Songhai capital of Gao. One of the eunuchs went into medical practice and became a fashionable physician. But, unfortunately, this whole story is open to grave doubts.

Although Christians were not normally tolerated in Islam, Jews to a large extent were, and probably most of Europe's knowledge of the Sudan and its gold came from Jewish merchants. One or two Christians, however, attempted to insinuate themselves into the profitable Saharan trade. Antonio Malfante of Genoa reached Tuat in 1443 on the track of the gold trade. He was protected by a wealthy citizen of that oasis-city, and wrote to a friend that he could 'go alone anywhere, with no one to say an evil word to me'. He failed to locate the gold, and his other commercial transactions were unprofitable, as he was forced to sell his goods at a loss. Whether he went farther south, and whether he ever returned to Genoa, nobody knows, but his report from Tuat did not discourage other Italian businessmen from following him. A Florentine, Benedetto Dei, appears to have visited Timbuktu in 1470, selling broadcloth and Lombardy serge, and there were almost certainly others of whom no record survives. The western Sudan in the 15th and 16th centuries may not have been so remote a place for Europeans as has been generally supposed.

Part of the mysterious ruins of the Great Zimbabwe, built at various times but much of it by the people of the Monomatapa, whose capital was frequently located there when the Portuguese opened relations with the kingdom in the early 16th century.

The Era of the Slave Trade

Since the time of Prince Henry, the Portuguese had faced competition in West Africa, chiefly from Spaniards and Italians. By the middle of the 16th century, more northerly nations were taking an interest in West African trade, and Portuguese influence dwindled before the incursions of the Dutch, the French, and the English. The newcomers concentrated on the coast between the Senegal and the Niger delta, while the Portuguese hold farther south remained unchallenged. As slave-trading replaced missionary endeavour as the chief Portuguese activity in Africa, Angola became the scene of their most energetic operations. Rising demands for labour in the Brazilian plantations rapidly turned Angola into what a recent historian has described as 'a howling wilderness'.

The merchants of England, France, and Holland, like their Portuguese predecessors, seldom ventured into the interior. They built a few factories and moored a few hulks at suitable points, but for the most part they were eager to complete their business as quickly as possible and get away from the dangerous Guinea coast. Few significant facts were added to Europe's knowledge of West Africa before the end of the 18th century, and most of the men who sailed to West Africa, or lived there temporarily in the course of business, were not greatly interested in the country.

There were, of course, a number of exceptions. Books about Africa, almost non-existent before the 17th century, began to appear in growing numbers, and by the middle of the 18th century had become commonplace, although their authors did not always write from personal experience. There were some men too who did travel a considerable distance into the interior, chiefly along the Gambia in the case of the British, and the Senegal in the case of the French. The travellers who are remembered are those who wrote about their experiences or made their knowledge known to contemporary historians: those who wish to engage the attention of posterity must ensure that their activities are well publicised in their own time.

One of the first Englishmen to write an account of West Africa was Richard Jobson, whose *The Golden Trade, or a Discovery of the River Gambia and the Golden Trade of the Aethiopians* has been called by J.H. Plumb 'one of the masterpieces of the literature of West African discovery'.

Jobson sailed to West Africa in 1620 in support of an expedition sent out by an English merchant company which had recently been granted a royal charter to trade in Guinea. He soon learned of the death of those he had come to assist, but travelled some three hundred miles up the Gambia and, partly through his friendly relations with a local merchant, Bucknor Sano, he was hospitably entertained, finding not the hostility he had been warned to expect but 'familiar conversation, fair acceptance, and mutual amity'. He was interested in gold, not slaves, and his attitude to slave-trading possibly helped to make him welcome. When offered slaves, he explained that 'we were a people who did not deal in any such commodities, neither did we buy or sell one another, or any that had our own shapes . . . If they had no other commodities, we would return . . .'

Jobson was a sensible and tolerant man without the narrow prejudices that warped so many African-European contacts. His description of the political, social, and economic affairs of the Mandingo shows him to have been a perceptive and careful observer, with an eye for detail, often surprised but seldom shocked. A scholarly caution hardly to be expected in a Jacobean sea captain is evident in phrases such as 'so far as we can perceive', with which he qualifies some of his statements.

Jobson often supported his generalisations with colourful stories. He writes, for example, of the abstemiousness of the 'Mary-bucks' (marabouts), who would not touch alcoholic liquor nor allow fruit or sweets even to their children, and illustrates this puritanism with a compelling incident. 'As I was travelling up the River in my boat, upon some occasions our people being in the water, and in the shallow, leading up to our boat, a sudden deepness, occasioned by a steep bank, brought them beyond their reaches, and enforced them to shift for themselves by swimming. My Alchade or Marybucke, being one of them, was . . . taken in a whirlpool, and in great danger of drowning, having been twice at the bottom, but at the second rise, one of our men took hold upon him, and with help, we presently got him aboard, being almost spent, and his senses gone. We earnest to recover him, fearing the agony we saw him in, got rosa solis (perhaps the drink made from that plant, which contained brandy) to put in his mouth, the scent whereof, as it appeared, made him close his lips, that we gave him none, but within a while he came perfectly to himself, and as it seemed retained the savour, so as he asked whether he had taken any or no. He was answered no. "I had rather", saith he, "have died, than any should have come within me", although I am verily persuaded, the very savour refreshed, and did him good.'

When it came to business, Jobson kept a cool head and exercised professional cunning. 'We never talked unto them of gold, the principal we came for, but waited opportunity, and notwithstanding as we saw it worn in their women's ears, warning was given, none of our people should take any great notice of it as a thing we should greatly desire, until occasion was given, by Bucknor Sano himself, who taking note of our gilt swords, and some other things we had, although but poorly set out, with some show of gold trimming, did ask if that were gold. He was answered yes. "It should seem", saith he, "you have much of this in your country". We affirmed the same, and that it was a thing our men did all use to wear, and therefore, if they had any, we would buy it of them, because we had more use than they for it'.

Whether Bucknor Sano was taken in by this generous offer seems doubtful. He was no innocent himself in these matters. He whetted the appetites of the English with a dubious tale about a city two months' journey away, 'the houses whereof are covered only with gold', which he claimed to have visited. But Jobson did learn some more reliable facts about 'the Golden Trade of the Moors', and asked Bucknor Sano if he would guide them to the town where the Moors traded. 'He stopped his nose between his finger and his thumb: and cried "Hore, Hore", which is the greatest oath they use among them that he would perform it.'

But that journey Jobson never made. He returned to England certain that he had laid the basis for breaking into the rich Saharan gold trade; but in spite of his optimistic account, published in 1623, others were not convinced. His employers had already spent a large sum for small return, and although Jobson did make at least one more attempt to return to the Gambia, he never reached it.

A number of Englishmen during the 17th century followed Jobson up the river in hope of discovering the source of the Golden Trade, but only one of them, Captain Cornelius Hodges in the 1680s, ventured farther than he had gone.

Hodges is a less attractive character than Jobson. His most notable characteristic was guts, and his account of the privations he endured and the dangers he overcame helps to explain why European traders accomplished so little in West Africa, a fact which would be hard to understand from the amiable pages of Jobson.

Unlike Jobson, Hodges failed to establish friendly relations with the Mande merchants of the upper Gambia. His avowed intent of visiting the gold mines – together with sixty-odd well-armed comrades – was not unnaturally regarded as hostile. But in spite of local opposition and a worrying shortage of supplies, he reached some gold mines in Bambuk (Wangara), which lies on the western border of the present republic of Mali. The mines were not being worked, according to Hodges, because of famine in the area.

He sent a party of his men on to a town called Tarra 'in the Moors' country'. Their arrival coincided with a Moroccan attack on the town, and the Englishmen elected to join the attackers. Reputedly, their action helped to ensure a Moroccan victory and thus endeared them to the Sultan, who expressed his desire to meet their leader. Hodges endeavoured to fulfill this request, no doubt foreseeing easy access to the Golden Trade under the Sultan's patronage, but his every movement was opposed by the Mande traders, and when he crossed the Senegal, he was ambushed by a body of horsemen. Undoubtedly he would have been killed but for the intervention of three marabouts. As it was, he lost all his goods and was compelled to give up his attempt to make contact with the Moroccans.

Forced to retreat through Bambuk with no supplies and no friends among the inhabitants, in a land desolated by famine, Hodges suffered and endured. For five months he lived on 'wild fruits, roots, such as I could get in the woods and never nearer starving in all my life'. Several of his men died of hunger before he reached Barracunda on the Gambia, over a year after he had left it.

Some further attempts were made to push into the Sudan from the Gambia in the early 18th century, most notably that of Captain Bartholomew Stibbs, who travelled some three hundred miles up the river in 1720. But when the African Association was founded in 1788, the British knew little more about this region than they had known a century earlier.

* * *

The French on the Senegal in the 17th and 18th centuries made rather more progress than the British on the Gambia. Once past the difficult entrance, the river proved navigable when in flood for a greater distance than the Gambia, and the country near the coast on both sides of the river was unsettled, presenting no attractions to make the exploring traders linger. However, it was not until the second half of the 17th century, soon after the founding of Fort St Louis near the mouth of the river, that serious efforts were made to follow the river deep into the interior, and real progress awaited the arrival at St Louis in 1697 of a remarkable character, André Brue.

Fat and sweating uncomfortably, but energetic, intelligent, and ambitious, Brue spent twelve years in Senegal, but in two widely separated tours of duty. He did not leave West Africa for good until 1720, and by that time he had established French posts far up the river and laid the basis for the future French colony. He made few long journeys himself, and not all his subordinates shared his determination and imperial vision, though one or two difficult journeys were performed under his direction, particularly that of the cool Compagnon, who explored Bambuk unmoved by threats to beat his brains out.

The first major journey up the Senegal was undertaken by Brue himself. Like Richard Jobson, he possessed the knack of getting on well with people of an entirely alien culture. Whether explaining the customs of Versailles to a slaving chief, chatting to the members of a harem as they bobbed along in all-enclosing baskets slung on camels, or extracting details of the route to Timbuktu from suspicious traders, Brue displayed tact and courtesy that disarmed potential opponents. His liberal distribution of good French brandy also helped to smooth his way.

Even Brue's efforts were not sufficient to get the French to Timbuktu; most of their trading posts in the interior did not survive for long. Trade with Senegambia was disappointing: the gold never flowed in any quantity and slaves were not easily obtained in this relatively thinly populated region. To supply their West Indian plantations, the French, like the English, came to rely on the more populous coasts of the Gulf of Guinea – the Grain (i.e. malagueta pepper) Coast, the Ivory Coast, the Gold Coast, and the Slave Coast between the mouths of the Volta and the Niger.

Besides the French and the British, the Dutch were active in Guinea, particularly on the Gold Coast where they had taken over former Portuguese posts, including the castle of Elmina. Willem Bosman, who spent many years in West Africa around the turn of the century, described one of the forts where he was stationed as 'not great, but neatly and beautifully built as well as strong and conveniently situated . . . with three good batteries besides breastworks, outworks,

A near-idyllic scene in a creek of the Niger delta. The estuaries of the great rivers of West Africa were the starting point for many European enterprises in the region.

and high walls on the land side and a sufficient quantity of guns. If it were well stored with provisions, it might hold out against a strong army of the natives'.

Bosman's *New and Accurate Description of the Coast of Guinea* was published in English in 1705. It was the most detailed and, as Bosman claimed, accurate description of the coast available, and it gives an interesting picture of international rivalry, current trade, and the wretched depraved existence of the European factors stationed permanently on the coast: the English garrison at Cape Coast Castle was made up of 'such miserable poor wretches that the very sight of them excites pity'.

Bosman was less informative about the interior, for the good reason that, except in limited cases, Europeans were prevented from entering it. Moreover, he was primarily interested in trade, not African society, although he does tell some good stories – for instance, his highly dramatic, perhaps romantic, account of the origins of a local war which brought the rising power of Ashanti into contact with the Europeans on the coast.

Perhaps the most valuable part of Bosman's account is his description of the slave trade, which is expert, detailed, and cool – if not, in the circumstances of the time, callous. 'I doubt not but this Trade seems very barbarous to you,' he admits. The slave ships came, loaded up, and departed in ever-increasing numbers. Many Europeans visited West Africa, but they knew nothing of the great plains and rivers, the mountains and forests; they saw only a gloomy coast, a crude fort, and a few stinking ships, with hundreds of young men and women, naked, branded, and filled with fear, packed into the ships' holds like dates in a box.

*   *   *

In the 18th century, the Muslim states of North Africa were reasonably well-known to Europeans, or to those who took the trouble to find out. Barbary was certainly not on the schedule of the Grand Tour. Religious animosity and guerilla warfare in the Mediterranean kept traditional hostilities simmering; but there were a number of Europeans who lived and travelled in North Africa, and several of them wrote books about their experiences. None apparently travelled beyond the Atlas in the west, or far into the desert. At least, not voluntarily: there were many Europeans in Barbary as captives of the Berber states. The Moroccan army that devastated Songhai at the end of the 16th century was chiefly Christian in composition; the standard language of command was Spanish.

Not much is known of most of the people who disappeared into Muslim captivity, but a few of them survived and returned to Europe to relate their experiences. Such accounts provided plenty of propaganda against the North African Muslims while adding little to what was known of North Africa from the accounts of Leo Africanus and others, although some of

*The oasis town of El Golea, about 400 miles due south of Algiers.
Once the capital of a Berber kingdom, El Golea and part of the oasis
is here seen from the mud-wall fortress built nearly 1,000 years ago.*

*The Niger east of Timbuktu. For much of its course the river does
not run between smooth and regular banks, but spreads itself lazily
over many miles of pool and swamp.*

The market place at Gao on the left bank of the Niger in what is now the republic of Mali. Gao enjoyed considerable importance and prosperity in the 15th century as the capital city of the Songhai empire. Little of the old city remains and the present one dates from the French occupation (French West Africa) in 1900.

46

Basutoland (Lesotho), and part of the Drakensberg mountain range
which became a defensive stronghold against the ambitions of Chaka,
the Zulu king. The northward trekking Boers settled in large numbers
on the rich Basutoland pastures.

them made exciting reading. A Cornish lad, Thomas Pellow, was captured in 1715 and spent over twenty years in Moroccan service. He adopted Islam and learned Arabic and, during his career as a soldier, he crossed the Sahara with an expedition that was guided, he says, by a blind man who could tell the route by smelling the sand (Leo Africanus has a similar story of a blind man saving a lost caravan by smelling the sand at every mile). Pellow escaped eventually and made his way back to England.

Egypt saw a somewhat greater number of European visitors. A few intrepid tourists risked insults and worse in pursuit of antiquarian inquiries in the 17th century. One or two travelled some way up the Nile, and in 1737 a Dane, Frederick Norden, reached Nubia. A French physician, C.J. Poncet, reached the Ethiopian court in 1698, and subsequently a number of French missionaries travelled the route from Cairo to Sennar and Ethiopia. Two Frenchmen, Savary and de Volney, published accounts of their travels in Egypt in 1787, but it was not until Napoleon's invasion eleven years later that Europe's fascination with Egypt really began, and drawing-room furniture began sprouting sphinxes' heads and lions' feet.

*   *   *

That part of the continent which was to prove most attractive to Europeans was farthest from Europe in distance. The Cape was also one of the last regions of European settlement, though it soon became the most populous. A supply post for Dutch merchant ships was built at the Cape in 1652, and although the Dutch East India Company had no desire to extend its operations beyond the station, in order to keep it operating it was necessary to encourage a few colonists to settle there. The colonists soon began to move east and west, searching first for minerals, later for good cattle-grazing.

Simon van der Stel, born in Mauritius and educated in Holland, was appointed governor of the Cape station in 1679. Not long after his arrival, rumours began to circulate concerning a people who were not Hottentots (the only Africans encountered at the Cape) and lived north of Namaqualand (on the borders of the modern Namibia). More concrete evidence, in the shape of copper ore, persuaded van der Stel to send an expedition to Namaqualand to make friends with the people and investigate the potential of the copper mines.

The expedition, which set out under the command of van der Stel himself in 1685, numbered fifty-seven white men plus a few Hottentot servants. Its size and scope makes it the first major, non-Portuguese expedition organized by Europeans in Africa. It was a formal, indeed a military, operation: on van der Stel's birthday, the company paraded and fired three salvoes in his honour.

After a march of about three hundred miles, which took two months, the expedition reached the Copper Mountains. As Eric Axelson has pointed out, van der Stel was fortunate in travelling through this rather dry region immediately after a particularly wet rainy season. The copper deposits seemed rich enough, but in the current state of the Cape colony, they might as well have been on the moon. No trace was found of the – presumably Bantu – people who were said to live in the north, but the Namaqua themselves were friendly enough. Informed of the reason for the three salvoes of musket fire, they insisted on offering their own acknow-

ledgement of the commander's birthday, and a concert was arranged.

'Their instruments were long hollow reeds to each of which they can give a different note, and the sound and beat compared with that of an organ. They stood in a ring, about twenty altogether, and in their midst was one who carried a long thin stick in his hand. He led the singing and beat the time, which they all correctly observed. They danced in a ring with one hand to their ear and the other firmly holding the reed to their lips. Outside this ring of musicians were men and women who danced to the music and reinforced it with hand-clapping. All this passed off very decently, considering that they are savages.'

It was a marathon performance for, according to van der Stel, it lasted the whole day, and no doubt both performers and audience were relieved when it ended. The Dutch commander gave orders that an ox should be killed for the musicians and performers. He also distributed some arrack, 'with which they made merry'.

There can be no doubt that the early Dutch colonists travelled much farther and more frequently than history records, nor that they encountered Bantu peoples long before the prolonged confrontation that began on the Great Fish River in the 1770s. He who discovered the habitat of a herd of

James Fort, Gambia, on a small island about twenty miles from the mouth of the river, built in 1664 and named in honour of the Duke of York (later James II). It superseded an earlier fort, nearer the coast, built by the Company of Adventurers of London Trading into Africa (chartered 1618), one of whose agents was Richard Jobson.

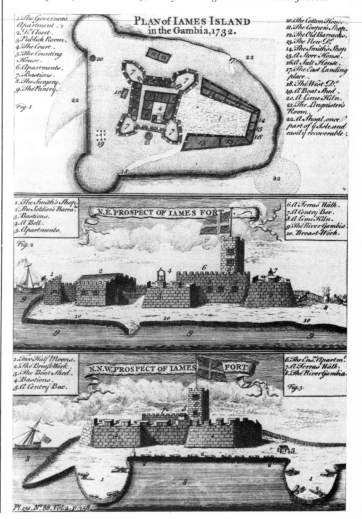

'An elephant enters the town of Elmina' – and receives a hostile reception from startled Dutch merchants. From Bosman's book on the Guinea coast, published in Amsterdam, 1709.

Cane bridge over the Wallia Creek (about five miles north of the Gambia). 'There is over this creek . . . a cane bridge, supported by two rows of forked stakes, on which are laid cross pieces; these are covered with small pieces of Bamboo, which, further strengthened by being interwoven with the smaller branches of the cane, affords a safe, though shaking passage for two or three people on foot. From the eastern bank . . . I had a very good view of the bridge, the village, and the surrounding country . . . Great numbers of evergreen trees and shrubs afford a pleasing and refreshing relief to the eye, wearied from beholding a light coloured sand reflecting the rays of a vertical sun unobstructed by clouds.' (Gray and Dochard Travels in Western Africa, *1825).*

elephants kept quiet about it for fear someone else should forestall him and gain the valuable ivory. In 1736, a party led by Hermanus Hubner made contact with Xosa beyond the Great Fish River and found white colonists already there, shooting elephants. Later they encountered some ship-wrecked English sailors engaged in the same activity, and with some success apparently, for Hubner's men bought five tons of ivory from them.

Van der Stel's expedition had stopped some way short of the Orange River, and although subsequent expeditions to the Copper Mountains heard stories of the *Garib* ('great water' or, to the Dutch, Groote-River), it was not discovered until Jacobus Coetsee crossed it in 1760. The following year, Hendrick Hop led a party from the Cape to investigate reports heard by Coetsee of a 'tawny' race living north of the river.

The expedition was troubled by scarcity of water, but reached the river in September 1761, 'without mishap, with all our wagons and about one hundred Little Namaquas, men, women and children, who were accompanying us to visit their friends among the Great Namaquas'. Continuing north, they reached Warmbad, where they found the 'ever-flowing spring of water, temperately warm, and thus always suitable to bathe in' that gave the place its name. They shot two giraffes and captured a young one which, however, 'died despite all efforts made to preserve its life'.

Across the river, the battered wagons rolled north again, and Coetsee (who was among the party of seventeen whites) rode on ahead, scouting for water and pasture. They crossed well-grassed veld and saw 'great herds of divers species of game such as rhinoceri, giraffes, buffaloes, witte eilde paarden, exels, quaggas, kudus, Gemsboks, Hartebeests, as well as "Auer-ossen" [wildebeest]'. An advance party reached the Fish River (not to be confused with the Great Fish River of Cape Province), but reported a dangerous shortage of water ahead. Hop believed in reaching important decisions by democratic means, and asked his men to give a night's thought to their future course of action. The morning brought a unanimous decision to turn back, and the linen-wearing 'tawny' people remained undiscovered.

During the last quarter of the 18th century, several notable travellers published accounts of their experiences in South Africa, though none of them broke any significant quantity of new ground. The Swedish naturalist, Anders (Andrew) Sparrman, spent a couple of years in South Africa restoring warmth to his bones after completing the circumnavigation of Antarctica under Captain James Cook. He undertook to provide 'a somewhat more accurate description of . . . the original inhabitants of the southernmost part of Africa, who are known by the name of Hottentots', and fulfilled his aim admirably. Later, he accompanied Carl Bernard Wadström in an abortive attempt to found a Swedish colony in West Africa, and in England he and Wadström gave the aboli-tionists some powerful ammunition against the slave trade.

Lieutenant William Patterson, whose *Narrative of Four Journeys in the Country of the Hottentots and Caffraria* was published in 1789, explored parts of the Orange River in company with Captain R. J. Gordon, a Dutch officer of British descent. By the end of the century, several missions were established on the Orange River, and expeditions from Cape Town had reached Bechuanaland. There were many others in South Africa, even more than in other parts of the continent, who for their exploits or their writings ought to be remembered, but there were no momentous journeys by outstanding individual explorers on the scale of Livingstone in 1852–56.

* * *

If a distinction may be drawn between facts available and facts known, then Europe's knowledge of Africa towards the end of the 18th century was not quite so insignificant as is often suggested. East Africa beyond the coast was virtually untouched, but in the north-east several men had travelled in and reported on Ethiopia, and in the south-east the Portuguese had penetrated several hundred miles beyond the limits of the present republic of South Africa in several places, though large areas within it remained unknown. Portuguese *pombeiros* (travelling slave dealers) had travelled through much of Angola. On the Guinea coast, as in North Africa, the hostility of the inhabitants largely prevented European penetration, but a good deal of information, much of it admittedly at second hand, was available on the Sudan, and the French had explored a long way eastward from the Senegal.

It is true that much of the information available was misleading, if not actually false, and that the true significance of many known features was not understood. There was, for instance, almost total ignorance of the four major rivers, although the lower Nile had of course been known since ancient times. The Portuguese knew the Zambezi several hundred miles from its mouth and the Zaire for a much shorter distance. The Niger was shrouded in mystery: it had not occurred to anyone that the web of streams, known as the Oil Rivers, which emptied into the Bight of Benin, was actually the delta of a single great river.

European exploration had been mostly incidental to other purposes, and even if it had been possible to gather all the available information together, large regions of the continent would have remained unillumined by a single known fact.

The extent of European knowledge can best be judged from contemporary maps, which immediately reveal the quandary in which their makers found themselves once past the coasts. Cartographers were compelled to use the utmost ingenuity to fill in the embarrassingly blank stretches that lay before them, and the results often justified Dean Swift's well-known jeer:

> Geographers in Afric-maps
> With Savage-Pictures fill their Gaps:
> And o'er unhabitable Downs
> Place Elephants for want of Towns.

Maps of Africa up to the 18th century were often beautiful, with hypothetical creatures painted in delicate colours and sharp detail, but accurate they were not. Lack of information also encouraged cartographers to make the most of the meagre details they did have and led them gently through exaggeration to pure invention. A 17th-century map of Africa such as that of Willem Jansz Blaeu, the official cartographer of the Dutch East India Company, at first glance displays a surprising quantity of detail – kingdoms, peoples, and towns plainly located, and set among rivers, lakes, and mountain ranges. Closer inspection reveals that many of the carefully drawn physical features are not just out of place or

Top: Christiansborg, a Danish fort near Accra. African towns inevitably gathered around the chief European strongholds, sometimes with disastrous effects. The town at Elmina, wrote William Bosman, was once 'very Populous, and eight times as strong as at present . . . but about 15 Years past the Small-Pox swept away so many' that, together with wars and 'Tyrannical Government . . . they have been so miserably Depopulated and Impoverished, that 'tis hardly to be believed how weak it is at present'.

Above: The beach where van Riebeeck, 'a thick-set, determined little man of thirty-three', landed in 1652 from Table Bay.

exaggerated in extent but altogether imaginary, not based on any traceable source. Moreover, even places that were comparatively well known were often widely misplaced: places on the coast were extended far into the interior, presumably in order to fill in empty space. Accuracy was further threatened by the tendency to stick to well-established traditions and to prefer classical authority to modern evidence. One reason why early Portuguese explorers received less than their due acknowledgement was that their information was widely disregarded by cartographers when it conflicted with a reputable authority like Ptolemy. One map of Africa, published as late as 1720, bore the statement that the discoveries of the Portuguese missionaries had been included, but the map itself revealed no trace of their influence, and the public was explicitly advised to put no trust in the maps of the Jesuits.

A tremendous advance in cartography took place in France in the 18th century. It is associated particularly with the names of Guillaume Delisle and his still more brilliant successor, Bourguignon d'Anville (1697–1782).

D'Anville published over two hundred maps, including an *Atlas Générale*. His map of Africa of 1727 was the first scientifically compiled map of the continent, less picturesque than many of its predecessors but much more useful.

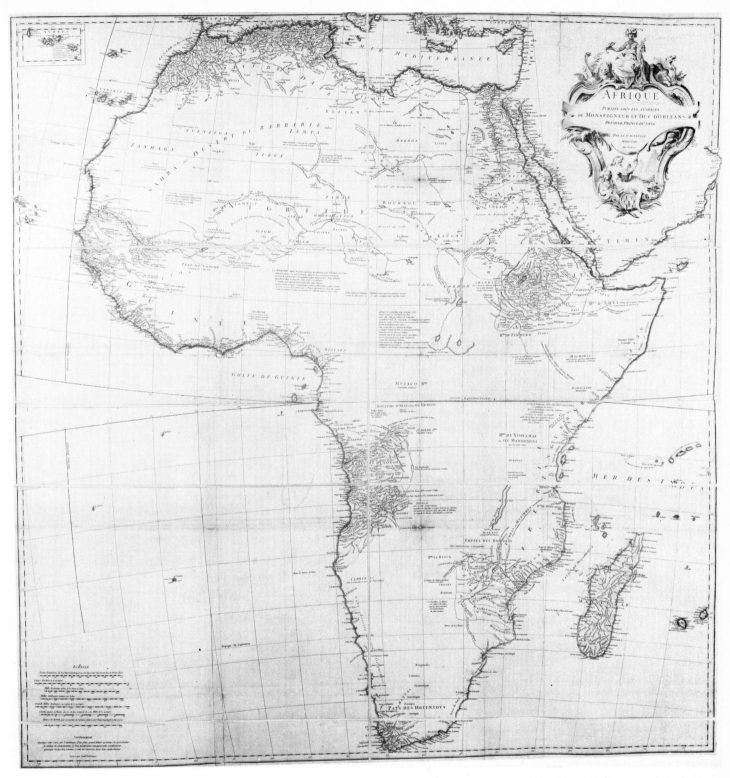

Opposite Page

Top left: Le Vaillant's camp beyond the Swartburg range.

Top right: Ivory being gathered by an expedition in South Africa in the mid-19th century.

Centre: 'Quagga – young male (most probably new and if so Equus Chapmanni)'. Thomas Baines' note on this sketch of what seems to be a species of zebra, the precise number of which remains a matter of argument. There is no Equus Chapmanni (Chapman was the man who shot this specimen). The quagga, which once roamed the plains of southern Africa in huge herds, became extinct when the last survivor died in London Zoo in 1872.

Bottom: In search of freedom and cheap land, the descendants of the Dutch colonists at the Cape 'trekked' north and east, driving off the Matabele and eventually clashing bloodily with the trained impis of the mighty Zulu nation. In the course of their migration, the Boers opened up regions previously unknown to Europeans.

An elegant map of 1749 by D'Anville, which shows at a glance the (rather slight) interior regions of Africa known to Europeans (the Maghreb, the Nile valley and Ethiopia, the lower Zambezi, the Cape, the lower Zaire and Angola, and Senegambia). D'Anville followed Ptolemy in placing the lacustrine sources of the Nile in the 'Mountains of the Moon'.

D'Anville adopted the simple but novel principle of excluding everything for which there was no reliable evidence; as he said, to destroy what is false is as much a contribution to the advancement of knowledge as to discover new facts. With ruthless dedication D'Anville swept away imagined mountains, banished hypothetical lakes, and revealed, on his stark but elegant page, the full extent of Europe's ignorance, which his more decorative predecessors had concealed.

In erasing the errors and misconceptions of earlier cartographers, D'Anville in effect did add new facts – by winnowing the chaff he revealed the true character of the grain, or at least some grains, although the size of the harvest was little larger for him than for Renaissance map-makers. Since the 16th century European maps, almost without exception, had made the Senegal and the Niger one river. D'Anville (benefiting, admittedly, from French exploration up the Senegal), concluded that they were separate as, indeed, Ptolemy had said. Of course D'Anville, in spite of his caution, did not avoid all errors: he added a mythical lake of his own to provide the Senegal with an appropriate source; but he did sum up the known geographical facts and so prepared the way for the more systematic exploration of Africa which, at the time of his death, was just beginning.

In the course of the 18th century, there were signs that Africa was coming to play a larger part in the thought and activities of Europeans. Perhaps it was little more than one aspect of the inquiring spirit of the age, part of the increasing interest that European man took in his environment, which was apparent in the founding of learned societies, the growth of natural science, and the rise of such amusements as gardening and zoo-keeping. But it cannot be said that the growth of interest in Africa was an especially notable feature of these general developments in society, and the number of people who took more than a cursory interest in the continent, who saw beyond the romance and the travellers' tales, remained very small.

Still, the signs were there. According to Robin Hallett, the total number of books about Africa published in Britain in the course of the 17th century was more than tripled in the first fifty years of the 18th. The rate continued to rise in the second half of the century, which also saw the publication of three books by West African authors: Ottobah Cugoana, a Fante, who wrote about the slave trade; Olaudah Equiano, an Ibo sold into slavery as a boy, who wrote an autobiography that included a vivid sketch of a West African village; and Ignatius Sancho, born on a slave ship, who eventually became a grocer in London and wrote plays and poetry when he was not weighing the cheese. The autobiographical works of Equiano and Sancho were very popular in the late 18th century, although they have attracted surprisingly little notice since.

The English have always been great readers (though not, alas, buyers) of books, and in the 18th century the number of readers and the amount of reading material available (newspapers and pamphlets as well as books) was increasing rapidly. People went to meetings and travelled about the country more easily. In the 1750s, it was possible to travel from Edinburgh to London in a steel-sprung stage-coach in ten days, God and the weather permitting.

The reading public was especially interested in tales of travel, as it still is. Daniel Defoe and Jonathan Swift attracted a larger public by setting their tales in foreign or imaginary places. Dr Johnson places his *Rasselas* in Ethiopia, though his Ethiopia would not have been easily recognized by James Bruce (neither did Johnson recognize Bruce's Ethiopia: 'when he first conversed with Mr Bruce, the Abyssinian traveller, he was very much inclined to believe that he had been there, but he afterwards altered his opinion'). William Dampier's accounts of his travels (he went three times around the world, taking eight years on one trip), published before the end of the 17th century, were one example of the kind of book that could rely on a good sale. Half a century later more serious explorers than Dampier were mapping the Pacific, and in 1768 James Cook, the greatest of British maritime explorers, set out on his first voyage. With Cook on the *Endeavour* sailed a young botanist, Joseph Banks, a man of enormous energy, both mental and physical, who was to become president of the Royal Society at the age of thirty-five, prime mover of the African Association and, by virtue of his position, capacity, and contacts, what J.C. Beaglehole called 'the Great Panjandrum of British Science'.

* * *

For most of the 18th century the relationship of Europe, and especially Britain, to Africa, was dominated by the slave trade. Everything else was insignificant when compared with the role of the trade in British society. It was the most valuable item in British commerce, and commerce was the main support of the nation.

The Atlantic trade was a triangular business: guns and cheap manufactured goods from Europe to West Africa; slaves from Africa to the American plantations; American products (especially West Indian sugar) from the Caribbean and mainland colonies to Europe. The whole, vastly profitable enterprise hung on slaves. The ports on England's west coast grew rich on Africa, and the actor who, hissed by a Liverpool audience, rounded on them with the charge that 'every brick in their detestable town was cemented by the blood of a Negro' spoke poetic truth. Moreover, the trade was growing throughout the 18th century; it reached its height about the time that slavery was declared illegal in England (1772).

In several ways the slave trade acted as a deterrent to European exploration of Africa in the 18th century. It had become such big business that it overpowered the 'legitimate' trade which, in the early years, had seemed quite promising. Such West African products as gum, mahogany, and pepper could be obtained in better quality elsewhere, and few merchants found it worthwhile dealing in such commodities when slaves were so much more profitable. The factors actually stationed at the coastal markets were a poor lot: their surroundings were inhospitable, their life expectancy low, their business beastly. Scientific curiosity, or even commercial enterprise, could hardly be expected from them.

The voracious demand for slaves could only be satisfied by raiding, and gave rise to fierce wars in the West African interior. The slave raiders who provided the slaves sold at the coast guarded their territory jealously against rivals, whether African or European, and to put it mildly, they discouraged trespassers on their preserves. The Europeans provided the means to enforce their own exclusion, being compelled to trade for slaves with people who would accept no other goods than guns: 'certainly', wrote Major Denham in Bornu, 'never were people so enamoured of gun-powder and smoke'.

The European slave traders were themselves anxious to exclude, as far as possible, any visitors to Africa with motives different from their own. Many of them had found their business a very unpleasant one when they had first embarked upon it, and although familiarity hardened their hearts and stilled their consciences, they were not unaware that opposition to slaving was growing in their home countries, and feared deleterious effects on their livelihood from the exposure of their activities. The Portuguese government permitted missionaries in its territories, but they were Portuguese missionaries and, although some individuals might

Below: British ambassadors received at the court of Ashanti, the warlike kingdom that expanded, partly on proceeds from the slave trade, in the 18th century. The Ashanti conquest of the Fante on the coast was acknowledged in the British treaty of 1807, and confirmed by Joseph Dupuis as consul in 1820. The latter treaty was disowned by the British government and the first of the Ashanti wars broke out as a result. From Dupuis Journal of a Residence in Ashantee, *1824.*

Bottom: Stowage plan of the Liverpool slaver Brooks. *An ocean crossing in a wooden sailing ship could be a rough experience for anyone; for slaves chained and packed between decks, no more horrible treatment could be imagined. A ship's surgeon wrote of the sick lying on bare planks under the half-deck: 'those who are emaciated frequently have their skin, and even their flesh, entirely rubbed off, by the motion of the ship . . . so as to render the bones . . . quite bare. And some of them, by constantly lying in the blood and mucus . . . have their flesh much sooner rubbed off, than those who have only to contend with the mere friction of the ship' (A. Falconbridge* An Account of the Slave Trade, *1788, quoted by R. Rotberg,* Tropical Africa*).*

Below: Europe's most valued gift: Africans at a British post in West Africa test the efficiency of their newly acquired weapons.

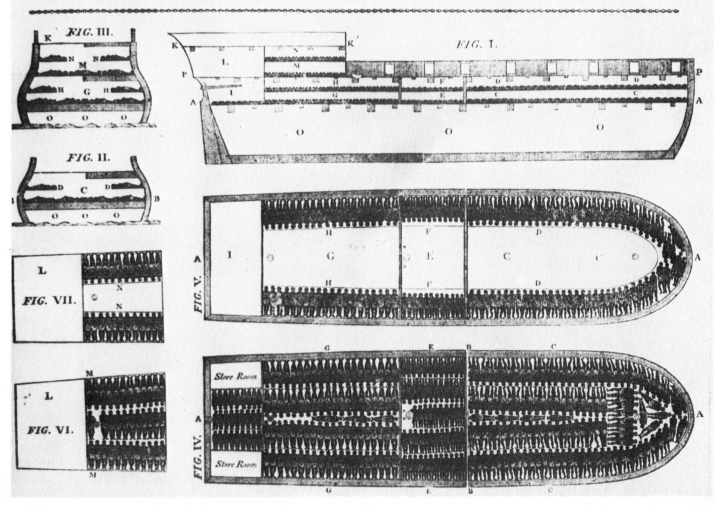

DESCRIPTION OF A SLAVE SHIP.

occasionally protest at the horrors they witnessed, they were ultimately under Portuguese control. When the Pope proposed sending out non-Portuguese missionaries, the government's attitude became thoroughly hostile.

As long as the slave trade prospered, virtually all other contacts with Africa were occluded. But while the trade continued to flourish, indeed expand, in the 18th century, by about 1750 the balance of public opinion was turning against it. The 'West India interest', which formed such a powerful lobby in Britain, was declining in influence. The decision to keep Canada rather than the French sugar islands (Guadeloupe and Martinique) at the Peace of Paris in 1763 was a sign of this decline, and the growth of industry made the traditional Atlantic trade less vital.

Considerations of world strategy, which had resulted in the retention of Canada rather than the West Indian islands, also affected West Africa. Until the Seven Years War, European governments had shown little interest in the region, and the slave traders had run their affairs without much interference from government. Yet the strategic importance of West Africa, on one of the main shipping routes, was obvious, and Senegambia became a pawn in the Anglo-French contest for world trade. (The first British colony in Africa was founded in Senegambia after the Peace of Paris, though it was a frail creation and lasted only twenty years.)

More important than these strictly commercial and political developments, however, was the rising tide of opinion, especially in Britain (the chief slave-trading nation), against slavery.

Of course, opponents of slavery and the slave trade had always existed, but they were to be found chiefly among a small intellectual class. More practical men might dislike the whole business, but regarded it as a regrettable necessity. Most people did not much care, and anyway regarded Africans and other dark-skinned people as barely human, more closely related to apes than to themselves.

In the 18th century, this attitude was changing. Rousseau, fathering the cult of the 'noble savage', suggested that the life of 'primitive' man in the wilderness might be superior to the life of 'civilized', decadent Europe. This Romantic idea had a considerable effect, but more important was the strong growth of humane concern in British middle-class society, a growing awareness of the plight of people in less fortunate circumstances, which in the case of the slave trade was to generate a moral passion of great force.

It was partly religious: the most determined opponents of slavery were to be found in the Wesleyan movement and the smaller but more influential evangelical group within the Church of England. Opposition was also found in intellectual, secular – even anti-clerical – circles. Wilberforce once wryly lamented that his strongest allies were Dissenters and free-thinkers.

Wilberforce is the most famous name among the British abolitionists. A man of great ability and personal charm, he led the campaign in parliament (it is often said that he would have been Prime Minister had he not devoted himself exclusively to the cause), and so attracted most public attention. An equally important figure was Thomas Clarkson, who collected (sometimes at risk to his life) the evidence on which Wilberforce built his case against the merchants of slavery.

The Abolitionists conducted their campaign skilfully and relentlessly against powerful and well-organized opposition. Wilberforce chose to sit for the county of Yorkshire rather than some safe borough, and he was returned to parliament time and again by the anti-slavery vote of the Yorkshire middle classes (things might have been different on the other side of the country: there were no big slaving ports in Yorkshire). 'The hold of Wilberforce and the antislavery movement on the solid middle class in town and country was a thing,' wrote G.M. Trevelyan, getting a bit carried away by patriotic Liberalism, 'entirely beautiful, English of the best, and something new in the world.' Petitions poured into parliament from towns up and down the kingdom (over five hundred in 1792), demanding an end of the slave trade.

In a test case in 1772, the institution of slavery had been declared illegal in England, and six years later a similar judgment was passed in Scotland, but the main fight – to put an end to the trade in slaves and end slavery in the colonies – had hardly begun. Not until 1807 was the slave trade declared illegal, and slavery was only abolished in the British empire in 1833.

Although Britain led the way in opposition to the slave trade, and after abolishing it put very heavy pressure on other countries to do the same, the people of other European countries were not, of course, sitting in smug idleness. Denmark abolished the trade three years earlier than Britain, though the significance of the act was slight in view of Denmark's limited activities in the trade. The French Revolution delivered a boost to abolition (Clarkson was greeted as a popular hero in Paris in 1789), though the ensuing reaction made the task of reformers more difficult. Intellectuals also contributed, notably the German scholar Johann Friedrich Blumenbach (1752–1840), who is regarded as the founder of the science of anthropology. Blumenbach attacked the common belief that African man, and other non-Caucasian peoples, belonged to a different species. 'I am acquainted with no single distinctive bodily character which is at once peculiar to the Negro,' he wrote, 'and which cannot be found to exist in any other nation.' Stating a fact does not make people believe it; indeed, some people cannot accept Blumenbach's conclusions even now. Still, Blumenbach and his disciples struck a good blow against the malign belief that black men were, at best, a kind of sub-species. Blumenbach was particularly interested in Africa and an admirer of the 'capacity for scientific culture [shown by] the Negro'.

Others, perhaps less learned but equally enlightened, were soon writing in a similar vein. The history of European-African relations in the century following perhaps suggests that their influence was not great, but the influence of ideas is hard to judge. Many closed minds were opened by Blumenbach and his successors.

Before the middle of the 19th century, the slave trade had been declared illegal in the northern hemisphere by all the European and North American slave-trading nations. That did not stop the trade, because as long as the institution of slavery existed, smugglers were ready to dodge the British gunboats for the sake of large profits, sometimes with the connivance of other governments. Nevertheless, the abolition of the trade opened the way for communications of a more amiable kind, while efforts to destroy slavery and slave-trading altogether, by Protestant missionaries especially, led to many of the greatest exploring expeditions of the 19th century, including the journeys of David Livingstone.

The Blue Nile

Of all the internal states and kingdoms of 16th-century Africa, Ethiopia was probably the best-known to Europe.

In the 16th century Ethiopia had entered into a sporadic relationship with Europe, or at least with Portugal. The movement of men between Ethiopia and Europe was small but almost continuous. A tiny Ethiopian monastery was founded in the Vatican; there had been a moment when Ethiopia had rejected its monophysite traditions and embraced the doctrines of Rome. This was a remarkable achievement by the Jesuit missionaries, but events proved they had overplayed their hand. A fierce reaction set in; the Jesuits were expelled in 1632, and the Ethiopians retired into their mountain fastness, more suspicious of foreigners than ever before.

In the one hundred and fifty years following, their isolation was not quite complete. The French doctor, Charles Jacques Poncet, was summoned to Gondar in 1699 to treat the king, and there were one or two other visitors of whom little is known. But with these few exceptions, Ethiopia was cut off from European contact as effectively as it was before the arrival of the Portuguese.

During this period of isolation, important advances were made in the study of Ethiopia. The man chiefly responsible was an immensely able scholar, Job (Hiob) Ludolf (1624–1704), who has been called the 'founder of Ethiopian studies in Europe'. Although he never visited the country, Ludolf formed a close working relationship with an Ethiopian monk resident in Rome, himself clearly a highly intelligent man. From this fruitful partnership emerged grammars and dictionaries of Amharic and Ge'ez (the classical Ethiopian language) as well as a lengthy history of the country in Latin.

After Poncet's visit, no European published any significant account of Ethiopia for many years. The centenary of that visit was not far off when there appeared, with a defiant flourish, the five hefty quarto volumes of James Bruce's *Travels to Discover the Source of the Nile*.

Bruce's contemporaries regarded him as a fantastic figure, and an air of fantasy clings to him still. Sheer size has something to do with it. It was entirely characteristic of Bruce that his account of his travels should be so vast a work. He was vast himself: six feet four inches in height and powerfully built – the 'Man Mountain', Fanny Burney called him. His description of Ethiopia was too much for many people to swallow – a blend of romance, grandeur, bestiality, and violence, devious intrigues and bold ploys – a weird combination of Machiavelli and Tolkien.

The youth of James Bruce, if not unhappy, was not particularly promising. He made a number of false starts in life. Born in 1730, eldest son of the laird of Kinnaird in the county of Stirling, he lost his mother when he was a child, and was sent to Harrow School in England, partly to get him away from troubled Scotland after the '45 and partly because he did not fit well into the rapidly growing family of his father's second wife. His first ambition, surprisingly, was to be an Anglican priest, but this was discarded in favour of law, which he studied at Edinburgh University. Law did not suit him either – he wrote Italian verses in his law books – and he was troubled by ill health, perhaps through out-growing his strength.

The professions discarded, there was nothing for it but commerce, and he went to London in hope of gaining a licence to trade from the East India Company. Instead, he married the daughter of a wine merchant and entered the family firm.

The girl was a consumptive, and after nine months of marriage she died in Paris, as the couple were on the way to a healthier climate in the South of France. Bruce was distraught. He was pestered by Catholic priests, which turned his solid Protestant prejudices into the fierce loathing of Papists apparent in his account of the Portuguese Jesuits in Ethiopia, and he had difficulty in getting his wife buried in consecrated ground. After the funeral, he rode like a madman from Paris to Boulogne overnight, with the elements thundering a symphony of despair and the torrential rain soaking his coatless form.

While continuing his father-in-law's wine business, Bruce exercised his lively talents by travelling around Europe, learning languages and studying art. He visited Portugal soon after the Lisbon earthquake and formed a poor opinion of the Portuguese. He was impressed by Moorish culture in Spain and tried, without success, to get permission to study Arabic documents in the Escorial. He visited the vineyards in France, collected Arabic books and the works of Ludolf in the Netherlands, and witnessed the battle of Krefeld in Germany. The death of his father brought him back to Kinnaird, but by this time he was convinced of the need to fulfil his ambitions in some more adventurous style of life than that of wine merchant or Scottish laird. He had contacts in Whitehall, and Pitt showed some interest in the plan he had evolved to attack the Spanish port of Ferrol.

Bruce intended to lead this expedition himself, but nothing came of it. Instead, he was offered the position of British consul in Algiers. The post would hardly require full-time attendance, and he would be able to further his Arabic studies in North Africa.

According to Bruce, the possibility of a journey to discover the source of the Nile was hinted at, as well as future rewards (never forthcoming) in the way of rank and a state pension.

In March, 1763, Bruce arrived at Algiers to take up his official position. As things turned out, it was no sinecure. The Dey of Algiers was hostile and unpredictable and Bruce, in his own opinion, received insufficient support from London. His French colleague was arrested and put to work in the stone quarries, and Bruce himself was attacked in the street. His calls for British warships was, perhaps not surprisingly, ignored, and he offered to resign. His resignation was accepted, leaving him free to pursue his antiquarian interests in North Africa.

On his travels among the archaeological sites, Bruce was accompanied by an Italian named Luigi Balugani. This young man was an artist, talented enough for the Bologna academy to have bent its rules in order to admit him below the minimum age. His function was to assist Bruce in recording the architecture they inspected. He remained with him for the next seven years, accompanied him on his many dangerous journeys, was with him when he reached the source of the Blue Nile, and died at Gondar soon afterwards. In his enormous and detailed account of his travels, Bruce never mentions Balugani's name.

It is the chief accusation against him, and it is a weighty one. Bruce does refer to Balugani indirectly on several occasions, and he says that Balugani died *before* he reached the source of the Nile, although it is certain from Bruce's own correspondence that he died *after* that notable occasion. This discrepancy,

James Bruce, from the portrait by Pompeo Batoni, 1762. Scottish National Portrait Gallery, Edinburgh.

together with Bruce's general neglect of Balugani, gave rise to suspicions about the manner of the Italian's death, but there is neither reason nor evidence to accuse Bruce of foul play. The explanation is probably a simple matter of explorer's jealousy, one of the most powerful emotions in human nature and highly developed in James Bruce. To discover the source of the Nile was always the spur for Bruce. His achievement had to be unique. A sophisticated European companion (one who might wish to write his own account of the event) would have diluted Bruce's triumph. Thus he wrote Balugani out of his description of the source of the Blue Nile by advancing the date of his death.

Paradoxically, the discovery of the river's source was one of the least important of Bruce's successes. In the first place, and in spite of Bruce's lengthy and fervent refutation, it had been discovered before, by the Spanish-born missionary Pero Paez early in the 17th century, and probably by several Portuguese also, including Manuel d'Almeida, a copy of whose map is in the British Museum. In the second place, the reason for regarding the source of the Little Abbai as the source also of the Abbai (Blue Nile) is slight: the former is merely one of several streams feeding Lake Tana, from which the Blue Nile flows. In the third place, the Blue Nile is not the true Nile but

a tributary. The parent river is the much larger White Nile, to which Bruce resolutely refused to attach the name 'Nile' at all (it is, however, the Blue Nile that causes the life-giving annual flood).

Such questions, so important to the explorer himself as to obliterate reason and common humanity from his arguments, do not matter very much to posterity. Amundsen beat Scott to the South Pole, but Scott's journey is the one most people remember. And it was Bruce who brought Ethiopia and the Blue Nile to the attention of Europe.

After various adventures, during which he twice escaped death by the barest margin (once from robbers, once from shipwreck), Bruce arrived at Alexandria in June, 1768. His great journey was about to begin.

* * *

The early stages were easy. From Cairo Bruce sailed up the Nile as far as Aswan, inspecting ruins on the way, then backtracked to Kena, where he joined a caravan to the Red Sea and embarked on a little boat captained by one Sidi Ali, 'the Ape'. His voyage down the east coat of the Red Sea was leisurely, or at least slow (conditions were not always comfortable), and he took every opportunity of collecting letters from influential persons which might raise his status in future encounters. This was his invariable practice, and a very wise one, as many later explorers would have testified (Gerhard Rohlfs was another inveterate collector of written references). It undoubtedly saved him from robbery and perhaps death on more than one occasion.

It took five days just to cross the Red Sea to Massawa, the ancient gateway to Ethiopia, where Bruce landed on 19 September 1769. The ruler here was a Muslim, the Naib, an unfriendly person 'of a most stupid, brutal appearance', who pretty obviously wished to murder Bruce and plunder his baggage. He was restrained by the traveller's influential contacts, especially Ras Michael, the effective ruler of Ethiopia, who was aware of Bruce's approach. Nevertheless, two months passed before Bruce, with the aid of the Naib's nephew and heir, managed to extricate himself from Massawa.

A hard journey with some steep climbing brought them to the ancient capital of Axum in January, 1770. It was shortly after leaving that city that an incident occurred which Bruce's contemporaries were to find hard to believe. The explorer's party encountered three men driving a cow, and Bruce's Ethiopian attendants engaged the three in conversation with the aim of buying the beast. The men explained that the cow was not wholly theirs, so they would not part with it; but they were willing to sell part of it. They 'tript up the cow, and gave the poor animal a very rude fall upon the ground, which was but the beginning of her sufferings. One of them

*Three Capuchin missionaries executed at Suakin on the Red Sea in
1648, by order of the king of Ethiopia.*

*D'Almeida's map of Ethiopia, about 1636, showing the Nile springing
from the 'fountains', flowing peacefully through Lake Tana and,
south-east of the lake, embarking upon the great curve that carries
it almost in a circle before it settles into its northerly direction,
towards what is now Khartoum.*

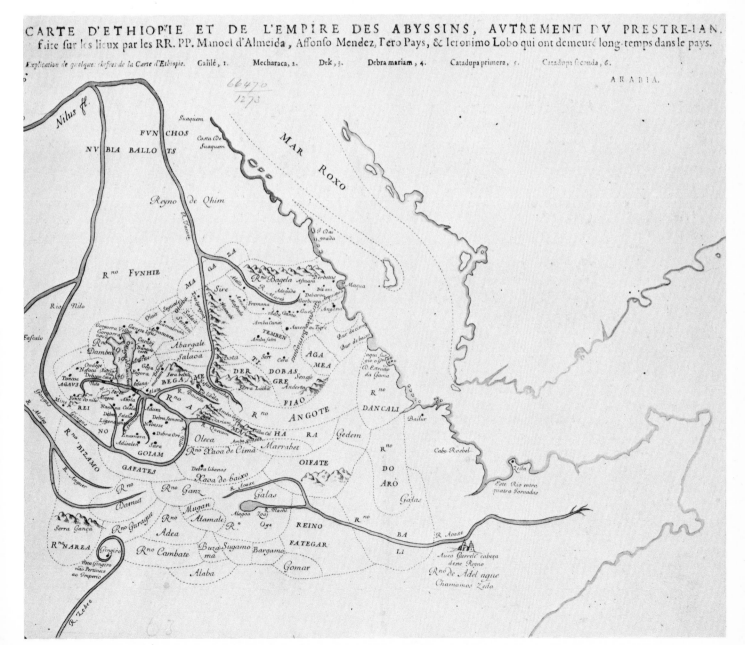

CARTE D'ETHIOPIE ET DE L'EMPIRE DES ABYSSINS, AVTREMENT DV PRESTRE-IAN.
faite sur les lieux par les RR. PP. Manoel d'Almeida, Affonso Mendez, Tero Pays, & Ieronimo Lobo qui ont demeuré long-temps dans le pays.

Explication de quelque chifres de la Carte d'Ethiopie. Galilé , 1. Mecharaca , 2. Dek , 3. Debra mariam , 4. Catadupa primera , 5. Catadupa seconda , 6.

Butchering a cow. From an Ethiopic manuscript of the 18th century.

sat across her neck, holding down her head by the horns, the other twisted the halter about her forefeet, while the third, who had a knife in his hand . . . got astride upon her belly before her hindlegs and gave her a very deep wound in the upper part of her buttock. . . . I saw, with the utmost astonishment, two pieces, thicker, and longer than our ordinary beafsteaks, cut out of the higher portion of the buttock of the beast. . . . One of them still continued holding her head, while the other two were busy curing the wound. This too was not done in an ordinary manner; the skin which had covered the flesh that was taken away was left entire, and flapped over the wound, and was fastened to the corresponding part by two or more small skewers, or pins. Whether they had put anything under the skin, between that and the wounded flesh, I know not; but at the river side where they were, they had prepared a cataplasm of clay, with which they covered the wound; they then forced the animal to rise, and drove it on before them, to furnish them with a fuller meal when they should meet their companions in the evening'.

Bruce goes on to say that when he first told this story of how to have one's steak and eat it, he had been disbelieved, and his friends had accordingly advised him to leave it out of

The Princess Esther. You could not see her for a few moments, said Bruce, 'without being attached to her for ever'. From Travels to Discover the Source of the Nile, *1790.*

his book, just as Thomas Shaw, an 18th-century traveller in Algeria, had been persuaded to omit his account of eating lion meat (though why that should have been thought so incredible it is hard to imagine). But, says Bruce, 'To represent as truth a thing I know to be a falsehood, not to avow a truth I ought to declare; the one is fraud, the other cowardice; I hope I am equally distant from them both.'

People believed stranger things in the 18th century, yet this incident, together with his account of a feast in Gondar where the meat was served cut straight from the living animal, aroused the sharpest mockery and shook the credibility of Bruce's whole colourful account of the violent kingdom of Ethiopia.

When Bruce arrived in Ethiopia, the country was spiralling dizzily into a period of anarchy that was to last nearly one hundred years. Ras Michael, the *de facto* ruler and governor of the powerful north-eastern province of Tigre, through which Bruce had passed, had been plotting to murder the Emperor while Bruce was at Massawa. Nor was he a novice at regicide, having killed the previous Emperor a short time earlier. Yet he apparently enjoyed the full confidence of the new and youthful Emperor, Takla Haymanot, in spite of the fact that the Ras's most recent victim had been the young man's father.

Though violent and cruel, the seventy-year-old Ras Michael was an able and, in Bruce's account, a not unattractive man – intelligent and on occasion humorous. When he read one of Bruce's introductory letters, which asked him to ensure the traveller's safety, he exclaimed, 'Safety! Where is that to be found? I am obliged to fight for my own life every day.'

Bruce was also favourably impressed by the young Emperor. According to his own account, what placed him firmly in the Emperor's favour was his boast, successfully fulfilled, that he could shoot a candle-end through a solid wooden door. The Ethiopians had firearms, but nothing as effective as Bruce's guns, and the traveller's proficiency in the martial arts – he was also a good horseman – astonished them.

With his usual carefully judged mixture of tactful courtesy and confident self-assertion (in Britain, it was the latter quality that predominated) Bruce made himself welcome to the two chief men in the kingdom and was honoured with a court appointment. Bruce, however, was a ladies' man: he was fond of women and justifiably proud of his ability to win their favour. In Africa, he says, he found that all his acquaintance with the fairer sex was to his advantage.

The most important women in Gondar were the Iteghe – the Empress Dowager – and the Princess Esther, her daughter, who was also the wife of Ras Michael (the relationships of the Ethiopian ruling family, it must be said, were as complex and unstable as Ethiopian politics, the two being, indeed, inseparable). The Empress Mentwab, an elderly but fine-looking lady whose political ambitions were far from dead, was, says Bruce, 'whiter than most Portuguese'. In fact she had Portuguese blood (so, naturally, did her daughter, who was also light-skinned). She was the first member of the royal family, apart from humbler relatives, whom Bruce had met, and she greeted him kindly, although puzzled at his presence in Ethiopia when he might have as easily gone to Jerusalem, which she so longed to visit. She welcomed Bruce's medical knowledge, which he had picked up from a doctor who had treated him during a long illness in Syria (Bruce absorbed knowledge like a sponge: his command of languages is not the least impressive aspect of his qualifications as an explorer).

But the person to whom Bruce felt closest in the royal court at Gondar was the beautiful Princess Esther. To know her, says Bruce in almost as few words, was to love her; but as his most recent biographer, the late J.M. Reid, said, his feelings for Esther were, in a sense, his feelings for Ethiopia. She was royal (Bruce admired royalty and himself claimed royal descent), she was splendid, she was beautiful, she was sometimes humorous and affectionate; she was also savagely cruel. For Bruce, writing nearly twenty years after he had first met her, she had become the personification of Ethiopia.

Bruce was soon established at Gondar, he says, as a favoured official, commander of a troop of Negro cavalry (which he came to consider the equal of any comparable force in Europe), and the valued adviser and friend of the Emperor and the Ras. Of course, he had opponents too, particularly the priests, who viewed him with deep suspicion and ascribed his accomplishments with horse and gun to magic. In spite of his emphatic insistence that he was not a 'Frank' (i.e. a Roman Catholic) and his care to avoid theological controversy, he never overcame this opposition.

The region that Ras Michael controlled was much smaller than the present area of Ethiopia, corresponding, very roughly, to the northern third of the modern state. South of Lake Tana, various provincial governors possessed effective autonomy, usually acknowledging the Emperor but not necessarily obeying him. The most powerful, Fasil, commanded a large area in the bend of the Blue Nile. Here lived the numerous Galla, a people regarded at Gondar as a savage, inferior race, who supported Fasil's resistance to the rule of Michael. (As recently as 1930, according to Evelyn Waugh, trains to Addis Ababa travelled only in daylight, so that the driver could see whether the Galla had ripped up the rails to make spear-heads).

In Gondar, Bruce was not much more than one hundred miles from his objective – the source of the Little Abbai. But the obstacles to be overcome in traversing that short distance seemed insurmountable. They were not so much physical, though the country was hilly and covered with dense bush, as political. The journey could not be accomplished through hostile territory, it seemed, unless with a guard the size of an army. However, after several weeks of bacchanalian feasting in Gondar, Ras Michael decided to march south in order to attack Fasil. The march would take the army near to the places that interested Bruce and, although he was not eager to witness at first hand the savageries of Ethiopian warfare (one custom was for the victors to cut off the testicles of their enemies and carry them off as trophies), he decided to follow the army to the south. Some of his friends advised against it. The Empress Mentwab still could not understand why he had forsaken Jerusalem to travel through 'vile Turkish governments, and hot unwholesome climates, to see a river and a bog, no part of which you can carry away were it ever so valuable'.

In the wake of Ras Michael's destroying army, Bruce travelled south, passing east of Lake Tana, with a few servants including a Greek called Strates, whose function seems to have been that of the clownish squire – the Sancho Panza to Bruce's Don Quixote (Bruce himself made this allusion). He was, says Bruce, 'an avowed enemy to all learned inquiries, or botanical researches'. Strates was sent on ahead, but re-

appeared some time later wearing nothing but a cotton nightcap and 'prancing and capering about in great passion', having had an unfortunate encounter with robbers.

Untoward military developments made it impossible for Bruce to reach the source of the Nile, but he did manage to make a trip to see the great waterfall some fifteen miles from the river's outlet in Lake Tana. 'The river had been considerably increased by rains, and fell in one sheet of water, without any interval, above half an English mile in breadth, with a force and noise that was truly terrible, and which stunned and made me, for a time, perfectly dizzy. A thick fume, or haze, covered the fall all round, and hung over the course of the stream both above and below, marking its track, though the water was not seen.'

The Tissisat (Alata) Falls, second only to Victoria Falls among Africa's great cataracts (though far less famous), had been seen by earlier travellers. The Portuguese Father Lobo had written a detailed description of them, with which Bruce took angry dispute. According to Bruce, Lobo had exaggerated the height of the falls, though in fact he had underestimated them. Lobo's story of how he had stood on a rock behind the falling water aroused Bruce's most scornful denunciations ('the lies of a grovelling fanatic priest'), but Colonel R.E. Cheesman, who visited the falls at low water in 1927, found that he could repeat Lobo's experience without too much difficulty.

After his brief visit to the falls, Bruce rejoined the disorganized army of Ras Michael and the Emperor. Fasil had not been defeated, but sent a herald to announce that he proposed to retire to the south. With the rains approaching, Michael was equally anxious to withdraw northward, and a compromise was reached in which Fasil, to Bruce's astonishment, was confirmed in all his offices. The campaign had not been a success for the Ras. At dinner, a black eagle flew into the tent, pursued by smaller birds; this was regarded as a bad omen.

While the Ras and the Emperor retired to Michael's province of Tigre, the source of his strength, Bruce remained at Gondar. He had secured from the Emperor the gift of the village of Gish and its environs, which included the source of the Nile, and the grant had been recognized by Fasil's ambassadors. But the constantly shifting political situation still threatened Bruce's plans. With Gondar virtually defenceless, two rebel chiefs who had gone over to Fasil during the recent campaign persuaded the Empress Dowager, no friend of Michael, to recognise a new emperor, Susenyos, an unattractive character whose royal descent was open to doubt. At the same time a captured Galla revealed details of the plot that had resulted in the death of the Emperor Joas in 1769, implicating an uncomfortably large number of people in ruling circles. Meanwhile, Michael sent news secretly that he would soon return with a larger army. It seemed to Bruce that events were drawing to a head: a greater conflict was imminent, and if he were ever to reach the source of the Nile, this might be his last chance. In October, 1770, he set out.

The first necessity was to gain the protection of Fasil, who was encamped with his Galla army not far away. Fasil received him ungraciously, and pretended to be astonished by Bruce's plan. 'The source of the Abai! Are you raving?' After some argument, Bruce finally lost his temper. '"Sir", said I, "I have passed through many of the most barbarous nations in the world; all of them, excepting this clan of yours,

61

James Bruce drinking the health of King George at the – romantically neat and tidy – source of the Blue Nile. Engraved by Gillray from the romantic painting by R.M. Paye, published in 1793.

The waters of Lake Tana.

have some great men among them, above using a defenceless stranger ill. But the worst and lowest individual among the most uncivilized people, never treated me as you have done today, under your own roof, where I have come so far for protection.'' He asked, "How?" "You have in the first place," said I, "publicly called me Frank, the most odious name in this country, and sufficient to occasion me to be stoned to death without further ceremony, by any set of men, wherever I may present myself. By Frank, you mean one of the Romish religion, to which my nation is as adverse as yours; and again, without having ever seen any of my countrymen but myself, you have discovered, from that specimen, that we are all cowards and effeminate people, like, or inferior to, your boys and women. Look you, Sir, you never heard that I gave myself out as more than an ordinary man in my own country, far less to be a pattern of what is excellent in it. I am no soldier, though I know enough of war, to see yours are poor proficients in that trade. But there are soldiers, friends and countrymen of mine . . . who would not think it an action of his life to vaunt of, that with five hundred men he had trampled all yon naked savages into dust . . . As to myself,'' continued I, "unskilled in war as I am, could it be now without further consequence, let me but be armed in my own country's fashion, on horseback . . . I should, without thinking myself overmatched, fight the two best horsemen you shall choose from this your army of famous men, who are warriors from their cradle . . .''

Whatever the effect on Fasil of this veritably Shakespearian speech ('passionate and rash' the orator admits), it had a dramatic effect on Bruce himself, for his passion burst a blood vessel in his nose, and he had to be hurried out of the tent with blood streaming on to his clothes. Later that night, however, Fasil sent servants to guard him from robbery and to tell him that he should be prepared to make an early start in the morning, in order to get well away before the un-governable Galla were released from camp. In spite of a dangerous practical joke by Fasil's groom, who recom-mended to him a horse that was 'too dull and quiet' for its master but turned out to be wild and unbroken, Bruce parted from Fasil on good terms and with a necessary escort of Galla warriors.

Under the guardianship of these colourful characters (one of them was called 'the Lamb' because of his absurdly charitable disinclination to massacre pregnant women during Galla raids), Bruce finally arrived at Gish. From a little church on a hillside, his guide pointed towards the valley. 'Look at that hillock of green and in the middle of that watery spot; it is in that the two fountains of the Nile are to be found.' Bruce threw off his shoes (this was holy ground) and with clothes flapping he pounded down the hill, twice tripping and falling headlong, until he came to an 'island of green turf, which was in form of an altar, apparently the work of art, and I stood in rapture over the principal fountain which rises in the middle of it.

'It is easier to guess than to describe the situation of my mind at that moment – standing in that spot which had baffled the genius, industry, and inquiry, of both ancients and moderns, for the course of near three thousand years. Kings had attempted this discovery . . . Fame, riches, and honour, had been held out for a series of ages to every individual of those myriads these princes commanded . . .' And so on. Bruce inserts a long paragraph of bombast that he deems

Warfare in Ethiopia. From a manuscript of the 18th century.

suitable to the occasion, but then, more interestingly, goes on to confess that upon the fulfilment of the task he had set himself, he was suddenly swept by a wave of depression, from which he took refuge in farcical fooling with his 'Sancho Panza', the Greek Strates. The details of these antics were certainly invented, but the manic mood may have been authentic.

At the fountains was an old, white-bearded man, who, Bruce was told, was the high priest of the Nile. He seems a rather romanticized figure, in spite of his eighty-five children (among them an attractive sixteen-year-old girl upon whom Bruce cast an approving eye). Bruce was in no hurry to get back to Gondar, in spite of a relayed request for medical attention from Princess Esther (who, as Bruce realized, was neurotic), but lingered over his botanical specimens, feeling intensely gloomy at the prospect of making his way out of the country without a compelling motive, like that which had

'A learned Abyssinian', drawn by Henry Salt. The Abyssinian, when a young man, had known Bruce in Gondar and told Salt that Bruce's status at the Ethiopian court was less exalted than the traveller himself had implied.

DOFTER ESTHER.

lured him in, to give him energy. At Gondar, nothing but bloody turmoil could be expected.

When Bruce arrived at the capital his worst fears were soon realized. The drunken puppet emperor sanctioned by the Empress still reigned. He plundered Bruce's house in one of his rampages. But Ras Michael was returning with Takla Haymanot and their army. The pretender and the Empress fled. Fasil also diplomatically retired to the south.

Michael arrived, bringing torture and death to those whose loyalty had wavered. There was no need for Bruce to feed his hunting dogs; they foraged among the corpses strewn about Gondar. 'Blood continued to be spilt as water, day after day . . . Priests, laymen, young men and old, noble and vile, daily found their end by the knife or the cord.' The young Emperor, hardened since Bruce had parted from him, could not understand why his Lord of the Bedchamber should be upset by the carnage. He knew Bruce was a brave man, yet he was 'as much disturbed by these things as the most cowardly woman or child'. At the court of Gondar, any display of pity or common humanity tended to be interpreted as a sign of weakness.

In these miserable circumstances, the arrival at Gondar of Guangoul, a minor chief of the Galla, provided light relief. Although many of his contemporaries found Bruce pompous – perhaps a symptom of shyness – he had a strong if erratic sense of humour. So did many of his Ethiopian friends; but his account of Guangoul's arrival at Gondar perhaps owes as much to Bruce's instinctive urge to spin a good yarn as to plain facts.

Guangoul, accompanied by five hundred men, came to pay his respects to the Emperor and Ras Michael. 'He was a little, thin, cross-made man . . . his legs and thighs being thin and

James Bruce's progress through Ethiopia, from the time of his arrival in Massawa in September 1769 to his departure for Cairo in December 1771.

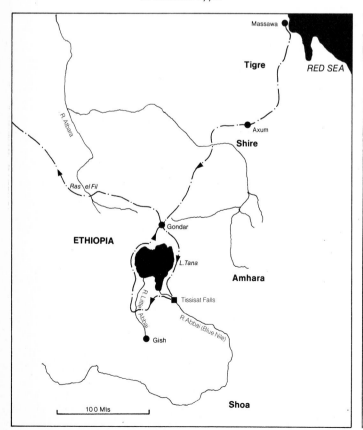

small for his body, and his head large; he was of a yellow, unwholesome colour, not black nor brown; he had long hair plaited and interwoven with the bowels of oxen, and so knotted and twisted together as to render it impossible to distinguish the hair from the bowels, which hung down in long strings, part before his breast and part behind his shoulder, the most extraordinary ringlets I have ever seen. He had likewise a wreath of guts hung about his neck, and several rounds of the same about his middle, which served as a girdle, below which was a short cotton cloth dipped in butter, and all his body was wet, and running down with the same; he seemed to be about fifty years of age, with a confident and insolent superiority painted on his face . . . He was then in full dress and ceremony, and mounted upon [a cow], not of the largest sort, but which had monstrous horns. He had no saddle on his cow. He had short drawers, that did not reach the middle of his thighs; his knees, feet, legs, and all his body were bare . . . Whether it was necessary for the poising himself upon the sharp ridge of the beast's back, or whether it was meant as graceful riding, I do not know, being quite unskilled in cowmanship; but he leaned exceedingly backwards pushing his belly forwards, and holding his left arm and shield stretched out on one side of him, and his right arm and lance in the same way on the other, like wings.

'. . . An insufferable stench of carrion soon made everyone in the tent sensible of the approach of this nasty sovereign, even before they saw him. The king, when he perceived him coming . . . could not contain himself from an immoderate fit of laughter, which finding it impossible to stifle, he rose from his chair, and ran as hard as he could into another apartment behind the throne.

'The savage got off from his cow at the door of the tent with all his tripes about him; and while we were admiring him as a monster, seeing the king's seat empty, he took it for his own, and down he sat upon the crimson silk cushion [a crime punishable by death], with the butter running from every part of him. A general cry of astonishment was made by every person in the tent: he started up I believe without divining the cause, and . . . they all fell upon him, and with pushes and blows drove this greasy chieftain to the door of the tent, staring with wild amazement . . . Poor Guangoul owed his life to his ignorance . . . The king . . . came out laughing, and unable to speak. The cushion was lifted and thrown away . . .'

When Princess Esther, who had not been present, heard about this remarkable scene, she insisted on a re-enactment. 'Doho, accordingly, a dwarf belonging to Ras Michael, very ugly, with a monstrous big head, but very sharp and clever, and capable of acting his part, was brought to represent the person of Guangoul: a burnt stick and a bad shield were provided; but the great difficulty remained, how to persuade Doho, the dwarf, to put on the raw guts about his neck and waist, and, above all, to plait them in the hair, which he absolutely refused . . . At last I suggested that several hanks of cotton, dyed blue, red, and yellow . . . oiled, greased, and knotted properly, and twisted among the hair, well-annointed with butter, would give a pretty accurate resemblance of what we saw in the king's tent . . . An old milk cow was found . . . and in came Guangoul into a great hall in [Princess] Esther's apartment.

'Never was anything better personated, or better received; the whole hall resounded with one cry of laughter; Doho,

64

encouraged by this . . . began to act his part with great humour and confidence: he was born in the neighbourhood of these very Galla, knew their manners, and spoke their language perfectly . . . The cow was brought into the middle of the room, and Guangoul descended with his lance and shield in great state; a cushion was not spared, nor did Doho spare the cushion; the butter showed very distinctly where he had been sitting: we all fell upon him and belaboured him heartily, and chased him to the door.'

Later the whole performance was repeated for the benefit of the Ras. Michael was told that Guangoul wished an audience. '"Poh!" says the Ras. "Guangoul is gone . . ." but he had no sooner done with speaking than in comes Doho upon his cow; neither man nor woman that had yet seen him ever laughed so heartily as the old Ras; he humoured the thing entirely; welcomed Doho in Galla language, and saw the whole farce, finished by his flight to the door, with the utmost good humour.'

But the days of this appalling, yet impressive, old warlord were numbered. During the next campaign, on which Bruce served in command of his cavalry troop, Michael was compelled to withdraw, and Gondar was surrounded by the rebels. The Ras was deposed, although the victorious rebels swore allegiance to the Emperor and behaved more generously to their opponents than Michael had done. Bruce as usual succeeded in staying friends with most of the people who mattered – no mean achievement. But he was increasingly anxious to get away.

He had decided to avoid another tense confrontation with the Naib of Massawa by taking the overland route back to Cairo. Like all Bruce's journeys, this path had been followed by Europeans before, but not often, especially in a south–north direction. He would have to pass through some unfriendly places and cross the Nubian desert to Aswan, where the Nile takes its great bend to the west. This, Bruce's last great journey, was to prove the most dangerous of all, and his account of it is one of the most exciting parts of his book.

He set out in the last week of 1771, making first for the small outlying province of Ras el Fil, of which he was the absentee governor. But on the way he stopped at the house of Princess Esther's son, a young man who had always been a good friend to Bruce. The magnetic Esther herself was there, together with several old friends, and the beautiful girl whom Esther had suggested Bruce should marry. For two weeks Bruce lingered, feasting, talking, and hunting game. Esther spoke half-seriously of going away with him to Jerusalem,

A rhinoceros, after a drawing by Bruce.

where she wished to end her days. It was a last, elegaic interlude. Soon, Esther was summoned to Gondar, while Bruce took the road to Ras el Fil. He never saw any of his Ethiopian friends again.

*   *   *

The most valuable aspect of Bruce's work is surely his report on Ethiopia – the brilliant, if distorted, spotlight that picked out in sharp detail a fascinating society of which Europe was almost utterly unaware. More vivid than any fiction, the events and characters of his story leaped from the page to astonish his readers so thoroughly that many of them concluded the whole work was invented and Bruce had never been to Ethiopia at all.

An explorer's impedimenta. Equipment carried by Bruce on his expedition to Ethiopia, including (foreground) dividers, lens, and compass. To the left of the telescope are a vessel made from a rhinoceros horn (very popular in the East because they were said to disintegrate in contact with poison) and Bruce's famous folding blunderbuss, which he was able to conceal under his robe, producing it, like a derringer from a gangster's sleeve, at a moment of crisis.

No one now would suggest that Bruce made it all up; but it is known that he exaggerated some events, that he made several mistakes that seem too serious to be the result of carelessness, and that he inflated his own role at the Ethiopian court.

Bruce did not begin work on his book until 1785, fourteen years after he had left Ethiopia. Much of it was dictated non-stop to a scribe (whom Bruce appears to have treated shabbily) in almost unbroken spells of twelve hours or more. As his most recent editor, Professor C.F. Beckingham, says, this method of composition was 'unlikely to promote accuracy, or even clarity'. Henry Salt, who travelled in Ethiopia in the first decade of the 19th century, was unable to find confirmation of many of Bruce's stories, but he seems to have made little allowance for the fact that the events about which he was enquiring had taken place nearly forty years earlier. And even Salt, though critical of Bruce, found him correct on basic matters. That he embroidered the story, invented details, and sometimes indulged in grooming his own vanity may easily be inferred from an unbiased reading of his book.

The way home lay through Muslim territory where central authority was in decline and local chiefs were likely to be hostile. At Teawa, a sinister sheikh held up Bruce and his party with a mixture of threats and promises. He believed (erroneously) that Bruce carried a large quantity of gold. Bruce and his party sat tight, weapons ready, and sent messages back to Ras el Fil and forward to Sennar, requesting help. When the Sheikh himself threatened Bruce with a sword, the hefty Scot turned the tables by whipping a blunderbuss from beneath his burnous. The arrival of a holy man from Sennar relieved the tension, and the Sheikh, whose only virtue was that he had sired, as Bruce observed, one particularly beautiful daughter, let his captives go. Bruce had promised a sign in the sky to demonstrate his importance in the world, and when the eclipse of the moon duly occurred, as, in that society, only Bruce could foretell, his prestige soared.

Sennar, once the capital of a large kingdom, now in decay, was inhabited by a 'horrible people', whose only employment seemed to be 'war and treason'. The King, in appearance not an impressive figure, put to Bruce the question that African explorers were so frequently asked: if he were such an important man, what was he doing wandering in the desert like an indigent, constantly in danger, when he might have been eating, drinking, and enjoying himself at home? The answer that Bruce came to rely on was that he was a dervish, a holy man, seeking the remission of his sins through renunciation of the world. The King remarked that, as Bruce said he had been travelling for twenty years, he must have been rather young when he committed these sins. No doubt they had all been with women? 'Part of them, I suppose . . .' replied the disconcerted traveller. The King also advised Bruce to rub himself down with elephant grease. A course of this treatment might have prevented his hair turning that unfortunate colour (Bruce's hair was red). The King's wives, to whom he was required to administer emetics ('I will spare my reader the recital of so nauseous a scene'), did not comment on the colour of his hair, but were repelled by the whiteness of his skin, a considerable area of which they insisted on inspecting. Bruce found the whole experience intensely disagreeable. The wives were not beautiful.

Bruce had arrived at Sennar at the end of April, 1772. He was unable to get away until the beginning of September, and then only by a ruse in which he was assisted by his one influential friend in the city, Ahmed, who held the curious official position (not unique in African societies) of official regicide-in-waiting – ready to perform his grisly duty if or when it should become necessary to get rid of the King.

A month later, Bruce and his party reached the junction of the Blue and the White Nile. The explorer gazed uneasily at the mighty stream from Central Africa, and passed on. At Shendi, he found a female ruler, a fact that he considered promising – and rightly. He flirted diplomatically ('Well, you are an odd man'), and his brief period here, waiting for a guide, was the most pleasant part of his rigorous journey.

Ahead of the little party, which included an elderly Egyptian sherif, a half-blind Greek, and several Africans, lay the three-week trek across the Nubian desert. Bruce makes the most of the dangers he encountered and the manner in which he overcame them, but this was not a trip to be lightly undertaken. Apart from the harsh physical conditions, above all the scarcity of water, they were in constant danger from marauding nomads. To save their camels, they walked most of the time, and Bruce's feet were soon in a terrible state. He had also picked up a guinea worm in the leg, which gave him increasing pain. This infection is usually caught in drinking water, and the parasite is extremely hard to remove. The traditional method, as related by William Dampier, is to pull out a small portion each day and wind it round a stick. As Bruce discovered, an attempt to extract it too quickly makes it break off.

After eighteen days, Bruce and his companions were in a desperate plight. They had to kill their camels, which refused to move farther, though this meant that they could at least drain the precious water from the animals' internal reservoirs. Bruce was forced to leave all his baggage, his drawings and notes, as well as his instruments, in a pile in the desert. But, two days later, they staggered into Aswan and saw the Nile again. After a few days rest, Bruce managed to borrow some fast camels to recover his abandoned possessions. They were still lying unharmed where he had left them.

Weary and far from well, Bruce sailed gently down the Nile. At Cairo there was one last occasion on which he was required to mount a display of bluff British bravado, in response to impertinent treatment by a group of the Bey's soldiers: 'Keep your distance, you insolent blackguard! Remember I am an Englishman: do not lay your hands on me. If the Bey calls me, he is master in his own country and I will go to him. But, hands off! Though I have not seen him these three years he knows what is due to his own character better than to allow a slave like you to lay his filthy hands on a stranger like me.' The interview with the Bey went well, and on his return Bruce found his escort properly respectful.

After ten years in Africa, Bruce showed a surprising lack of eagerness to return to Britain. He went first to France, where he always received much better treatment than in England, and luxuriated in the hospitality of the great naturalist, the Comte de Buffon. Then he went to Italy for treatment of his leg, and while there picked an absurd quarrel with a Roman *marchese*, who had married a Scottish girl once unofficially engaged to Bruce. It is a common mistake of explorers, as of all people who move away from home for a long time, to suppose that nothing changes during their absence. It was foolish of Bruce to think that this young woman would wait for him for over a decade, with no evidence for much of that time to prove he was still alive. Fortunately, the tactful behaviour of the *marchese* avoided an unpleasant incident, but rumours of this affair reached England and helped to encourage a view of Bruce as a somewhat ridiculous figure.

In London, where he arrived fifteen months after leaving Alexandria, Bruce was a sensation. He was not taken very seriously perhaps, but London society was not very serious, especially about travellers' tales, and he was not, at first, frankly disbelieved. But as Professor Beckingham says, 'Bruce was not at home in the world of Lady Sneerwell.' He tended to withdraw, to grow aloof, to become heavier and more serious or, worse, aggressive. People began to treat him as a bit of a joke. After a while he withdrew to Kinnaird to busy himself with domestic affairs, which largely consisted of arguments and lawsuits. He married a neighbour's daughter in 1776 and, in his grief after her death nine years later, he was persuaded, at last, to get to work on his book. It was published in 1790, and the arguments began again. However, the book was popular, and Bruce was working on the second edition in April, 1794, when he slipped and fell down some steps. Gallant as ever, he was escorting a lady to her carriage. He struck his head and died some hours later without regaining consciousness.

The Niger I

The foundation of The Association for Promoting the Discovery of the Interior Parts of Africa in London in 1788 introduced a new era in African exploration. It marked the beginning of the systematic exploration of the continent: the Association made plans, it identified specific geographical problems, and it organized scientifically conducted expeditions.

The African Association was created by the energy and foresight of Joseph Banks, supported by an informal group of prominent men (most of them titled) whose motives were altruistic. 'Of the objects of inquiry which engaged our attention the most', said the Association's prospectus, 'there are none, perhaps that so much excited continued curiosity, from childhood to age; none that the learned and unlearned so equally wish to investigate, as the nature and history of those parts of the world, which have not, to our knowledge, been hitherto explored. To this desire the voyages of the late Captain Cook have so far afforded gratification, that nothing worthy of research by Sea, the Poles themselves excepted, remains to be examined; but by Land, the objects of Discovery are still so vast, as to include at least a third of the habitable surface of the earth: for much of Asia, a still larger proportion of America, and almost the whole of Africa, are unvisited and unknown.

'. . . Notwithstanding the progress of discovery on the coasts and borders of that vast continent, the map of its Interior is still but a wide extended blank, on which the Geographer . . . has traced, with a hesitating hand, a few names of unexplored rivers and of uncertain nations.'

The original aims of the Association were thus primarily inquiry and exploration, although other motives, notably the battle against the slave trade, later became equally important. Commercial possibilities were not neglected; but the expeditions sent out under the auspices of the Association were more purely exploratory than most previous expeditions. Political motives were usually absent, commercial considerations secondary, missionary fervour suppressed. The breath of exploitation could barely be detected.

The African Association approached Africa from two directions: the north, usually from the neighbourhood of Tripoli, which is the starting point of the shortest trans-Saharan route; and the west, the traditional route following in the footsteps of the early explorers up the Senegal and the Gambia. The results of expeditions in both areas were, at first, disappointing.

Simon Lucas, the middle-aged Oriental interpreter at the Court of St James, was chosen chiefly because he could speak Arabic. In February 1789 he set out from Tripoli with an Arab caravan. After a pleasant night camping in the sub-urban garden of a Tripoli merchant, Lucas and his companions travelled eastward along the coast to Misurata, a journey of four days. There, reports of a revolt against the Pasha of Tripoli convinced him that it would be dangerous to go any farther, and he brought his expedition to a none-too-triumphant conclusion.

While Lucas was still preparing for his excursion along the Mediterranean, the African Association hired another hero, John Ledyard, an American with a rather chequered career as a world traveller, who had served in the marines on Cook's ship and been thrown out of Russia while attempting to walk to Canada. Henry Beaufoy, the enthusiastic secretary of the African Association, was impressed by Ledyard's willingness to rush off to Africa. Asked to name a date when he would be ready to set out, he replied, 'Tomorrow morning.' Carrying an Arabic dictionary, he departed breezily for Cairo. There he bustled about energetically if untactfully, but became ill and unfortunately overdosed himself with medicine. A regretful letter from the British consul informed Ledyard's employers of his demise.

The scarcity of potential explorers who could speak Arabic drove the Association to hire a Moroccan Berber, who accepted an advance in order to equip himself and then disappeared; but a more likely candidate soon turned up in the person of Daniel Houghton, an Irish major who had spent several years on the West African coast, where he had picked up a smattering of Mande.

The fate of Major Houghton partakes more of tragedy than farce. He was a middle-aged man and a somewhat desperate one, striving to escape the demands of his exigent family and the penurious boredom of his situation as an unpensioned officer. As far as he went, he showed himself a determined and capable servant of the African Association. He advanced up the Gambia, lost his supplies in a fire, was wounded by his gun misfiring, and robbed by an unsympathetic ruler. He kept going, sending back a report that, according to local information, the Niger flowed eastward, but soon afterwards his letters ceased. Rumours of his death percolated down the coast. The African Association had lost another agent.

By the time of Houghton's expedition, the aim of exploration was narrowing on to a specific target – the course of the River Niger. It was known that a great river flowed through the western Sudan, but not where it started or finished, nor where or how it flowed. Powerful opinion still held that it flowed to the west and became the Senegal; some (including, it later appeared, many Africans) supposed it was connected with the Nile; others suspected that it was a tributary of the Zaire. Many other hypotheses were aired concerning the great river's destination. Not one of them was correct.

A modern map suggests that the obvious point to start looking for the Niger was from the Guinea coast. But apart from the various hazards of the coastal region, which had helped to prevent penetration of the forest belt, no one suspected that the Niger was to be found in that part, and exploring expeditions continued to use the northern or the western approach.

Apart from its sad end, Houghton's expedition was encouraging. The African Association was eager to build on his work, but for some time looked about in vain for a suitable candidate. Then in 1793 a young ship's surgeon, who had recently gratified the members of the Linnaean Society with a paper on 'Eight Small Fishes from the Coast of Sumatra', offered his services. Sir Joseph Banks, the driving force of the African Association, knew him well and, although he lacked many of the qualifications desirable in a West African explorer, the committee of the Association decided that he would do. They had, in fact, picked a winner.

*   *   *

Like so many of the most capable explorers of Africa, Mungo Park was a Scot. His background was closer to that of Livingstone than that of Bruce, for he was one of thirteen children of a farmer from Selkirk. He had studied medicine at Edinburgh, but without taking a degree, and had sailed to the East Indies as a ship's surgeon. Beside his medical knowledge, he was a fairly keen naturalist, and he had a talent for languages; at any rate, he was able

Mungo Park. From the first edition of his Travels in the Interior of Africa, *1799.*

to learn some Mande while staying in 'the hospitable mansion of Dr Laidley', a commercial representative stationed some two hundred miles up the Gambia.

But the young man who arrived in West Africa at the age of twenty-four in 1795 was primarily interested not in geographical exploration but in self-advancement, and his chief qualification as an explorer was not knowledge – of medicine or geography – but great physical stamina and strength of will. Through illness and ill treatment, ambition drove him on.

He began his journey towards the east in December 1795, five months after his arrival. He was accompanied by an interpreter and a young slave who proved a loyal servant, plus one or two others. His equipment was minimal and his supplies few, as it was feared that lavish accoutrements would prove too tempting to thieves. His instructions were, as he says, simple: 'to pass on to the Niger . . . ascertain the course, and, if possible, the rise and termination of that river. That I should use my utmost exertions to visit the principal towns in its neighbourhood, particularly Timbuctoo and Houssa'.

In the course of his journey, Park was to encounter many different peoples. They could be broadly divided into 'Moors' and 'Negroes', and he found that on the whole he was treated well by Negroes ('whatever difference there is between Negro and European in the confrontation of the nose and the colour of the skin, there is none in the genuine sympathies and characteristic feelings of our common nature'), and badly by Moors ('they hissed, shouted, and abused me; they even spit in my face, with a view to irritate me, and afford them a pretext for seizing my baggage'). Religion was only part of the explanation, for many Negroes were Muslims, although in general less fanatical and prejudiced than the Moors.

As he travelled, he was warned that the people he would meet as he moved east would be less friendly, and this proved all too true. He encountered trains of refugees from Moorish raids, and personally witnessed a cattle-stealing episode.

The people he met found it difficult to comprehend what he was doing in their country. A Fulani king, to whom Park made a much-appreciated present of his umbrella 'asked if I wished to purchase any slaves, or gold: being answered in the negative, he seemed rather surprised'. After Park had tried to explain the object of his journey, the King seemed 'but half satisfied. The notion of travelling for curiosity was quite new to him. He thought it impossible, he said, that any man in his senses would undertake so dangerous a journey, merely to look at the country, and its inhabitants'. All African explorers had to deal with this problem. In a country already potentially hostile to strangers, the explanation sounded a bit thin.

The wives of this king manifested other common reactions to European explorers in Africa. 'They rallied me with a good deal of gaiety on different subjects; particularly upon the whiteness of my skin, and the prominency of my nose. They insisted that both were artificial. The first, they said, was produced when I was an infant, by dipping me in milk; and they insisted that my nose had been pinched every day, till it had acquired its present unsightly and unnatural conformation'. Park was himself no mean hand at this kind of railery: a sense of humour, plus a willingness to flirt, were desirable qualities for West African travellers and in this respect Park was not lacking. At one of his worst moments when a captive of the Moors, he agreed to their demand that he should prove himself to be uncircumcized provided he was allowed to demonstrate the fact to the prettiest girl present.

Against advice, Park pushed on to Jarra, in Bambara, where he fell into the hands of an unpleasant individual named Ali, 'the chief or sovereign of Ludamar', who kept him in virtual captivity for several weeks and refused to release his 'faithful boy' who was earning his freedom by serving Mungo Park. Ali's people practised a crude form of psychological warfare on Park, presumably with the intention, as he guessed, of provoking him into some hostile act which would give them an excuse to retaliate. 'It is sufficient to observe that the rudeness, ferocity and fanaticism, which distinguished the Moors from the rest of mankind, found here a proper subject whereon to exercise their propensities. I was a *stranger*, I was *unprotected*, and I was a *Christian*; each of these circumstances is sufficient to drive every spark of humanity from the heart of a Moor; but when all of them, as in my case, were combined in the same person, and a suspicion prevailed withal, that I had come as a *spy* into the country, the reader will easily imagine that, in such a situation, I had everything to fear. Anxious, however, to conciliate favour, and, if possible, to afford the Moors no pretence for ill treating me, I readily complied with every command, and patiently bore every insult; but never did any period of my life pass away so heavily: from sunrise to sunset, was I obliged to suffer, with an unruffled countenance, the insults of the rudest savages on earth.' He was gradually stripped of all his equipment, though he regained his compass from Ali by a skilful ruse. Ali wanted to know why the needle always pointed to the desert (i.e. north). Rather at a loss, Park eventually explained the phenomenon of magnetism by saying that the needle was a guide that always pointed to his mother, who lived beyond the great desert. Ali was disconcerted by this piece of magic, and returned the compass to its owner as something too dangerous to have around.

Park got away from this horrid situation at last. That he survived the ordeal – made worse by attacks of fever and doubt of his ever escaping – argues a tough character. That he, apparently without considering any other course, continued his journey towards the Niger argues a man of exceptional courage. He was now quite alone, unable to speak the languages in the region, lacking supplies, with almost no clothes except what he was wearing (plus a cloak of which he was soon robbed), and no food for himself or his horse.

Assisted occasionally by people he met on his way, he finally reached the Niger at Segu, capital of Bambara, over five hundred miles from his starting point, on 20 July 1796. 'I hastened to the brink and, having drank of the water, lifted up my fervent thanks in prayer, to the Great Ruler of all things, for having thus far crowned my endeavours with success.'

As for Segu, 'the view of this extensive city; the numerous canoes upon the river; the crowded population, and the cultivated state of the surrounding country, formed altogether a prospect of civilization and magnificence, which I little expected to find in the bosom of Africa'. Unfortunately, however, there were many Moors there, and Park was refused permission to cross the river to the city. He was directed instead to a village some way off, but on arriving he was met with 'astonishment and fear'. No one would open a door to him. He was hungry, exhausted, and far from well. A storm was blowing up, and Park was utterly despondent at the prospect of spending the night in a tree to avoid wild animals. But at this gloomy point, there occurred one of the most attractive incidents in the whole of his story.

'A woman, returning from the labours of the field, stopped to observe me, and perceiving that I was weary and dejected, inquired into my situation, which I briefly explained to her; whereupon, with looks of great compassion, she took up my saddle and bridle, and told me to follow her. Having conducted me into her hut, she lighted up a lamp, spread a mat on the floor, and told me I might remain there for the night. Finding that I was very hungry, she said she would procure me something to eat. She accordingly went out, and returned in a short time with a very fine fish; which, having caused to be half boiled upon some embers, she gave me for supper. The rites of hospitality being thus performed towards a stranger in distress, my worthy benefactress (pointing to the mat and telling me that I might sleep there without apprehension) called to the female part of her family, who had stood gazing on me all the while in fixed astonishment, to resume their task of spinning cotton; in which they continued to employ themselves [a] great part of the night. They lightened their labour by songs, one of which was composed extempore; for I was myself the subject of it. It was sung by one of the young women, the rest joining in a sort of chorus. The air was sweet and plaintive, and the words, literally translated, were these. – "The winds roared and the rains fell. – The poor white man, faint and weary, came and sat under our tree. – He has no mother to bring him milk; no wife to grind his corn. *Chorus* Let us pity the white man; no mother has he etc., etc." . . . In the morning I presented my compassionate landlady with two of the four brass buttons which remained on my waistcoat; the only recompense I could make her.'

Such an incident almost made up for the beastliness of the Moors. It was not the first time that Mungo Park had benefited from an entirely arbitrary act of kindness at the hands of a woman, and other explorers relate similar stories. If the European heroes of African exploration are obvious, so too are the heroines. Time and again, a black female hand was extended to the benighted white traveller, sometimes in circumstances that made the gesture dangerous. James Bruce used to say that he had always found women kind and generous, and others echoed his sentiments. Perhaps Richard Lander acknowledged the debt most gracefully:

'I take this opportunity of expressing my high admiration of the amiable conduct of the African females towards me; in sickness and in health; in prosperity and in adversity – their kindness and affection were ever the same. They have danced and sung with me in health, grieved with me in sorrow, and shed tears of compassion at the recital of my misfortunes. Through whatever region I have wandered, whether slave or free, I have invariably found a chord of tenderness and trembling pity to vibrate in the heart of African women; and I never in my life knew one of them to bestow on me a single unpleasant look or angry word.'

Park's next objective was Jenne, but he had small hope of reaching it. 'Worn down by sickness, exhausted with hunger and fatigue; half-naked, and without any article of value, by which I might procure provisions, clothes, or lodging; I began to reflect seriously on my situation.' The result of his reflection was a decision to return – this time by a more southerly route in hope of avoiding 'those merciless fanatics'. Having attempted to gather all the information he could about the course of the Niger farther east – it did not amount to much – he set out on the long journey back to the Gambia.

Limping and staggering at times, he made his painful way west, surviving river crossings, wild animals, and another encounter with thieves (who fortunately gave back his hat in which he kept his notes) on the way. He waited out the rainy season at Kamalia, and there a slave-dealing merchant named Karfa Taura, whose brother had assisted him on an earlier occasion, took him under his wing. This man, a

A bridge over one of the tributaries of the upper Senegal, based on a sketch by Park. The bridge, though sagging wearily, looks more substantial than the explorer's description of it as formed by trees growing out of each bank and tied together at their tops, with bamboos laid over them. 'This bridge is carried away every year by the swelling of the river in the rainy season.' No wonder the people levied a toll; the continual painting of the Forth Bridge seems an easy labour by comparison.

Muslim Negro, probably saved his life. For the remainder of his journey, Park marched with Karfa's *cafila* of slaves, and although this was a miserable way to travel, it was a good deal safer than travelling alone. In June 1797, he was greeted by an amazed Dr Laidley, who had never expected to see him again, on the Gambia. An American slave-ship took him to the West Indies, whence he sailed on an English vessel that landed him at Falmouth just in time for Christmas.

He was ecstatically welcomed by the African Association and entertained by London Society, the ornaments of which, however, found him a bit dull. His account of his travels ('a plain unvarnished tale'), published in 1799, was an immediate success and has been constantly reissued ever since. Park pocketed his royalties and returned to Scotland, where he married a local girl and, after a while, settled down as a doctor in Peebles.

*   *   *

Meanwhile, the northern route had not been neglected. Friedrich Hornemann arrived in Cairo a few months after Park left the Gambia. He intended to overcome the difficulties that beset Christians in Muslim Africa by travelling as an Arab, and although he knew some Arabic already, he wanted to do some concentrated study in Cairo before venturing farther.

Hornemann was one of the most accomplished travellers of the first phase of European exploration. Though not initially well qualified – he had studied to be a minister at the University of Göttingen – he was intelligent, fit, and thorough. Perhaps more important, he had a vocation for African travel. He was recommended to Banks by a famous scholar, J.F. Blumenbach, a professor at Göttingen, and the African Association subsidized his Arabic studies in Germany.

Hornemann was kept longer in Cairo than he intended by plague, then by the French invasion of Egypt, which finally toppled the power of the Mamelukes; but in September 1798, he accompanied an Arab caravan into the Fezzan. A year later he was in Tripoli, whence he set off southwards across the desert. In seven weeks he was in Murzuk, compiling an excellent account of travel with an Arab caravan, clear and detailed in its description of domestic arrangements. He was still in Murzuk on 6 April, when the caravan was on the point of setting out for Bornu. To Banks, Hornemann wrote on that day: 'Being in an excellent state of health, perfectly inured to the climate, sufficiently acquainted with the manners of my fellow-travellers, speaking the Arabic language, and somewhat of the Bornou tongue, and being well-armed and not without courage, and under protection of two great Shereefs, I have the best hopes of success in my undertaking . . . Being the first European traveller undertaking so long a journey into this part of the world, *I will not put my discoveries to the hazard, by exposing myself to the casualties of long and unnecessary residence and delays in any one place . . .*'

He went on to report that, according to a man who had passed through the region farther south, 'the communication of the Niger with the Nile was not to be doubted', although in the dry season the Niger was so low that the link was insignificant. Finally, he commended himself to the remembrance of his patron. And then, sad to say, Friedrich Hornemann disappeared.

Although nothing more was heard from him, there is no doubt that he succeeded in reaching Bornu and possibly went a good distance beyond. He probably reached the Niger south of the modern town of Niamey and followed it downstream a short distance (which would have made him revise his opinion of the connection between Niger and Nile) before succumbing to one or other of the tropical diseases for which no prophylactive had yet been found. Something of his progress was learned by Lieutenant G.F. Lyon, who journeyed south of Murzuk in 1818 and published a beautifully illustrated account of his journey three years later (having first, by way of a change from the Sahara, spent a winter in the Arctic with Parry), and by Denham and Clapperton, who followed the same route in 1822.

*   *   *

When Mungo Park arrived back in Britain in 1797, he had accomplished what he had set out to do. He had achieved fame and some fortune. But was it enough? His book sold well, but he was far from a rich man. His name was known,

A doctor in demand. Mungo Park in Bondu: 'I had no sooner entered the court appropriated to the ladies than the whole seraglio surrounded me; some begging for physic, some for amber: and all of them desirous of trying that great African specific, blood-letting.'

but he was not such a sensation as James Bruce nor such a hero as James Cook. For a time he resisted the blandishments of Sir Joseph Banks, who wished to employ him on other projects. When Banks accused him of being too mercenary, he snapped back, 'Pecuniary considerations, however contemptible in themselves, serve as a good interest by which to judge the importance of any office or any pursuit.' On the other hand, there was not much profit in lugging lancet and plaister ladle over the hills of Peebles (as a physician, Mungo Park might be described as unmotivated; on his travels, he seems to have made less use of his medical knowledge than most less qualified explorers). He was soon offering proposals for further exploration in West Africa, and in 1803 he accepted an invitation to lead a new expedition to the Niger. The expedition was supported by the government, apprehensive of French expansion from the Senegal, and it was military in character, Park being commissioned a captain.

It is a law of human activity that successful enterprises tend to expand; but it does not follow that size equals success. Mungo Park was but one of many explorers who operated better on his own than as the leader of a large party (Livingstone was another). His second expedition began with disaster and ended with disaster, although enormous progress was made in between.

With his brother-in-law as second-in-command, Park reached the Gambia with thirty-five soldiers – of poor quality as there was a war on – in April, 1805, at the end of the dry season. Plans were more than a little sketchy. Park's instructions were to follow the Niger, if he were able, to its mouth, or rather its end, for no one knew if it had a mouth and the commonest theory held that it ended in lakes. Park himself had a rather ill-founded but fixed notion that he would end up at the mouth of the Zaire (Congo).

They were no more than half-way to the Niger when the rains started, and the soldiers began to sicken. All suffered from fever and by 13 June, after five weeks' marching, half the party were 'either sick of the fever or unable to use great exertion, and fatigued in driving the asses'. Their numbers dwindled as, one by one, soldiers were left behind at friendly villages, protesting their inability to go farther (one of them was a veteran of thirty-one years' service). Their officer, Lieutenant Martyn, had a fondness for African beer, ('Whitbread's Beer is nothing to what we get here') and a

View of Kamalia, where Mungo Park was 'delivered, by the friendly care of [Karfa Taura] from a situation truly deplorable'.

dangerous tendency to use his fists in an argument. Minor pilfering diminished the stores. The donkeys tended to wander off. The only man who could keep up with the vigorous, though feverish Park was their invaluable guide, Isaaco, who was nearly lost in a nasty accident while driving the donkeys across a river: 'When he had reached the middle of the river, a crocodile rose close to him, and instantly seizing him by the left thigh, pulled him under water. With wonderful presence of mind he felt the head of the animal, and thrust his finger into its eye; on which it quitted its hold, and Isaaco attempted to reach the farther shore, calling out for a knife. But the crocodile returned and seized him by the other thigh, and again pulled him under the water; he had recourse to the same expedient, and thrust his fingers into its eyes with such violence that it again quitted him; and when it rose, flounced about on the surface of the water as if stupid, and then swam down the middle of the river.' Park patched up Isaaco's gaping wounds and got him to the next village, where they waited for five days. At the end of that time the courageous Isaaco, incredibly enough, was ready to continue.

On 19 August they reached the Niger. 'After the fatiguing march which we had experienced, the sight of this river was no doubt pleasant, as it promised an end to, or to be at least an alleviation of our toils. But when I reflected that three fourths of the soldiers had died on their march [two more died that night], and that in addition to our weakly state we had no carpenters to build the boats, in which we proposed to prosecute our discoveries; the prospect appeared somewhat gloomy.' The explorer drew some comfort from his belief (or illusion) that in spite of everything, 'I had always been able to preserve the most friendly terms with the natives.' He drew the doubtful conclusion that a trade route between the Gambia and the Niger was perfectly feasible, and 'that if this journey be performed in the dry season, one may calculate on losing not more than three or at most four men out of fifty'. Why, then, had Mungo Park undertaken it in the wet season?

Mansong, the king of Segu, who had refused to allow Park into his city on his first expedition, was again unwilling to see him, but promised that he should be allowed to travel down the river in peace. (Many Sudanic rulers, while friendly towards white explorers, displayed a certain hesitation in their attitude towards them. Their descendants would find these misgivings justified.)

The camp where Park was held prisoner. 'It presented to the eye a great number of dirty looking tents, scattered without order, over a large space of ground.'

The depleted party prepared for their voyage down the Niger. Some difficulty was encountered in obtaining serviceable canoes, and it proved necessary to take the good half of one canoe and join it to the good half of another, discarding the rotten parts of both. As these barge-like canoes tended to be leaky vessels at the best of times, this was not an ideal solution; nevertheless, 'eighteen days *hard labour*, changed the Bambara canoe into *His Majesty's schooner Joliba*; the length forty feet, the breadth six feet; being flat-bottomed, draws only one foot of water when loaded'.

The death of Alexander Anderson, Park's brother-in-law, not long before they set off on about 19 November, thrust the explorer into unwonted gloom. Only five white men were left in the party: Lieutenant Martyn, durable in spite of, or because of, the beer, and three of his men, besides Park himself. Isaaco was sent back to the Gambia with Park's letters, and thereafter communication ceased. The precise manner of the death of Mungo Park and his companions remains unclear, but the place and circumstances were discovered by Isaaco himself, sent on a mission of inquiry several years later.

Park's policy, no doubt a wise one in the circumstances, was to get down the river as fast as possible, ignoring the places they passed (including Timbuktu) and rejecting attempts to communicate with them. Probably Park was right in considering it safer to ignore the customs and tolls of the river than to become involved with people who in some cases were bound to be hostile, although his policy seems to have resulted in resisting attempts to delay them by force, and there is evidence that Lieutenant Martyn, if not the others, was rather quick on the trigger.

The end came at Bussa, perhaps as the result of a deliberate ambush laid by an insulted ruler, perhaps through chance encounter and misunderstanding. At Bussa the river narrowed and large rocks appeared in midstream, offering excellent opportunity for ambush. The canoe came under attack and was wrecked. The Europeans – apparently only two of them fit (Park and Martyn, it scarcely needs saying) jumped into the river and were drowned.

The echoes of Park's fate lingered for many years. Later explorers in the region reported a marked disinclination to talk about the incident, and Clapperton was forbidden to visit the spot because it was 'a bad place'. Fifty years later, Heinrich Barth found that Park was still remembered on the lower Niger, though rapidly passing into the realm of myth. It is said that the legend exists to this day, and that the Emir of Yauri uses Park's silver-topped cane as his staff of office.

The Niger II

Apart from the second expedition of Mungo Park, little advance was made in the exploration of Africa in the first two decades of the 19th century, a period in which the energies of Europe were largely devoted to war. Meanwhile, other changes were taking place. Sir Joseph Banks was growing old and gouty, and though he lived until 1820, his place as unofficial dean and patron of British exploration had by that time been assumed by John Barrow, second secretary at the Admiralty, perhaps better known for his sponsorship of Arctic exploration. Barrow visited South Africa himself, and wrote a book about it which was published in 1806. Thereafter, he not unnaturally tended to regard himself as an expert on Africa as a whole.

The function of the African Association as the engine of exploration gradually declined (Park's second expedition was a government enterprise). The fight against the slave trade was beginning to affect the motives of exploration and the attitudes of explorers; a private hobby was becoming a state concern. The African Association itself ceased to exist as an independent body when it was merged with the new Geographical Society, of which Barrow was the chief founder, in 1831.

The efforts of explorers sponsored by the African Association had, by the beginning of the 19th century, led to some important adjustments and additions in the map of Africa. Further details came from elsewhere, for the Association was not the only organization concerned with Africa.

The commercial and political agents stationed at various places in the north and west, though few of them travelled more than a few miles from the coast, reported what they knew or were told. Merchants and others visiting the newly founded entrepôt of Mogador described conditions in Morocco. Officials of the Sierra Leone Company, which ran the colony established for Africans freed from slavery, travelled in the territory of the rising Fulani dominion and pioneered the first part of the route that René Caillié was to follow in the 1820s. A curiously reticent man named William George Browne, inspired by the example of James Bruce, set off on a solitary expedition to seek the sources of the Nile and was marooned in Darfur for three years. A succession of visitors to South Africa saw enough to provide them with the material for an interesting travel book.

Perhaps the most interesting – and most attractive – explorer of the relatively uneventful period of the Napoleonic wars was an Anglophile Swiss, Johann Ludwig Burckhardt, another protégé of J.F. Blumenbach. Having failed to land a job in the British Foreign Service, he was encouraged by Banks to volunteer his services to the African Association. He was a sensible young man with an urge to do something worthy in the world; lacking personal ambition, he regarded European society (and, ultimately, African society also) with a somewhat puritanical disapproval. A natural linguist, he learned Arabic at Cambridge University and marched assiduously across the fens without a hat on warm summer days. Like Hornemann and René Caillié, he intended to pass himself off as a Muslim, and he spent nearly three years in Syria perfecting the language as well as exploring some of the less well-known regions of the Middle East. In the summer of 1812, he made his way to Cairo, visiting Petra on the way; but disturbances in upper Egypt held him back for another year.

Eventually, he joined a caravan passing through the Nubian desert to Sennar – the route followed in the opposite direction by James Bruce. He endured some fairly rough treatment from his companions as a result of his current pretence that he was a Turk. Burckhardt was one of the not very numerous class of explorers who was directly and genuinely interested in the societies he visited, and his description of economic and social conditions in the province of Sennar was to be of great value. From Shendi, Burckhardt

When a bride leaves her father's house, 'a camel is sent for her with a jaata, or sedan chair of basketwork, on its back, covered with skins of animals, shawls from Soudan, Cairo, and Timbuctoo: she steps into this, and so places herself as to see what is going forward, and yet to be entirely hid from the view of others'. (Denham)

travelled with a caravan through an entirely unknown region to the Red Sea at Suakin, all the time observing, enquiring and making notes. He crossed over into Arabia, and changed his guise again, now appearing as a 'reduced Egyptian gentleman'. He visited the holy places of Mecca and Medina before making his way back to Cairo and Alexandria, where he wrote his account of his travels.

Although he had been out of Europe for over five years, Burckhardt was in no hurry to go home – even to see the parents to whom he wrote fond and frequent letters. He was waiting to join a caravan to the Fezzan on the first stage of a projected expedition to West Africa when he suffered a recurrence of the illness that had nearly killed him in Arabia. He died and was buried in Cairo as a Muslim.

Since Mungo Park's discovery of the river in 1795, little progress had been made in mapping the course of the Niger. The German geographer, C.G. Reichard, had proposed as early as 1803 that the river's outflow would be found in a delta on the Bight of Benin, but this skilful piece of scholarly inference was largely ignored. The most popular theory in England was still that the river ended in a large lake, or lakes, in the centre of the continent.

*   *   *

The disappearance of Park and the comparative failure of the Gray-Dochard expedition, which followed the same route (reaching no farther than Segu) in 1818, helped to tilt the balance in favour of the northern approach pioneered by Hornemann. In the same year, Lieutenant G.F. Lyon had travelled from Tripoli to Murzuk, where his companion, Dr Ritchie, died. The amiable young naval officer went some way farther south before lack of funds compelled his return. He reported that everyone he spoke to said that the Niger was somehow linked with the Nile. It was not yet generally realized that in Africa what appear to be proper names are sometimes used generically. When people mentioned the Nile they may have meant no more than 'great river'. This custom also caused confusion over the location of gold-producing 'Wangara', and of 'Medina' – a name applied to several towns in Muslim West Africa.

Other factors in favour of the northern approach were the friendly relations that existed with the Pasha of Tripoli, whose influence extended beyond the desert to the Sudan (though not as effectively as the British imagined) and the presence in Tripoli of an influential and colourful, though conceited, British official, Consul Warrington. It was the Pasha's offer of a large bodyguard, plus pressure from Warrington in Tripoli and Barrow in London, that resulted in the Denham-Clapperton-Oudney expedition to Bornu, which set out in 1822.

The organization of the expedition was a shocking muddle, for which the Colonial Office in London, in particular Lord Bathurst, the secretary of state, and Barrow were chiefly to blame. The man originally appointed to lead it was Dr Walter Oudney, a young ex-naval surgeon currently practising as a doctor in Edinburgh. He was a quiet, conscientious, and pleasant man, a considerable naturalist, but not strong. He became ill at an early stage in the expedition and must have known then that he would never get back alive. But he

'A Slave Kaffle', after G.F. Lyon. A Negro girl, weak from fever and privation 'was lashed on the camel she rode. She continually asked for water and complained of a severe pain in her side . . . Her master troubled his head very little about her; and her voice was, in consequence of her sufferings, so feeble, that had I not rode near her, and supplied her with water, she would have perished from thirst . . . I persuaded the girl's master to let her remain under my care until she was a little recovered, as I should then be enabled to bestow more attention on her than he could, or was inclined to do: at this time she was very cold, quite speechless, and unable to swallow. I wrapped her up in my carpet, and made two of her fellow slaves chafe her hands and feet; but our efforts to save her were useless, and she breathed her last at eight o'clock, having, poor girl, suffered much agony' (Lyon's account of his return journey to Tripoli).

preferred to go on. Probably he knew he would not have lived much longer if he had stayed in Edinburgh.

Oudney was allowed to pick a companion, and he made what turned out to be an excellent choice in Lieutenant Hugh Clapperton, a rugged native of Dumfries, recently returned from naval duties in Canada and on the lookout for a challenging job. He was ready to go to Africa without pay.

This looked like a good team; but independently, an English officer teaching at Sandhurst had volunteered for the expedition. This was Major Dixon Denham, a rather arrogant fellow, even for a Regency army officer striving to conceal a humble background, with a streak of ruthless self-interest. He formed a low opinion of Oudney and Clapperton, whom he scarcely met before they all gathered in Tripoli, and they liked him no better. According to Clapperton, Denham was not even capable of taking celestial bearings.

It is still not clear why the Colonial Office felt that both Clapperton and Denham had to be appointed; what was worse at the time, it was not clear who was in charge. The revised plans required Oudney, on arrival in Bornu, to become consul there (something he had no desire to be – he wished to travel), whereupon Denham would become leader of the expedition. This was hardly very satisfactory from Clapperton's point of view, and it left the leadership of the expedition during the Sahara crossing open to some doubt.

None of these problems appear in the published account of the expedition which was written by Denham (it is, in fact, highly readable) largely for purposes of self-glorification. When it was published, Oudney was dead and Clapperton was out of the country, but at Barrow's urging Denham did permit Clapperton's account of his journey to Sokoto to appear at the end. Otherwise, Oudney and Clapperton receive hardly more mention than the tough ship's carpenter, William Hillman who accompanied them to Bornu.

Reaching Murzuk, an unhealthy place where Dr Ritchie had died, in April 1822 the travellers were baulked from further advance by the Bey. Denham returned to Tripoli to request help from the Pasha in overcoming the Bey's hesitations, while Oudney and Clapperton made an excursion to Ghat, west of Murzuk, discovering on their way the Roman ruins at Germa (Garama), and receiving a friendly reception from the dreaded Tuareg. Meanwhile Denham was behaving

Top: Dixon Denham, from an engraving published in 1830.

Above: Hugh Clapperton, from the portrait by Gildon Manton. National Portrait Gallery, London.

oddly. From Tripoli he sailed to Europe in order to lay his complaints before the Colonial Secretary. Probably he hoped to secure undisputed command of the expedition. But at Marseilles he heard that the expedition was about to set off again, with a smaller escort, under the protection of a respected merchant Bu Khallum ('an excellent man', according to Oudney). Denham thereupon hurried back.

It was a large party that made the desert crossing, including two hundred soldiers and a number of Arab merchants anxious to travel to Bornu in the safety of an armed party. The physical hazards – excessive heat by day, sandstorms, rocky hills, choked-up wells – were on the whole less frightening than the human hazards. The route was lined with the bones of slaves who had not survived the journey north. Any caravan was liable to attack by the nomadic, though fortunately gunless, Tebu, and safety was unreliably procured by bribes to various minor chiefs through whose territory they passed.

After two months of very hard going, the harsh frown of the desert began to fade: a few 'miserable bushes' put new spirit into the travellers, inspiring Hillman to compare the scene with a valley near his home in the west of England. Soon, date trees appeared, and then 'grass in abundance'. Denham could have 'stayed here a week with pleasure'. But the desert had not quite finished with them. On 30 January they were confined to their tents all day by a sandstorm. Denham was unwell, but he derived comfort from being rubbed with oil by the wife of his Negro servant. 'It is an undoubted fact', he remarked, 'and in no case better exemplified than in my own, that man naturally longs for attention and support from female hands, of whatever colour or country, so soon as debility or sickness comes upon him.'

The scenery continued to improve and at last, on 4 February, Denham was able to record the first notable discovery: 'The great lake Tchad, glowing with the golden rays of the sun in its strength . . . within a mile of the spot on which we stood. My heart bounded within me at the prospect . . .' On the shores of the vast but shallow lake, there were prosperous little villages, most of the houses having a cow or two, some goats, and chickens in the yard; and the lake itself was thronged with birds and animals, easy victims for the explorers' guns. All was not, however, as peaceful as it seemed, for the villages were subject to constant raids, not only by the Tebu in the north, but from the warlike people who inhabited the islands of Lake Chad and controlled the waters from their battle canoes.

Travelling down the western border of the lake, the travellers came to Kuka (Kukawa), the capital of Bornu, and were received, with some reserve, by the Sheikh, El-Kanemi, a highly capable ruler who had succeeded in preserving his independence from the expanding power of the Fulani in the west. On learning the object of the explorers, he bade them welcome, and provided them with generous quantities of food: 'In England a brace of trout might be considered as a handsome present to a traveller sojourning in the neighbourhood of a stream, but at Bornu things are done differently. A camel-load of bream, and a sort of mullet, was thrown before our huts on the second morning after our arrival; and for fear that should not be sufficient, in the evening another was sent.'

Though interested in what they had to tell him of affairs in Europe, and vastly impressed by the military rockets they demonstrated for his amusement, the Sheikh was unwilling to let them travel beyond his dominions, giving as his reason his fear that he would be blamed by the Pasha of Tripoli if harm should come to them. Doubtless he had other reasons. He was aware that the British ruled India (it is notable that Sudanic rulers usually knew far more about Europe's affairs than Europe knew about them), and the Arab merchants, as always resenting European commercial competition, suggested that the purpose of the travellers in Bornu was less than peaceable.

The personality problems that had threatened to disrupt the conduct of the expedition from the start burst out in a major row at Kukawa. Already Clapperton and Denham had taken to exchanging critical letters. Later they were to restrict their communications for a time entirely to this medium. Now Denham wrote to Clapperton charging him with 'extreme impropriety of conduct'. After some prodding, Denham revealed that his startling complaint referred to Clapperton's indulgence in homosexual relations with his Arab servant. All recent writers agree with Dr Oudney that this charge, apparently originating in the idle gossip of the caravan, 'has so much improbability that the most disinterested would pronounce it a vile and malicious report'. Even Denham blandly remarked later that he had discounted the rumour. It does not seem particularly dreadful now, and to the Arabs it probably did not seem particularly dreadful then, while post-Freudian readers might consider Denham a more likely homosexual than Clapperton. But it made the breach between the naval and the army officer complete and permanent. They split up. Denham went off with the Arabs on a slave-raiding campaign in Mandara (they were defeated; Denham's account is vivid, though at some points unintentionally humorous), while Clapperton and Oudney discovered the River Shari, flowing into Lake Chad in the south. In view of prevailing opinions, they might have guessed the Shari, a mile wide where it entered the lake, to be the Niger, but this mistake they did not make.

After another short journey from Kukawa, on which the three were again united, Clapperton and Oudney, reluctantly released by Sheikh el-Kanemi, set off towards Hausaland in December 1823. Oudney seemed to think that travelling would improve his health, but the cold nights (one morning the waterskins were frozen) and hot days made him worse. He died after two weeks on the road. Clapperton, gloomy and feverish, continued alone.

On 20 January 1824 Clapperton reached the city of Kano, known to Europeans by name only and located on contemporary maps far out of its correct place. After the glowing reports of the Arabs, Kano, though large, was a disappointment, the houses 'scattered into detached groups, between large stagnant pools of water'. Clapperton had smartened himself up and put on his naval uniform, but no one paid any attention to him. He estimated the city had 30–40,000 inhabitants, more than half of them slaves. There was a large and well-stocked market, where the butchers were 'fully as knowing as our own, for they make a few slashes to show the fat, blow up meat, and sometimes even stick a little sheep's wool on a leg of goat's flesh'. At the market 'I bought, for three Spanish dollars, an English green cotton umbrella, an article I little expected to meet with, yet by no means uncommon' (in Sokoto he was sent food on pewter dishes with a London trademark and was once served meat in an English china basin; on his second expedition he observed an English toby-jug for sale at a market near Bussa).

In spite of almost incessant fever, Clapperton continued westward from Kano to the city of Sokoto, seat of the powerful Fulani sultan, Muhammad Bello. This was the son of the able leader, Usuman dan Fodio, who had led the *jihad* against the pagans of Hausa and established Fulani predominance over an area roughly as large as the modern state of Nigeria. Bello was 'a noble-looking man, forty-four years of age, although much younger in appearance, five feet ten inches high, portly in person, with a short curling black beard, a small mouth, a fine forehead, a Grecian nose, and large black eyes . . . The Sultan bade me many hearty welcomes, and asked me if I were not much tired with my journey . . .' They discussed theology, and poor Clapperton soon found himself out of his depth ('I was obliged to confess myself not sufficiently versed in religious subtleties to resolve these knotty points'). The Sultan then produced some books which Denham had lost during the disastrous Mandara raid, and requested that Clapperton should read some of them, as he wished to hear the language. On the next visit, according to protocol, the presents were produced. 'He took them up one by one. The compass and spy-glass excited great interest; and he seemed much gratified when I pointed out that by means of the former, he could at any time find out the east to address himself in his daily prayers. He said, "Everything is wonderful; but you are the greatest curiosity of all!"'

When the Sultan politely inquired what he could do for the king of England in recompense for these presents, Clapperton boldly suggested putting a stop to the slave trade. '"What?" said he, "have you no slaves in England?"' None, Clapperton explained, and added a brief and somewhat rosy description of labour conditions in Britain. The Sultan listened with interest, 'God is great!' he mused, 'You are a beautiful people.'

At a later interview with this impressive ruler, an awkward incident occurred to show that the Sultan's amiable attitude concealed a certain healthy distrust of the curious alien. Clapperton wished to demonstrate how he took an observation of the sun, but he had lost the key to the case containing the artificial horizon. He asked the bystanders for a knife to force the lid, but the one he was given was too small, 'and I quite inadvertently asked for a dagger for the same purpose. The sultan was instantly thrown into a fright: he seized his sword, and half drawing it from the scabbard, placed it before him, trembling all the time like an aspen leaf'. Very

The Libyan Desert, forty miles north of Ghat.

sensibly, Clapperton pretended not to notice the alarm he had caused, and the incident passed off harmlessly.

The question that Clapperton was asked most often in Sokoto was: Why had he come? He would reply that he came to see the country, 'its rivers, mountains, and inhabitants, its flowers, fruit, minerals, and animals . . . [for] the people of England could all read and write, and were acquainted with most other regions of the earth; but of this country alone they hitherto knew scarcely any thing, and erroneously regarded the inhabitants as naked savages, devoid of religion, and not far removed from the condition of wild beasts: whereas I found them, from my personal observation, to be civilized, learned, humane, and pious'. It is doubtful, however, if this tactful and generally accurate explanation (disregarding the exaggeration of the state of literacy in Britain) entirely satisfied his inquisitors.

The geographical purpose of the expedition – to seek the termination of the Niger – had not been forgotten by Clapperton, and he made diligent inquiries from the Sultan, who might have been expected to know its course fairly accurately. Whether he did or not, the map he gave Clapperton was thoroughly misleading and contradicted what the Sultan himself had said on an early occasion. It has been suggested that this showed a deliberate intent to deceive, but whatever misgivings Bello may have had about encouraging Europeans to enter his domain, it seems more likely that he was simply ignorant of aspects of geography that had no strategic importance for him.

In fact, the Sultan seemed keen to establish commercial links with England, foreseeing increased power from such a connection: but the Arab merchants in Sokoto understandably viewed the prospect less favourably. It may have been partly their influence that made the Sultan somewhat less than receptive when Clapperton contacted him during his second expedition.

It was particularly important for Clapperton to learn all he could about the course of the Niger while he was in Sokoto, for it soon became clear that he would get no farther. He could hardly have reached the city in safety if the Sultan had not provided him with a military escort through the hostile region of Gobir, and everyone in the capital agreed that travelling to the west was out of the question. Clapperton had done very well, and had learned more than any explorer since Mungo Park. Carrying a letter from Muhammad Bello to George IV ('Your Majesty's servant, Ra-yes-Abd-Allah [i.e. Clapperton] came to us, and we found him a very intelligent and wise man; representing in every respect your greatness, wisdom, dignity, clemency, and penetration'), he started his return journey to Kukawa after a stay of over eight weeks in Sokoto. From Kukawa he and Denham (briefly achieving a degree of co-operation) with the hardy Hillman and the invaluable Columbus, a much-travelled West Indian who had accompanied the expedition throughout, trekked across the desert back to Tripoli (Denham's daft idea of going via Egypt having been scotched). They arrived on 26 January 1825.

In Tripoli Clapperton, who had promised Sultan Bello he would be back next year via the Niger (which he had become certain must flow into the Bight of Benin), was disconcerted to learn that another British explorer had already been commissioned to strike across the desert to the south-west. This was Major Alexander Gordon Laing, another Edinburgh man, author of a book about his travels in the interior of Sierra Leone, and eager to prove his theory that the Niger and the Nile were separate rivers.

In certain respects, Laing resembled Denham: he could be almost as wilfully egoistic and his courage was equally great. In other respects he made a better explorer, being more experienced and more intelligent. As he died on his travels, and as his achievements were paralleled by others who, more fortunate, returned to write the customary account, Laing is not well remembered. As he was apparently the first European in modern times to succeed in reaching Timbuktu by his own efforts, the neglect seems unfair.

The usual delays occurred in Tripoli. The Pasha demanded ever-increasing bribes for his patronage of British explorers, and Laing fell in love with Consul Warrington's daughter (they were married in a civil ceremony 'under the most sacred, and most solemn obligation', reported the father of the bride, 'that they are not to cohabit till the marriage is duly performed by a clergyman of the established Church of England'). In July 1825 Laing at last set off, under the protection of a sheikh from Ghadames who was proceeding, by a much longer route than Laing would have chosen, to Timbuktu. As the direct distance is roughly 1,500 miles, Laing made the longest Saharan journey ever accomplished by a European up to that time (and one seldom equalled since). The land through which he passed was wilder and more dangerous than the road to Bornu. Life for all who lived here was a fierce struggle for survival in which the human qualities that we take for granted counted for little.

Nevertheless, the early part of the journey, via Ghadames to Tuat, went reasonably well. Laing was well treated at the desert camps and oases, though the constant necessity of making presents severely depleted his resources. Waiting at a place in Tuat for a large caravan to assemble, Laing was accused, by a man who had been wounded during the encounter at Bussa, of being none other than Mungo Park, a suspicion that at first seemed absurd, then embarrassing, finally rather dangerous. At one point the entire caravan, frightened by rumours of conflict on the road south, was prepared to turn back, but when Laing announced that he would go on alone, they changed their minds. Nevertheless, 'we were in a constant state of alarm . . . every acacia tree in the distance being magnified or rather metamorphosed by the apprehensive merchants into troops of armed foes'. Laing was loudly blamed for leading them into danger. Soon afterwards they were joined by some friendly Tuareg, and the outlook improved: 'I have little time at present to say more, than that my prospects are bright, and expectations [of reaching Timbuktu] sanguine.'

Nothing more was heard from Laing for some months, and disquieting rumours of an attack on the caravan reached Tripoli. Then, after three months silence, Mrs Laing received a letter in which her husband explained his bad writing as the result of a cut finger. The truth, related later by one of the camel-drivers, was far worse. A party of Tuareg from Ahaggar, ostensibly acting as escort, attacked Laing in his

The way south from the desert. From a drawing by Dixon Denham.

tent by night, having first gained possession of his ammunition. Laing was 'cut down by a sword on the thigh, he . . . jumped up and received one cut on the cheek and ear, and the other on the right arm above the wrist which broke the arm, he then fell to the ground, where he received seven cuts the last being on his neck'. His attendants were killed.

This was in February. In May word was sent by Laing him-

Reception of the Denham-Clapperton mission by the Sheikh of Bornu. 'Previous to entering into the open court, in which we were received, our papouches, or slippers, were whipped off by . . . gentlemen of the chamber; and we were seated on some clean sand . . . [The Sheikh] was seated in a sort of cage of cane or wood, near the door of his garden, on a seat which at the distance appeared to be covered with silk or satin, and through the railing looked upon the assembly before him . . .' From a drawing by Dixon Denham.

self, amazingly still alive in spite of his appalling wounds; but his letter took two years to reach Tripoli and by that time Laing was dead.

An unexpectedly charitable sheikh sheltered Laing while he recovered somewhat from his wounds, and generously provided a strong escort to assist him to Timbuktu. That city was in dispute between two uncompromising forces, a Fulani host inspired by preaching of a *jihad*, and Tuareg raiders who, at this time, were trying to isolate the city. Laing entered Timbuktu and appears to have explored it thoroughly, disregarding friendly warnings to keep within the walls and being generally well received by the inhabitants. After a month in the city he set out on 22 September with an ostensibly friendly sheikh towards the Senegal, which seemed to him the shortest route to safety. They had not gone far when the Sheikh murdered him as an infidel. The skeletons of Laing and an Arab boy travelling with him were exhumed by the French authorities in 1910 and reburied in Timbuktu.

So died Alexander Gordon Laing, deprived of the fame that would have been his had he lived to write down his adventures (even his journals, which rumour reported were sold to the unprincipled French consul in Tripoli, have never turned up). 'For resolute courage in the face of acute sufferings and incalculable perils,' wrote E.W. Bovill, 'Gordon Laing was a hero whom none could approach.'

*　　*　　*

When Hugh Clapperton left Sokoto in 1824 he told the Sultan that he would be at Whydah (Ouidah) on the coast in July of the following year. As he did not arrive in England until June 1825, that schedule had to be abandoned.

But Clapperton strove to return to West Africa as soon as possible, spurred on by the fear that Laing would discover the secret of the Niger before him. By the end of August he was on his way.

His instructions from the Colonial Office required him to establish firm relations with Muhammad Bello with a view to suppressing the slave trade and opening a less objectionable commerce. The tracing of the Niger's course to its termination was 'highly desirable' though not, so far as the Colonial Office was concerned, the primary task of the expedition. The Colonial Office was not in the exploring business; nor was it interested in acquiring colonies – especially in West Africa.

Clapperton was accompanied by six people. There were four Europeans, the West Indian Columbus, and an African, Pascoe, a native of Hausa and thus useful as an interpreter. Like many men on whom nature has seen fit to bestow an unusually ugly countenance, Pascoe was a tremendous womanizer, and that, plus his light fingers, were to be sometimes a source of trouble, though in the end he proved utterly invaluable. Columbus died soon after the ship reached West African waters, and three of Clapperton's four European companions were also dead before he reached Katunga (one went to Dahomey and disappeared). The sole survivor was Clapperton's personal servant, a Cornish youth not yet twenty-one named Richard Lemon Lander who, in the opinion of Professor Lloyd, is 'the most attractive of all African explorers'.

Richard Lander's most charming quality was perhaps the complete absence of pretension from his character. He is the one explorer it is easy to call by his first name – an unthinkable liberty in the case of a Livingstone or a Stanley. One of the numerous children of a Truro innkeeper, he ran away from home at the age of nine and travelled to the West Indies as a servant when he was only eleven. He had no education worth speaking of (he could barely write; his published writings were 'edited' by his brother John, a smooth stylist), yet in some ways this 'very humble but intelligent individual', as John Barrow later described him, was more sensitive to African society, and more sensible in his approach to the task of exploration, than most explorers. He liked Africans (at least, he liked Negroes – not Arabs), and usually got on very well with them. His lack of racial prejudice was possibly a happy result of his unprivileged background, though such an amiable, straightforward man could never have been a bigot, whatever his social environment. Richard Lander entertaining a Yoruba village with tunes on his 'bugle horn', which always accompanied him on his travels, makes one of the most pleasing scenes in the drama of European exploration of Africa.

Richard Lander, the son of a Truro innkeeper who was Hugh Clapperton's devoted friend and servant on his second expedition to West Africa. After Clapperton's death at Sokoto in 1827 Lander became an explorer in his own right (1830): it is to him that the credit must go for determining correctly the lower course of the great Niger river. From an engraving published in 1832.

Not surprisingly, no messengers from Bello were waiting at Whydah, and on the advice of a relatively knowledgeable trader, Clapperton decided to make his start from Badagri (about twenty miles west of Lagos), which was reached in November 1825. Once past the unhealthy climate of the coast and the forest, where Clapperton suffered severe bouts of fever that probably weakened him permanently, they entered the land of the Yoruba, and were pleased to find a warm welcome among the people, whom they had expected to be hostile.

With the entire population of villages turning out to sing songs of welcome and wave their hands in greeting, it is tempting to fall into the romantic trap of ascribing these pleasant scenes to the innocent, hospitable, happy-go-lucky nature of the people – a racial stereotype that is as misleading as most others. The Yoruba were not simple farmers and wood-carvers living in a tropical Eden, and the welcome they gave to Clapperton's expedition was not the way they greeted all visitors. Few, if any, of them had seen a European, but they had heard many stories of the wealth and the firepower of the white men on the coast. The advent of one of these half-legendary creatures, well-equipped with guns and goods and manifesting a desire for their friendship, promised power and prestige.

Like other explorers in other parts of Africa, Clapperton found that it was easier to enter a place than leave it. Every ruler wanted to believe that he was the man the Europeans had come to see. At Katunga, it took six weeks for Clapperton to extricate himself from the hospitality of the king and, more than most, Clapperton's expedition was hazarded by local war and politics. The Yoruba were at war with the Fulani, but it was the Fulani sultan with whom Clapperton hoped to cement an agreement. However, since the Bornu expedition, the uneasy relations between Bello and Sheikh El-Kanemi of Bornu had degenerated into war, and Clapperton also bore letters and presents for the Sheikh of Bornu. Naturally, the rulers that Clapperton visited were not at all pleased to learn that he proposed to visit their enemies also.

A week's march from Katunga, Clapperton and his party arrived at Kaiama, an important market town, the ruler of which was attended by an unusually attractive bodyguard of 'six young female slaves, naked as they were born, except a strip of narrow white cloth tied around their heads, about

A warrior of the Sheikh of Bornu, from a drawing published in 1826.

79

six inches of the ends flying out behind; each carrying a light spear in the right hand . . . Their light form, the vivacity of their eyes, and the ease with which they appeared to fly over the ground, made them appear something more than mortal as they flew alongside of his horse, when he was galloping . . .' The king of Kaiama believed that women should go about naked as a sign of their inferiority to men.

On the way to Bussa, where Mungo Park had died, they visited the large town of Wawa. There the two Britons became involved in a well-known, comic-pathetic entanglement with the widow Zuma.

This wealthy lady was of Arab descent and fair-skinned. She therefore required a white husband, but they were in short supply in Borgu. Clapperton and, more particularly, the young and attractive Lander therefore arrived like gifts from heaven, and she brought her whole impressive armoury to bear upon the target. Though Clapperton, at first, treated her as a joke (chiefly because she was grossly fat, 'just like a walking water-butt'), he later remarked that she had been a 'very handsome woman' and would have been thought a beauty 'in any country in Europe'. Lander found the widow's attentions less of a joke, and was 'positively afraid, from the warmth and energy of Zuma's embraces, I should actually be pressed to death between her monstrous arms'.

Finding she made no progress with Lander, she turned to Clapperton, bestowing a beautiful female slave on the insatiable Pascoe to secure his co-operation as match-maker. Paralysed by her determined affection, Clapperton thought 'this was carrying the joke a little too far'. The widow sent for a mirror in which she examined herself and then passed it to Clapperton, remarking 'to be sure she was rather older than me, but very little, and what of that?' The co-operation of the Sultan was required to extricate the explorers from Zuma's massive clutch.

They were now close to the Niger, the great river that was the object of Clapperton's quest, which he had failed to reach on his first expedition. He first saw it on 31 March 1826, though his journal merely notes the event cryptically – Clapperton's health was so poor that he was not always capable of writing lengthy notes.

The Niger was crossed by ferry on 10 April, and the expedition advanced along the well-travelled road to Kano, finding themselves in a more cosmopolitan environment with markets frequented by merchants from North Africa. Clapperton was so ill that he was carried a large part of the way in a hammock. At river fords, the stocky Lander carried him over on his back.

Kano was no more attractive than it had been on Clapperton's previous visit, and both men were ill in the fly-blown city. Clapperton's journal was reduced to brief and depressing comments:

Wednesday 27 July – ill
Thursday 28   – ill all day
Friday 29   – a little better
Saturday 30 [Lander's handwriting] – Verey hill, unable to [eat] anything

Finally, the daily entries ceased altogether.

Towards the end of August Clapperton, though still in 'very bad health', was able to drag himself over the 240 miles to Sokoto. He was kindly received by Bello, but it soon turned out that the Sultan was no longer so favourably disposed towards him as he had been nearly three years earlier. No doubt the Arab merchants had helped to turn him against Europeans, and perhaps he had had further thoughts about British expansion in India and the French conquest of Egypt, which had made a strong and unfavourable impression on the whole world of Islam. Worse still from Bello's point of view was the discovery that Clapperton carried letters and presents (arms, it was rumoured) for his enemy, the Sheikh of Bornu. The presents were taken away, along with other possessions, in spite of Clapperton's – in the circumstances, bravely spirited – protests that the Sultan's people were behaving like a nation of robbers.

Lander had been left at Kano, but in December he arrived at Sokoto, summoned thither by the suspicious Bello. The two men were both in poor condition and their supplies, through time and depradation, were low. They still had some cigars left, and the last pleasant scene of Clapperton's life is of the two friends – still master and servant but nonetheless devoted to each other – telling each other stories of home or singing Scottish and English songs as the companionable smoke drifted lazily into the warm evening air.

In March, Clapperton again became seriously ill, and soon he realized that he was dying. Richard Lander described his master's final instructions to him in a letter made all the more affecting by its innocence of punctuation and its curious spelling (corrected in the published version). Clapperton died on 13 April 1827. He was thirty-nine.

Although he was, perhaps, the greatest British explorer of Africa between Mungo Park and David Livingstone, Hugh Clapperton has received little attention by comparison with those much-discussed travellers. He became an African explorer more or less by chance, though the continent and its mysteries soon gripped him as they gripped many later travellers. He was obviously a man of great courage and strength (of character as well as body), hearty, patriotic, religious, basically conventional, occasionally rather rash (though usually for a good reason). His less likeable characteristics, such as his inclination to shoot anything that moved, are also those of his time: 19th-century explorers could hardly be expected to behave like 20th-century conservationists. His own writing about his travels is on the whole excellent: he was reasonably tolerant, observant, and sensible, and although the published *Journal* of his second expedition is inferior to his account of the earlier mission to Sokoto, that can be ascribed partly to illness and partly to the fact that death prevented him preparing his notes for publication, while the man who did (Barrow) was rather unsympathetic to Clapperton as a result of their contrary theories concerning the Niger (Barrow was weirdly determined that it should flow east and be linked with the Nile). Few personal feelings, bar the most obvious and predictable, emerge from Clapperton's writings, though he is unusual in admitting by implication to sexual relations with an African woman. Otherwise, he is reticent, and E.W. Bovill has suggested that his reputation 'suffered from his modesty and extreme reserve which, as an explorer, he carried to a fault'.

*   *   *

The death of Clapperton left the young and inexperienced Lander in an unenviable predicament. He was a man of immense resource, yet he could hardly have extricated himself from the middle of the continent if he had been entirely alone. In Kano, the frequent misdemeanours of Pascoe had caused endless trouble, but now Pascoe showed his worth. Declining to settle in his Hausa homeland, he accompanied Lander throughout his journey, and was still at his side when the intrepid young Cornishman reached England.

Clapperton had advised his servant to return by the northern route to the Fezzan, where he would be able to contact Consul Warrington in Tripoli, but so meagre were his resources that, at Kano, Lander found he would be unable to pay his way so far and elected instead to return southwards to the coast. As it turned out, the fears that made Clapperton advise against this route were unfounded. Lander encountered no resentment at his visit to the enemy capital of Sokoto, merely surprise that he had escaped with his life from so abominable a place. Those who had given him and Clapperton a friendly welcome on the way north were still friendly, and sorry to hear the news of Clapperton's death. The journey was not completed without frightening incidents, and Lander was revolted by the prevailing diet of roast dog, stewed rat, and fried locusts, but at least he did not have to run the gauntlet of a hostile population. He arrived at Badagri in November, 1827 two years all but nine days since he had left it.

Chiefly as a result of generations of contact with European slave-traders, life on the coast was often more violent and more dangerous than in the interior. No one paid much attention when two women had their throats cut in Lander's horrified sight. Moreover, the Portuguese-speaking half-castes who controlled the slave trade at Badagri were, not surprisingly, hostile to any member of the nation that was trying to close down their business. Having completed a long journey which no one, including himself, had really believed he would survive, Lander found himself, at the end of it, in a worse situation than any he had encountered on his travels. At the instigation of the slavers, he was called before the chief men and accused of being a spy preparing the way for a British invasion. He was forced to undergo trial by ordeal, which in this case consisted of drinking a quart of some liquid which, he was assured, would only kill him if he were guilty. Seeing no alternative, he swallowed the lot and, before an astonished throng, marched out of the place and back to the privacy of his hut, where he hastily took a powerful emetic that emptied his stomach.

Having survived without harm an ordeal which, he was told, 'almost always proved fatal', he rose sharply in the estimation of the local people, although the slavers made no secret of their continued hatred, and he was warned by the now-friendly king not to go out unarmed. It was a grim conclusion to all that Lander had endured, for it was not until early in the New Year that a British skipper, hearing rumours farther down the coast of a white man marooned at Badagri, put in to investigate. He was on patrol looking for slave ships, and Lander had, perforce, quite a voyage through the Atlantic before he arrived home. Among other places, they called at Fernando Po, where Lander met Colonel Dixon Denham, recently appointed governor of Sierra Leone. No record of their conversation exists, and Denham died not long afterwards.

Early in 1830, Richard Lander was again at Badagri. This time among his companions was his younger brother John, as well as that likeable tough egg, Pascoe.

The organization of the expedition seems to have been a shade casual. ('With a bundle of beads and bafts and other trinkets, we could land him somewhere about Bonny and let him find his way,' Barrow had suggested.) Expeditions to the Niger were no longer popular with the government, and the Landers' journey would probably never have taken place but for the tireless needling of John Barrow and the modest requirements of the two explorers. Richard Lander said he would go for £100; John said he would go for nothing, and nothing was approximately what he got (a modest payment was later authorized to compensate for his ruined health). The object of the expedition, however, was clearly stated: to take Clapperton's route to Bussa, there to embark in canoes and follow the river to its termination, wherever that might be.

Badagri was as beastly as ever, and the King demanded a large payment in gold for allowing the party to pass into the interior. They got away just in time to avoid witnessing the sacrifice of three hundred people that the king, with some relish, was planning.

Moving north on foot and horseback, they encountered familiar faces and the accustomed welcome, though less ecstatic than before as white men were no longer novelties. The peril from fever was no less, and John Lander in particular found the constant attention of the noisy populace a dreadful strain. They had little peace until they reached Katunga, where the king proclaimed that no one was to bother them, on pain of execution. Among the presents this sovereign received was no less valuable an item than Richard Lander's 'bugle horn'. At Kaiama, they witnessed an exciting horse race and observed that the king was still attended by naked virgins. On the way to Bussa, John Lander was very ill with fever and 'scarcely able to stand'. He grew worse and poor Richard feared that he was on the point of death when, quite suddenly, he recovered, showing a resilience comparable to that of his brother, who had a remarkable ability to throw off a serious illness in a day or two.

At Bussa they received a visit from 'the noted widow Zuma'. She had suffered a decline in her fortunes as a result, the brothers suspected, of unwise dabbling in the politics of Wawa. Nevertheless, she expounded on her misfortunes 'with great good humour'. She had grown even fatter, so that 'it was with the utmost difficulty she could squeeze herself into the doorway of our hut, although it is by no means small'.

The Niger at Bussa looked unimpressive, 'not more than a stone's throw across at present'. The Landers, 'knowing the jealousy of most of the people with regard to the Niger', did not reveal their intention to travel down it, but said they were on their way to Yauri and Bornu. The king promised them safe conduct to Yauri and, in answer to their inquiries about Mungo Park, produced a book that had belonged to that famous traveller. The excited Landers had hoped it might be Park's journal, but it turned out to be merely an almanac that he had carried. (It was purchased nearly thirty years later by Lieutenant John Glover, the first governor of Lagos, and is now at the Royal Geographical Society.) The only personal item was a slip of paper inviting Mr Park to dine with a Mr and Mrs Watson in the Strand in November 1804. Later, the Landers retrieved other relics of Park, but they lost them in the course of their homeward journey.

What made African exploration such a time-consuming

business was not so much the slow traversing of great distances but the inevitable long delays at place after place, which were often the result of political or economic circumstances of which the explorers comprehended little. The Landers on the Niger in the summer of 1830 had the utmost difficulty in equipping themselves with a canoe: 'There is infinitely more difficulty and greater bustle and discussion in simply purchasing a canoe here, than there would be in Europe in drawing up a treaty of peace, or in determining the boundaries of an empire . . .' At Yauri, where their reception was rather cool, they had no luck at all, so returned to Bussa and Wawa. They arranged to buy a suitable vessel from the king of Wawa, and travelled to the spot where it was to be picked up in two smaller canoes lent by the kindly ruler – 'a little round, fat, jolly-looking old man' – of an island just south of Bussa. On their arrival, the canoe was not there, and they therefore decided to keep the canoes they had already – although without much hope that the king of Wawa would hand over the price to their island benefactor. 'It grieves and saddens us beyond expression to do this thing . . . But what can we do?'

One of the gates of the city of Kano. Clapperton estimated that the city contained thirty or forty thousand residents, more than half of them slaves. 'The city is rendered very unhealthy by a large morass, which almost divides it into two parts, besides many pools of stagnant water, made by digging clay for building houses.' His own health was poor at the time, which perhaps exacerbated his poor opinion of the city.

The boatmen, provided with the canoes, naturally protested at what amounted to a theft from their master, and the brothers 'were actually ashamed to look them in the face'.

So far, they had been moving in territory already known to Richard Lander; now they embarked upon their epic cruise on the unknown Niger – to wherever the river should lead them. They were, of course, reasonably certain that the river would end in the Bight of Benin, and they knew it would not carry them to Lake Chad, as Barrow still believed. It seems strange, perhaps, that none of the people they asked could tell them for certain where the Niger flowed, but this part of Africa was inhabited by a confusing variety of people, most of them on bad terms with their neighbours and not interested in the river beyond their particular stretch. The Landers were warned of the many dangers that would assail them (and events were to show that the direst predictions were not much exaggerated), especially when they passed into the country of animistic peoples, where Islam had not penetrated, beyond the borders of Nupe.

John Lander's descriptions of the Niger scenery as they travelled downstream ('with considerable velocity') verged on the poetic: '. . . both banks presented the most delightful appearance. They were embellished with mighty trees and elegant shrubs, which were clad in thick and luxuriant foliage, some of lively green, and others of darker hue; and little birds were singing merrily among their branches. Magnificent festoons of creeping plants, always green, hung from the tops

of the tallest trees, and dropping to the water's edge, formed immense natural grottoes, pleasing and grateful to the eye, and seemed to be fit abodes for the Naiades of the River!' All the same, 'there is something wanting in an African scene to render it comparable in interest and beauty to an English landscape'.

At Zagozhi, south of Rabba, they obtained a canoe big enough to take their whole party. They nearly lost it the same evening, first when 'an incredible number of hippopotami . . . came plashing, snorting, and plunging all round the canoe', then as a storm made their craft unmanageable. The next day they stopped at a village on an island and, for the first time, were unable to make themselves understood, although the members of their party could speak, between them, five local languages including the *lingua franca*, Hausa. Another storm compelled them to take shelter in the swampy reedbeds fringing the river, but 'no sooner had we got into the morass, and were congratulating ourselves on our deliverance, than a frightful crocodile, of prodigious size, sprang forth from his retreat, close to the canoe, and plunged underneath it with extraordinary violence, to the amazement and terror of us all: we had evidently disturbed him from his sleep'.

On 19 October, three weeks after leaving Bussa, they reached the 'large, handsome town' of Eggan, the last town of Nupe. Here they were earnestly advised not to go farther south where the banks were 'inhabited by people who were little better than savages'. The venerable chief of Eggan had 'to all outward appearances lived at least a hundred years', but was still active, and 'instead of the peevishness and discontent too often the accompaniment of lengthened days, [he possessed] all the ease and gaiety of youth'. As elsewhere, the travellers were put to some inconvenience by the curiosity of the inhabitants, which kept them confined to their huts. 'The people stand gazing at us with visible emotions of amazement and terror; we are regarded, in fact, in just the same light as the fiercest tigers in England. If we venture to approach too near the doorway, they rush backwards in a state of the greatest alarm and trepidation; but when we are at the opposite side of the hut, they draw as near as their fears will permit them, in silence and caution.'

To the astonishment of the people, the Landers insisted on going forward in spite of the fears of their boatmen and the warning that they would undoubtedly be captured and plundered. 'Go we must,' said the brothers, 'if we live or die by it, and that also tomorrow.' They agreed to pass one notorious trouble spot by night, but even so, 'the poor natives gazed at us with astonishment, no doubt expecting that we should never be seen or heard of more'.

Two days later, the direction of the river, running between high hills, changed to SSW. 'At five o'clock this morning, we found ourselves nearly opposite a very considerable river, entering the Niger from the eastward; it appeared to be three or four miles wide at its mouth . . . We first supposed it to be an arm of [the Niger], and running from us; and therefore directed our course for it. We proceeded up a short distance, but finding the current against us . . . we were compelled to give up the attempt . . . We conclude this to be the Tshadda . . .' It was, of course, the river now known as the Benue (i.e. 'mother of waters'), not seen before by Europeans, the existence of which no doubt helps to account for the persistence of the theory that the Niger ran east–west in this region.

The same day, 25 October, the language difficulty was

Tuareg. They 'are no agriculturalists [and] have a sovereign contempt for inhabitants of cities and cultivators of ground. They look upon them all as degenerate beings.' (Oudeney). 'The appearance of three or four Tuareg is sufficient to strike terror into five or six villages.' (Caillié). From a 19th-century lithograph.

responsible for a crisis which might have ended in the death of the whole party but for the sensible and courageous behaviour of the Landers. They sought food from a village, but the women of the village (the men being absent) were terrified by the appearance of strangers and ran away. The explorers set up camp nearby, and were preparing for sleep when an alarm was given. A large party of armed men was approaching the camp, their aggressive intentions in no doubt. The Landers resolved 'to prevent bloodshed if possible – our numbers were too few to leave us a chance of escaping by any other way'. Pascoe and the others (except for two who fled) were ordered to have their guns at the ready but not to fire unless first fired upon. The Landers threw down their own pistols and walked towards the leader of their attackers, making all the signs they could think of to indicate a desire for peace. 'His quiver was dangling at his side, his bow was bent, and an arrow, which was pointed at our breasts, already trembled on the string, when we were within a few yards of his person. This was a highly critical moment – the next might be our last. But the hand of Providence averted the blow; for

A palaver. 'Had Job, amongst his other trials, been exposed to the horrors of an interminable African palaver, *his patience must have forsaken him.' (John Lander).*

just as the chief was about to pull the fatal cord, a man that was nearest him rushed forward, and stayed his arm. At that instant we stood before him, and immediately held forth our hands; all of them trembled like aspen leaves; the chief looked up full in our faces, kneeling on the ground – light seemed to flash from his dark rolling eyes – his body was convulsed all over, as though he were enduring the utmost torture, and with a timorous, yet undefinable, expression of countenance, in which all the passions of our nature were strangely blended, he drooped his head, eagerly grasped our proffered hands, and burst into tears. This was a sign of friendship – harmony followed, and war and bloodshed were thought of no more.'

Later, an old man was found who could translate into Hausa, and through him the chief explained that the travellers had been mistaken for enemies from the other side of the river, 'and when you drew near me, and extended your hand towards me, I felt my heart faint within me, and believed that you were "Children of Heaven".' Both misconceptions having been disposed of, the meeting ended happily with the provision of a large quantity of yams and kola nuts. Next morning, after 'our usual scanty breakfast of a roasted yam and some water from the river', the travellers said goodbye with three cheers and a couple of musket shots.

They found themselves passing through a heavily forested, little-populated region: 'Our canoe passed smoothly along the Niger, and everything was silent and solitary; no sound could be distinguished except our own voices and the plashing of the paddles with their echoes; the song of birds was not heard, nor could any animal whatever be seen: the banks seemed to be entirely deserted, and the magnificent Niger to be slumbering in its own grandeur.'

Soon they entered a country where Europeans were no longer cause for astonishment or dismay – a hopeful sign that they were nearing the coast. Many of the people even had a smattering of English. At Adamugu, a hospitable ruler ('one of the worthiest fellows whom we have yet met') gave the two brothers a smart canoe, as he regarded their presence in the battered old craft occupied by the rest of their party as undignified for such important persons. He offered the worst rum the Landers had ever tasted, but kindly devoted the attention of himself and his priests for several hours to the entrails of a chicken, an examination which revealed that the omens were inauspicious. 'Our determination of departing, however, was not to be shaken by such means.'

Perhaps they should have been less bold. They were

The confluence of the Rivers Niger and Chadda (or Benue). 'Far as the eye could reach, over miles and miles, the ground teemed with exuberant vegetation; seeming often in the fantastic appearance of its wild growth to revel in its exemption from culture. Such a fruitful soil . . . would yield support and employment to countless thousands, and long ere this have proved a source of untold wealth.' W.B. Baikie, writing in 1854.

approaching the delta region – where the Niger, as if exhausted by its long run to the sea, loses itself in a bewildering morass of streams and swamps – when they were attacked by Ibo river pirates. Their possessions were plundered (most of Richard's journal was lost permanently) and they were captured, which meant, in effect, enslaved. After a long palaver, it was resolved that the Landers' goods – those that had not gone to the bottom of the river during the attack – should be given back, but that they should remain prisoners of the Obi, an Ibo king. They had lost nearly everything of value and their situation was unpromising, to say the least. However, 'we quickly resumed our former cheerfulness' and looked forward eagerly to the trip down to Aboh, where the Obi was holding court. They do not seem to have realized that they were no more than the spoils of war to the Obi, though he soon enlightened them. It was a sad contrast to the favoured position they had enjoyed in Yoruba towns.

They were eventually extricated from their predicament by a minor chieftain with the charming and, as his father was ruler of Brass, not inappropriate name of king Boy. He ransomed them from the Obi and transported them down the Nun (one of the main streams of the delta) to Brass, where he hoped to make a reasonable profit by turning them over to an English ship anchored there. In fact, the drunken and coarse Captain Lake at first refused to let them on board. However, he was short-handed, and when he realized the Landers' party included several able-bodied African boatmen, he agreed to take them all. When king Boy arrived to collect his ransom, however, Captain Lake turned his guns on him and refused to pay a single cowrie. The Landers were shocked by this shabby trick, but they could do nothing about it. (The money was eventually paid to king Boy by the British government, and Richard Lander brought presents to the somewhat mollified chief when he returned to the Niger in 1832).

*   *   *

The problem of the Niger had been solved at last (although John Barrow, his theory in ruins, refused to accept that the river *was* the Niger), and while some long stretches remained almost or entirely unknown, the course had been followed by Europeans from the upper reaches to its mouth. The cost in lives had been high; indeed, the casualty rate for Europeans (including Park's unfortunate soldiers) was nearly 90 per cent. The results were less easy to calculate, and apart from the satisfying settlement of a great geographical problem, the immediate benefits, to Africans or Europeans, were slight. In the longer term, however, the exploration of the lower Niger was of immense significance, leading eventually to the colony and federation of modern Nigeria.

Richard Lander next appeared on the Niger a year later, as

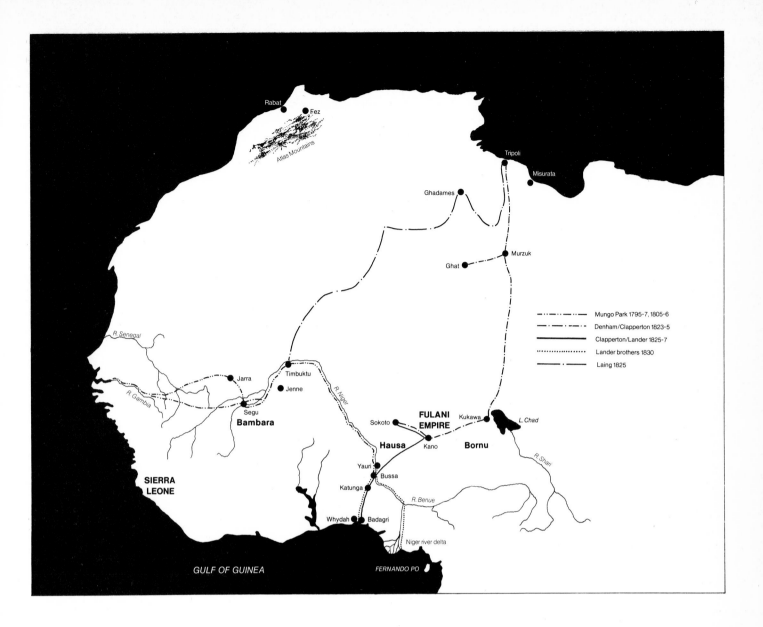

Mungo Park 1795-7, 1805-6
Denham/Clapperton 1823-5
Clapperton/Lander 1825-7
Lander brothers 1830
Laing 1825

captain of the steamer *Alburkha* (a Hausa word meaning blessing) in the commercially oriented expedition of a young shipbuilding magnate, Macgregor Laird. In the course of the expedition (1832–34) both Laird and Lander travelled independently a considerable distance up the Benue, but their expedition was not a success. Although palm oil was an increasingly important product on the old Slave Coast, slaves were still the most profitable merchandise.

The chief hazard remained, as it had always been, malaria. Only nine of the forty-eight Europeans on the Laird expedition returned safely. Lander could still fight off fever, but in January 1834, while canoeing upstream laden with valuable goods, he was ambushed, and in the fight received a shot in the buttock. Though unpleasant, it did not seem serious, but the wound festered and he died at Fernando Po two weeks later. His brother John never recovered altogether from the effects of his African travels, and died in 1839, still only thirty-two years old.

A further attempt to open up Nigerian commerce, this time with the primary aim of suppressing the slave trade, was made by the large expedition led by Captain William Allen and others (including the African missionary Samuel Crowther, later consecrated a bishop in England), in 1841. Heavy mortalities (35 per cent of the Europeans) made the

expedition a disaster, although one notable advance was made in the dawning realization of the effectiveness of quinine against malaria.

The final conquest of the disease was made by an Edinburgh-trained doctor, William Balfour Baikie, a protégé of Sir Roderick Murchison, who travelled as surgeon on the Niger expedition of 1854, penetrating a long way up the Benue. Thanks to Baikie's use of quinine, not one of the twelve Europeans died of fever on this expedition.

Along with Samuel Crowther and Lieutenant Glover, Baikie returned to the Niger in 1857, intent on proving his belief that trade was the best means of communication with the people. Near the junction of the Niger and the Benue, Crowther established the first Christian mission in Nigeria, and Baikie settled down for a stay of six years, acting as part British consul, part district governor for the Emir of Nupe, part doctor and part merchant. Though at first resentful at his neglect by the British government, when an order came for his recall he politely declined to go. By the time he did agree to return, in 1864, he had become more African than European. He had shown beyond doubt that Europeans could live without undue danger on the banks of the Niger but, by grim paradox, the courageous doctor died at Sierra Leone on the way home.

Roads to Timbuktu

Richard Lander was the first but not the last young man born with few advantages who was impelled by the lure of strange places and the desire for fame to impress his name upon the roll of African explorers. The great journey of René Caillié began in the same year that Lander went to West Africa with Clapperton, and was completed late in 1828, two years before the Lander brothers paddled down the Niger to the coast.

Caillié was a baker's son from Poitou, born in 1799, the year that Napoleon returned from Egypt to overthrow the Directory. Since his earliest infancy, says Caillié in the introduction to his *Travels*, he had cherished a strong desire to become a traveller. Though aware of his lack of qualifications ('the want of a good education') he was always hopeful of exploring some unknown part of Africa; in particular, 'the city of Timbuctoo became the continual object of all my thoughts, the aim of all my efforts, and I formed a resolution to reach it or perish'.

His preparations for his journey were lengthy but somewhat sporadic, largely as a result of the necessity of earning a living. He spent a long time in West Africa, but it is not always clear exactly what he was doing there. He first visited Senegal as a boy of sixteen, but after his application to join Major Gray's expedition up the Gambia (1819) had been rejected, he took ship for the West Indies. Three years later he was back in West Africa and made a journey into the interior. He became ill and returned to France, where for a time he worked as a clerk in Bordeaux, but returned in 1824, this time set firmly in his intention of reaching Timbuktu. An additional incentive was provided by the Geographical Society of Paris, which in 1824 offered a substantial cash prize to the first person to deliver an eye-witness report of the famous desert city.

Caillié made up for his lack of financial resources, and to some extent for his inexperience too, by a certain personal charm which attracted Europeans and Africans alike. He was, he tells us, 'an unpresuming traveller', and there was something about him – a youthful air of enthusiasm, combined with a courteous deference – that made people anxious to assist him. (There were some, however, who were immune to Caillié's charm.)

He decided to travel as a Muslim. Other explorers had adopted this method of avoiding the hostility of narrow-minded religious fanaticism, but Caillié's disguise was more thorough and was sustained longer than any except Burkhardt's. His story was that he was an Egyptian Arab who had been captured by Christians at an early age, taken to Europe (this excused his stumbling Arabic), and was now travelling as a pilgrim, anxious to regain the religious culture into which he had been born.

Many writers have expressed astonishment that he managed to get away with his pose, and although he appears to have escaped suspicion in Timbuktu, it is likely that he was frequently recognized for what he was. He records numerous examples of suspicion, and it is clear, for instance, that his first guide, Ibrahim, while accepting the story on the surface and faithfully repeating it to everyone they met, did not really believe a word of it. However, at times when it mattered most, Caillié's disguise seems to have been effective.

For a time Caillié worked in Sierra Leone as manager of an indigo factory, and though he failed to secure the governor's support for his projected journey, he managed to save from his wages the not inconsiderable sum of 2,000 francs. 'This treasure seemed to me to be sufficient to carry me all over the world.' He gave up his job, exchanged most of his cash for suitable trade goods, and moved a few miles up the coast to the Rio Nunez in order to establish his 'cover' in a region where his background was not so well known. Assisted by a French merchant, he made friends with a small group of Mande merchants who were preparing to travel to Timbuktu.

With Caillié's guide, Ibrahim, and his wife, plus one porter, besides the merchants and their women, the party of a dozen or so set out on 19 April 1827. They had gone but a mile or two when Ibrahim announced he was afraid that Caillié's fair skin would prevent his getting through. 'This reflection appeared to come a little too late,' said Caillié, noting ironically that it was followed by an exploratory request for a piece of cloth, a feeler that Caillié sensibly rejected. Ibrahim reluctantly swallowed his doubts with his avarice.

They were joined on the road by some Fulani travellers. They 'had been told that I was an Arab, shewed a sort of veneration for me, and were never weary of looking at me and pitying me: their extreme devotion renders them very charitable: they came and sat by me, taking my legs upon their knees, and rubbing them to relieve my fatigue. "Thou must suffer sadly," said they, "because thou art not used to such a toilsome journey." One of them went and fetched some leaves to make me a bed. "Here!" said he, "this is for thee; for thou canst not sleep upon the stones, as we do." Lying upon my bed of leaves, I felt as happy and as much at my ease as if I had been in my own apartment. The sky was serene. The heat of the day had been succeeded by a refreshing breeze, and everything was exceedingly pleasant'.

When he wanted to make notes, Caillié retired 'to the woods', or anywhere out of sight, and took care to rest his paper on a leaf of the Koran, which he would pretend to be studying if disturbed.

Like other travellers in Africa, Caillié was constantly called upon to exercise his presumed skills as a doctor: 'The traveller obliged to turn physician' is the way he puts it in a chapter sub-heading, for it was a task he embarked on with the greatest reluctance. Not only was he aware of his lack of medical skill, he was a trifle squeamish in face of the more horribly disease-ruined creatures brought to him. Some cases would indeed have puzzled the most brilliant product of the medical schools of Montpellier or Paris, and required magic rather than therapy. On these occasions Caillié, if forced to prescribe, would advise his patient that the cure would not begin to work for twenty days. By that time he hoped to be far away. His prescriptions were sometimes very plausible even though based on premises far removed from medical science. One man complained of impotence. 'As ginger grew in the environs, I advised him to eat plenty.'

Considering the difficulty of making notes on his journey, Caillié's account of people and places is at times remarkably detailed and perceptive, and his book is the more enjoyable for the inclusion of intimate details which an explorer like Clapperton rigorously excluded. He has a lot to say, for example, on the subject of food, of which he was fond. He found Ramadan, when Muslims fast until nightfall and then eat only sparingly, a severe trial. Fortunately, it was often not strictly observed, and those who did observe it did not expect him to do so. A hospitable Fulani who invited him to his camp and brought him milk in a calabash ('which he washed, an extraordinary ceremony in this part of the world') with some fried meat, would not join him at the meal. 'Pointing with his finger to the moon, he said, smiling, and with an air of timidity, "I fast; it is the Ramadan."'

René Caillié, the first European to visit Timbuktu – and return to tell of it.

They reached the Niger at Kouroussa in mid-June, and advanced through Bambara, where Caillié's health, which had been growing increasingly frail, broke down and plunged him into the worst crisis of his journey. He had reached a place called Tiémé, nearly halfway to Timbuktu, at the beginning of August, when his journey was interrupted for five months. His troubles began with an ulcerated foot, but he was soon attacked by a disease that he recognized as scurvy: 'The roof of my mouth became quite bare, a part of the bones exfoliated and fell away, and my teeth seemed ready to drop out of their sockets. I feared that my brain would be affected by the agonizing pains I felt in my head . . .' He prayed for death to release him from his misery. An old Negro woman looked after him, forcing him to drink rice-water twice a day. Another woman plied him with medicine made from a 'red wood' which may or may not have assisted his recovery. Meanwhile, his stock of trade goods dwindled away as he was bound to give presents to those who sheltered him and, unfortunately, they were convinced that he was rich.

Not until the New Year (1828) was he able to resume his journey towards Jenne, where he spent two weeks. He was well received by the chief men, for whose benefit he revised his cover story yet again. 'The Moors asked me numerous questions about the Christians and the way in which they had treated me. They all inquired whether I had been beaten and treated like a slave; whether I had been prevented from praying; and whether I had eaten pork or drunk brandy.' Caillié answered their faintly prurient questions with a mixture of truth and fantasy, endeavouring in a small way to further the cause of religious toleration without blowing his cover. He denied that the Christians kept slaves, but was naturally asked why, in that case, he had remained so long in their company. 'My master . . . who had no child, regarded me as his son and would not part with me. "His fortune," added I, "could not tempt me. I despised it when I thought of a future life and the paradise of Mahomet." They congratulated me on these praiseworthy feelings.'

If there seems to be something a little distasteful about Caillié's deceiving these eager inquirers, it ought to be remembered that, as the experiences of other travellers had shown, a different course would have subjected him to extreme danger, possibly death. To speak well of Christians invited trouble. In Timbuktu, when he attempted to defend the reputation of Christians from calumny, he was asked the unanswerable question, 'If the Christians are so very good, why did you not stay among them?'

After a very uncomfortable journey down the river in a hundred-foot punt, wrapped in a blanket to keep his fair skin from the sight of the greedy Tuareg (to whom it would have been a sign of wealth), Caillié arrived at Timbuktu on 20 April 1828, a year almost to the hour since he had started on his journey. In that time, five months of it stationary through illness, he had travelled about 1500 miles, two thirds of them on foot.

'At length, we arrived safely in Timbuktu . . . I now saw this capital of the Soudan, to reach which had so long been the object of my wishes. On entering this mysterious city, which is an object of curiosity and research to the civilized nations of Europe, I experienced an indescribable satisfaction. I never before felt a similar emotion and my transport was extreme . . . With what gratitude did I return thanks to Heaven, for the happy result which attended my enterprise.'

But, having given thanks to God, Caillié began to look around him and found that the sight before him did not answer his expectations. 'I had formed a totally different idea of the grandeur and wealth of Timbuctoo. The city presented, at first view, nothing but a mass of ill-looking houses, built of earth.'

So much for the great desert metropolis, with its roofs of gold and its libraries of learning! Whether or not Caillié was as surprised as he says he was to find it such an undistinguished-looking place, the legend was at last dead (although it took a long time to lie down). Like many legends, perhaps it was never believed quite so widely as now appears; perhaps people merely liked to preserve a harmless myth until the myth was thoroughly exploded by reported fact. Within a year of Caillié's entry into Timbuktu, and before the publication of his book, an undergraduate named Tennyson at Cambridge University wrote a prize-winning poem on the subject, in which he addressed Africa as follows:

> . . . Or is the rumour of thy Timbuctoo
> A dream as frail as those of ancient time?
> . . . the time is well-nigh come
> When I must render up this glorious home
> To keen Discovery: soon your brilliant towers
> Shall darken with the waving of her wand;
> Darken, and shrink and shiver into huts,
> Black specks amid a waste of dreary sand,
> Low-built, mud-wall'd, barbarian settlements.

(Quoted by Brian Gardner, *The Quest for Timbuctoo*.)

With his usual knack, Caillié found an influential and hospitable patron at Timbuktu. This generous host told him he could stay as long as he wished. 'You will gratify me by so doing; you shall want for nothing.' When two others were lodged in the house where he was staying, making it difficult for him to write his journal, he mentioned to his host that he would prefer being alone, and was immediately given another house (directly opposite the one where Gordon Laing had stayed). 'I found myself much more comfortable in my new lodging . . . The slaves who lived in the house were ordered to wait on me, and they brought me twice a day couscous and rice seasoned with beef or mutton.'

There were others in the town who treated the poor traveller generously: 'When I was at the mosque, a middle-aged Moor stepped up to me gravely, and without saying a word slipped a handful of cowries into the pocket of my coussabe. He withdrew immediately without affording me time to thank him.'

Caillié naturally devoted a substantial part of his book to a description of Timbuktu. He estimated the inhabitants at ten or twelve thousand, not counting the transient Arab merchants (Barth said thirteen thousand, with between five and ten thousand transients). He noted the precarious economic situation of the city, which had to import nearly all its food, and remarked on its dependence upon the trade in salt (the gold trade had long died out). If the Tuareg interrupted the river traffic, as they were undoubtedly capable of doing, the city was helpless. It was therefore customary to pay 'protection' money to the Tuareg as and when demanded: 'I was assured that, if the crews dared but to strike one of these savages, they would forthwith declare war against Timbuctoo, and intercept all communication with the port' (i.e. Kabara, the port of Timbuktu, some seven miles from the city; Caillié guessed Timbuktu had once been closer to the river). There was no communication along the Niger to the east; nevertheless, Caillié was again correct in suggesting that it turned south and flowed into the Gulf of Benin.

In spite of Timbuktu's disadvantages and the generally disappointing spectacle the city presented, Caillié's description is of a more attractive place than that seen by later visitors: higher living standards than most places he had visited; neatness and cleanliness; less personal violence ('the women . . . are not . . . subject to the punishment of beating'); reasonably good food, at least for the better-off; no tobacco-smoking, except by visitors; full warehouses and a well-stocked market. There was, Caillié concluded, 'something imposing in the aspect of a great city raised in the midst of sands, and the difficulties surmounted by its founders cannot fail to excite admiration'.

No prize was more justly earned than René Caillié's award from the Geographical Society of Paris, even though he was not the first European in modern times to visit Timbuktu. That strange, doomed adventurer, Gordon Laing, had been there two years earlier, but he had not returned, his journals were lost, and his only communication from the city was notably uninformative. Moreover, a man calling himself 'Robert Adams' (a *nom-de-plume*) had published in 1816 an account of a visit to Timbuktu several years earlier. Adams was an American sailor of part-African descent (it is therefore somewhat incongruous to call him a European; however, as far as Africa was concerned, he was a 'European'). He was shipwrecked on the coast south of Morocco in 1811, captured by 'Moors' and taken to Timbuktu as a slave. He was not the least interested in Timbuktu, or any other place in Africa. Very naturally, he wanted only to go home, and he eventually did, after nearly three years' slavery, being ransomed by the British consul at Mogador, Joseph Dupuis.

Although one or two influential men, including the well-informed Dupuis, accepted Adam's story without serious reservations, the consensus of opinion was against him. Part of his story, it was said, was no doubt true, but his visit to Timbuktu was an invention. According to Heinrich Barth, Adam's description of Timbuktu 'does not reveal a single trait which can be identified with its features'. One reason for doubting Adams may well have been his description of Timbuktu as a relatively poor and unattractive place. Later, this description would become a point in his favour, yet Adams' story has been doubted ever since. He was a poor man without powerful friends, with little interest in exploration, and his account, much edited (Adams was apparently illiterate), does contain some oddities. In his excellent book *The Quest for Timbuctoo* (1968), Brian Gardner devotes a chapter to Adams' adventures: he argues most convincingly for the truth of Adams' story, and the fact that Adams rapidly disappeared from the scene without making any effort to refute the accusations of fraud seems to be additional cause for believing that, bar a few touches where invention may have supplied the lapse of memory, Adams' story was genuine.

*   *   *

From Timbuktu, a thousand miles of deadly desert – where caravans hundreds strong had disappeared without a trace – stretched before the 'unpresuming traveller'. René Caillié chose this route, rather than returning by the way he had come, because there was always a chance that if he reappeared at his starting place, sceptics would say he had never been to Timbuktu at all. By crossing the whole great western bulge of Africa he would forestall such attacks. Caillié was by no means a 'professional' explorer in the modern sense; in fact, he was unable to fulfil all the requirements of the Paris Geographical Society, which included 'a geographical map founded upon celestial observations'. Fortunately, no one quibbled over this.

It is clear also that Caillié seriously underestimated the difficulty of the trans-Sahara journey. Wells were few and unreliable and, as more recent Saharan travellers have discovered (Geoffrey Moorhouse for example), the terrible stresses of the long desert journey tend to bring forth the unpleasant aspects of the character of one's companions.

He travelled with a caravan bound for Fez. The first landmark on the journey was the spot where Laing had been murdered, pointed out by Caillié's companions without regret while Caillié successfully dissembled his own feelings. They paused for a week in the uninviting desert town of Arouan (Arawan), waiting for others to join them, and set off again on 19 May. Some way north of the town, they came to the last wells for 200 miles. All stopped to pray. Then they pressed forward, through a landscape in which nothing at all was to be seen except an 'immense plain of shining sand, and over it a burning sky'.

It was like travelling across a vast mirror under a relentless spotlight. Caillié was possessed by the idea of water – oceans, rivers, streams, waterfalls. Lakes appeared shimmering before him, constantly retreating and vanishing before his tortured eyes. Nothing else in the world mattered: water was all.

As a strong wind arose, gritty blankets enveloped them, tearing down tents and hurling men and animals together. They marched on slowly, the camels faltering, and after 200 painful miles reached the wells, where Caillié thrust himself among the thirst-crazed camels to lap at thin black mud.

They passed the bleak salt mines of Taoudeni, a place of grim simplicity consisting of nothing but salt and sand. Caillié was unable to eat, but there was not much food anyway, except for the meat of the camels that had been slaughtered on the journey. In the night, large snakes slid from their holes and slithered among the bones that marked the road. Caillié was taunted by the Moors, who called him 'Christian' and threw rubbish at him. But, weak and injured in a fall, he was allowed to ride a camel while others walked. The days passed slowly, and the caravan advanced, though sometimes by no more than four or five miles a day.

After six weeks in the desert, blessed signs of vegetation appeared. At Tafilet they saw the first palm trees since leaving the Sudan. As they entered the valleys of the Atlas, villages became more frequent. The end of the journey was in sight.

While death from thirst no longer threatened, there were other dangers. Entering the world of the Maghreb, they encountered more intelligent and well-informed people, who showed a close interest in the fair-skinned traveller claiming to be an Arab. But Caillié blandly maintained his air of innocence, and on 12 August he limped into Fez.

His difficulties were not quite over then; he was weak and ill – he could not climb on to a donkey without help – and he had almost no money left. With cruel exertion, he reached Rabat, only to find the man acting as French consul there thoroughly unhelpful. After hanging about helplessly for a week or two he decided to press on to Tangier, clinging to the back of an overburdened donkey.

The first reaction of the Consul at Tangier was equally unpromising. Apparently he doubted the truth of Caillié's story – the traveller's appearance was certainly not in his favour – and it was several days before the Consul allowed him to stay at his house, where Caillié could at last discard his tiresome disguise. Having played his role as an Arab for so long, a sense of unreality descended on him when he reverted to his true self.

That night he lay in a good bed for the first time in over a year; but he could not sleep, 'so much was I agitated by the remembrance of the perils I had passed through'.

The nervous Consul at last got him a passage on a French ship, and at the beginning of October he landed in Toulon, thankful to be out of that 'frightful country'. He found he had brought glory to France, something that was perhaps as important to him as any other motive for his journey. In Paris he was championed by the foremost Africanist in the Geographical Society, E.F. Jomard, and in spite of the almost inevitable doubters (especially among the jealous British), his place in history was assured.

For all the relief he felt at escaping from Africa, where he had suffered such trials, Caillié was not immune to the addictiveness of exploration, which is especially powerful in the case of Africa. He put forward various schemes intended to get him back there, but nothing came of them, and he died at the age of thirty-eight in the spring of 1838. The circum-

Sierra Leone. Freetown harbour in the mid-19th century.

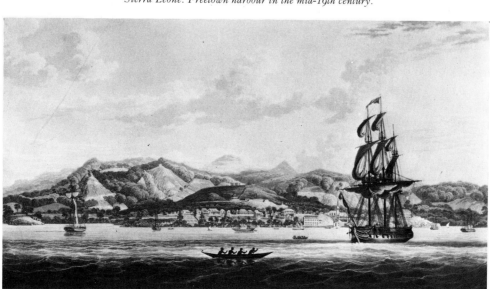

stances of his journey, without any kind of official sponsorship, without financial backing, and the manner of his description of it, make it one of the two or three outstanding journeys by Europeans in unexplored Africa.

* * *

In books about African explorers, accounts of Dr Heinrich Barth are usually prefaced by the remark that he is the most neglected of major African explorers. This was true in his own time (certainly Barth himself thought so) and for about one hundred years after his death, but although no biography in English has yet appeared, it is hardly true now. For Barth's reputation has been rising: his scholarly accomplishments and his scientific approach to geographical problems are now valued more highly than the tales of less weighty travellers. In some senses, Barth was the first 'modern' explorer, the antithesis of a romantic adventurer like René Caillié in his painstaking studies of African languages, his beautifully detailed maps (criticized in one contemporary review of his published account as unnecessarily elaborate!) and his acute historical sense.

Barth was the contemporary of Livingstone. The two met in London in the 1850s, and Livingstone later presented Barth with a copy of his *Missionary Travels* admiringly inscribed (the gesture was reciprocated). The glamour of Livingstone, and the associated shift in public interest away from the Sudan towards southern Africa partly accounted for the neglect of Barth. Another reason was that Barth, though working for the British, was a German, and a rather prickly, self-centred character, who utterly lacked Livingstone's popular appeal. Moreover, his travels, though vast and encompassing some important new geographical studies (to say nothing of his invaluable contributions to the history of northern Nigeria), seemed far less spectacular than Livingstone's march across Africa or the discovery of the Victoria Falls.

The tendency to dismiss Barth as a plodding, pedantic German professor has been responsible for some long-lasting misconceptions. His book, though enormous (five volumes of over 600 pages each) is seldom dull, and though no one could reasonably suggest that Barth's was a sparkling wit, he was not utterly lacking in humour. Indeed, it is hard to imagine how anyone could travel in West Africa and get on as well with the people as Barth generally did without possessing a sense of humour.

The leader of the expedition in which Barth took part was a deeply religious stalwart of the Anti-Slavery Society named James Richardson. He had already made one trip to Murzuk and Ghat, which had persuaded him that there was a chance of rescuing the Western Sudan from slavery and from what

Heinrich Barth, the German explorer whose written accounts of his travels set a standard of accuracy and observation rarely equalled.

he called 'the fake Prophet', and establishing Christianity in the heart of Africa. The foreign minister, Lord Palmerston, was sympathetic to these aspirations, and the government was still interested in opening up trans-Saharan trade. It was felt, however, that the expedition should include a man of science.

The name of Barth was put forward by the Prussian ambassador and recommended by August Petermann, the German cartographer, then working in London, and by the geographer Karl Ritter, a former teacher of Barth at the University of Berlin.

At this time (1849) Barth was twenty-eight years old, an experienced traveller and linguist, who carried in his leg a Bedouin bullet, painful reminder of a fracas in Egypt three years before from which he had been lucky to escape with his life. He had subsequently been appointed to the Department of Archaeology in Berlin, but had found the academic life unsuitable: one course of his lectures had to be cancelled because so few students turned up to listen.

The British government accepted Barth on condition that he paid £200 towards the expenses of the expedition. Barth agreed, but insisted on his own, not inconsiderable, condition: that geographical exploration should be the chief, not a secondary, object. Then a setback occurred. Barth's father, a stern Lutheran farmer to whom he was devoted, persuaded his son to withdraw from so perilous an enterprise. Another German, Dr Adolf Overweg, was appointed, but at the same time the government insisted that Barth was already under contract. The eventual result was that both Barth and Overweg accompanied Richardson across the Sahara (Richardson died near Kukawa early in 1851, Overweg near Lake Chad in the autumn of 1852).

The expedition also carried – in pieces – a boat which, reassembled and named the *Lord Palmerston*, was later sailed by Overweg on Lake Chad.

Barth landed at Tunis in December 1849. He sailed from Tripoli in September 1855. An idea of the territory he covered between those dates is given by the accompanying sketch map. His track often lay close to the routes of earlier explorers, and except for the area south of Lake Chad, Barth did not open up any very large regions that were wholly unknown. Yet he covered an immense amount of ground and, in his linguistic and historical inquiries particularly, he penetrated far more deeply than his predecessors into Sudanic culture.

Not the least remarkable of Barth's achievements was his success in simply staying alive for more than five years during his travels through the desert, swamp, and savanna. Yet an incident early in the expedition, between Murzuk and Ghat, did not augur well for his chances of survival.

In spite of the refusal of any guide to accompany him,

The mosque at Jenne. The original, 13th-century building disappeared long ago, and the present structure dates from the beginning of the 20th century.

Barth was determined to visit a rocky protuberance some way off where he expected to find some rock drawings and carvings (in which he was perhaps the first explorer to take a serious interest). But the distance proved to be greater than he had originally imagined, and when he at last reached a crest, 'in a state of the utmost exhaustion', not only was there no sign of rock carvings, rather worse, there was no sign of the caravan he had left. Nothing gave shelter from the sun, and he had very little water. After waiting for a time, and drinking the last of his water, he set out to find the camp. But, 'at length I became puzzled as to my direction'. He fired his pistols as a signal, but listened in vain for an answering report (the shots were not heard at the camp). He found some huts,

but they were abandoned and held no water. 'I sat down on the naked plain . . . and with some confidence expected the caravan.' His confidence was misplaced. A string of camels appeared, shimmered, and vanished with the mirage. Night fell quickly. Barth could not find the strength to gather wood for a fire: 'I was broken down and in a feverish state.' As dawn approached, he fired more shots, again without reply. Then 'the sun that I had longed for, half looked forward to with terror, at last rose'.

The Bedouins said a man might last in the desert without water for twelve hours. Barth had already lasted longer. He crawled about, desperately seeking shade, under a stunted, leafless tree. Desperate with thirst, he sucked blood from his own veins, then fell into 'a sort of delirium'. Some time later he regained consciousness and heard nearby the cry of a camel – 'the most delightful music I ever heard in my life'. A solitary

Tuareg, searching for him over the pebbly ground where there were no footprints, heard his croaking call for water and hastened to his aid.

The incident is not typical of Barth (though perhaps it would have occurred to few men in such a predicament to drink their own blood), but it may well have been fortuitous. Barth was a big man, immensely strong and immensely fit. Perhaps this adventure which so nearly ended in disaster taught him not to overestimate his own strength. 'It is, indeed, very remarkable,' he observed in his journal after his rescue, 'how quickly the strength of a European is broken in these climes.'

Further tests of endurance were not long delayed. On the way to Aïr it looked for a time as though the Europeans were to be murdered because of their religion. They sat in grim silence, awaiting the decision of their Tuareg escort. 'Let us talk a little,' said Richardson. 'We must die; what is the use of sitting so mute?' Fortunately, it was decided that they should be allowed to live after all.

Although, unlike Caillié, Barth did not consistently adopt the pose of an Arab, he usually managed to blend into the African background quite well. His usual dress was the tobe, a garment like a nightshirt common in the Sudan, though when approaching Timbuktu he appeared as an Arab, and in the desert he sometimes wore the baggy trousers favoured by the Tuareg. He used indigo to stain his skin darker (Barth is sometimes described as blond and blue-eyed, but this seems to be founded on the popular English conception of Prussian characteristics rather than solid evidence). On one memorable occasion, at Gao, Barth was asked by his inquisitive escort to wear his European clothes, and he obligingly appeared in the splendour of full evening dress – a gesture worthy of Beachcomber's hero of the Raj, Big White Carstairs. The Arabs thought his black tail suit was some kind of armour.

On the way south Barth separated from his companions to make an excursion to Agades, a desert town that 'by mere accident,' said Barth, 'has not attracted as much interest as her sister town, Timbuktu'. This was his first major discovery: the town was unknown to Europeans before Barth; he provided a detailed description of its current circumstances and earlier history.

At the beginning of the New Year, the three Europeans decided to split up again, arranging to meet at Kukawa in April (Richardson died before then). Barth pressed on towards Kano, a place that had loomed in his thoughts ever since a Hausa slave whom he had met near Tunis on an earlier journey, impressed by the interest Barth showed in his homeland, had told him, 'Please God, you shall go and visit Kano.'

He reached it in February, and remained a month – a month in which he acquired an astonishingly detailed knowledge of the city and its environs. He had hoped to travel on to the south, towards Adamawa, but was embarrassed by a lack of funds – a frequent complaint during his travels. However, if he intended to keep his rendezvous at Kukawa he would anyway have been compelled to go first to Bornu. Difficulties confronted him: 'there was no caravan; the road was infested by robbers; and I had only one servant upon whom I could rely [Muhammad El-Gatroni, who remained with him for five years and later served Duveyrier, Rohlfs, and Nachtigal, among others], while I had been so unwell the preceding day as to be unable to rise from my couch. However, I was full of confidence; and with the same delight with which

A grim prospect in the central Sahara. Bleached camel bones – the only sign of man's passing in the pitiless waste of sand.

a bird springs forth from its cage, I hastened to escape from the narrow, dirty mud-walls into the boundless creation'. For all his scholarly interests, Barth was really happiest on the move.

To travel virtually alone (mounted on 'my unsightly black four-dollar nag') was certainly dangerous, though occasionally, as in this case, unavoidable. In the event, the journey passed without serious mishap, and with excellent

Caillié's view of Timbuktu. Heinrich Barth, observing from the flat roof of his house, 'became aware of the great inaccuracy which characterises the view of the town as given by M. Caillié; still, on the whole, the character of the single dwellings was well represented by that traveller, the only error being that in his representation the whole town seems to consist of scattered and quite isolated houses, while, in reality, the streets are entirely shut in, as the dwellings form continuous and uninterrupted rows'.

timing Barth entered Kukawa on 2 April. For the next two and a half years, Bornu was his main base, where letters and supplies could be received and despatched. From there, he set out on the journeys that resulted in his most notable discoveries.

*　　*　　*

Towards the end of April, the Sheikh left for a visit to Ngornu, near Lake Chad, and Barth accompanied him. His first excursion to the lake was, however, something of a disappointment. 'I mounted on horseback early next morning in order to refresh myself with a sight of the lake, which I supposed to be at no great distance, and indulged beforehand in anticipations of the delightful view which I fondly imagined was soon to greet my eye . . . But no lake was to be seen, and an endless grassy plain without a single tree extended to the furthest horizon. At length, after the grass had increased continually in freshness and luxuriance, we reached a shallow swamp, the very indented border of which . . . greatly obstructed our progress. Having struggled for a length of time to get rid of this swamp, and straining my eyes in vain to discover the glimmering of an open water in the distance, I at length retraced my steps, consoling myself with the thought that I had seen at least some slight indication of the presence of the watery element . . .' Later visitors to Lake Chad would have sympathized with his frustration.

The following day he had better luck, finding, with the aid of a Kanem chief, 'a fine open sheet of water, encompassed with papyrus and tall reed'.

On 7 May, Overweg arrived from Zinder, looking 'greatly fatigued and much worse than when I left him, four months ago [and] having no clothes with him except those which he actually wore'. The two Germans conducted negotiations for a commercial treaty between Britain and Bornu, one of the chief objects of the expedition. Arab opposition made their task harder. Then Barth turned his attention to the next place on his agenda – Adamawa. 'I had been cherishing the plan of penetrating into those unknown countries to the south for so long a time, that I felt the utmost gratification in being at length able to carry out my design'. By a lucky chance, two messengers were about to set out from Bornu to Adamawa. The Sheikh also sent with the party a man named Billarma, who proved a good friend then and later.

In the villages through which they passed, Barth strolled about with his usual amiable curiosity. 'These simple people were greatly amused when they saw me take so much interest in them; but while they were pleased with my approval, and behaved very decently, they grew frightened when I set about sketching them . . . Two unmarried girls busy at housework . . . were in ecstasies when I made them some little presents, and did not know how to thank me sufficiently.'

Anthony Kirk-Greene, the foremost British authority on Barth, quotes this passage as evidence to support his suggestion that Barth's greatest quality as an African explorer was empathy – his genuine and friendly interest in the people he met, combined with an unassuming tolerance not evident in his dealings with Europeans.

Hardly less important was his rapid command of languages. He appears to have learned enough Hausa on the road from Ghat to carry on a conversation in that language by the time he reached Agades! He was of course fluent in Arabic, and he was later to publish extensive vocabularies of eight African languages besides Hausa.

The difficulty of sketching people ('This is the misfortune of the traveller in these regions . . . that he will very rarely succeed in persuading one of [the people] to stand while he mades an accurate drawing of him') was to trouble Barth, and other explorers, frequently. There are very few portraits among the many lithographs that embellish his published volumes.

Entering Adamawa in mid-June, Barth stopped at several villages where, his companions were surprised to discover, Fulani settlers had moved in since they had last passed by. A well-known passage in Barth's *Travels* describes his reception at one of these villages, Mbutudi:

'While resting here I received a deputation of the heads of families of the Fulbe [Fulani], who behaved very decently, and were not a little excited by the performances of my watch and compass. I then determined to ascend the rock, which commands and characterizes the village, although being fully aware of the debilitated state of my health, I was somewhat afraid of any great bodily exertion . . But it was well worth the trouble, although the view over an immense expanse of country was greatly interrupted by the many small trees and bushes which are shooting out [a rare Germanism in Barth's careful English prose] between the granite blocks.

'After I had finished taking angles I sat down on this magnificent rocky throne, and several of the natives having followed me, I wrote from their dictation a short vocabulary of their language . . . These poor creatures, seeing, probably for the first time, that a stranger took real interest in them, were extremely delighted in hearing their words pronounced by one whom they thought almost as much above them as their god . . . and frequently corrected each other when there was a doubt about the meaning of the word. The rock became continually more animated, and it was not long before two young Fulbe girls also, who from the first had cast a kindly eye upon me, came jumping up to me, accompanied by an elder married sister . . .

'At length I left my elevated situation, and with a good deal of trouble succeeded in getting down again; but the tranquility which I had enjoyed was now gone, and not a moment was I left alone. All these poor creatures wanted to have my blessing; and there was particularly an old blacksmith, who, although he had become a proselyte to Islam, pestered me extremely with his entreaties to benefit him by word and prayer . . . The eldest of the unmarried girls made me a direct proposal of marriage, and I consoled her by stating, that I should have been happy to accept her offer if it were my intention to reside in the country. The manners of people who live in these retired spots, shut out from the rest of the world, are necessarily very simple and unaffected; and this poor girl had certainly reason to look out for a husband . . .'

The picture of the learned doctor, seated notebook in hand on that rock as it became 'continually more animated', is one of the most pleasant and memorable scenes in his *Travels*.

Four days later, the travellers received a poorer welcome at a place called Sulleri. The chief would not answer the door in spite of loud knockings so, as it was pouring with rain, Barth's party forced their way into the chief's son's house. Barth spread his carpet on the floor and 'indulged in comfort and respose after the fatiguing day's march, while outside the tempest, and inside the landlord, were raging'. They left early next morning, having had no food, which put Barth's companions in a bad temper. But 'as for me, I was cheerful in the extreme, and borne away by an enthusiastic and triumphant feeling; for today I was to see the river'.

The river was, of course, the great 'mother of waters', the Benue. The Lander brothers had first seen it at its junction with the Niger, and some two hundred miles of it had been explored during the Macgregor Laird expedition. But apart from that short stretch, the river was unknown to Europeans.

'The appearance of the river far exceeded my most lively expectations. None of my informants had promised me that I should just come upon it at that most interesting locality . . . where the mightier river is joined by another of very considerable size . . . As I looked from the bank over the scene before me, I was quite enchanted . . . The principal river, the Benuwe, flowed here from east to west, in a broad and majestic course, through an entirely open country . . . while just opposite to my station, behind a pointed headland of sand, the Faro rushed forth, appearing from this point not much inferior to the principal river, and coming in a fine sweep from the south-east . . .

'I looked long and silently upon the stream; it was one of the happiest moments in my life.'

After a somewhat rash bathe (his companions thought he was looking for gold), Barth set about the difficult task of driving his camels and horses and transporting his luggage in dug-out canoes across the fast-flowing river, which was about half a mile wide. The job was accomplished without serious loss, and he pressed on towards the town of Yola, which he reached on 20 June.

Although the people were friendly – and, inevitably, inquisitive – Barth's reception from the ruler of Yola was cool. He had hoped to follow the river downstream, but he was not allowed to proceed beyond Yola (Dr Baikie approached Yola from the opposite direction two years later). Barth's health was in a poor state too, and he was only a little consoled by conversations, with an Arab who had seen Lake Nyasa and visited India, and with two 'very handsome and amiable' young Fulani (Barth got on especially well with intelligent young men.) Soon a message came from the ruler instructing him to leave the town. By the end of July, Barth was back in Kukawa.

* * *

During the sixteen months following his return from Yola, Barth made a number of shorter excursions to the east, in the approximate neighbourhood of Lake Chad (it is interesting to note that he never completed the exploration of the eastern shores of Lake Chad, which Major Denham has often been blamed for neglecting). With Overweg he visited Kanem in late 1851, then accompanied the Sheikh on a raid against Mandara. Early in 1852, he set out towards Masena, where he was held by the ruler for some time and spent several days in leg irons. He was back in Kukawa in August, but his plans to make a further thrust around Lake Chad were postponed, and finally abandoned, because of the illness and death of Overweg. This grim event, made worse by the ghastly delirium of the young geologist's last days and perhaps by Barth's feeling of guilt for deserting him (inexplicably) when the young man was obviously near to death, impelled the great traveller far

from Bornu. He decided to begin his long journey westward through Hausa and Songhai to Timbuktu.

There had been talk of Barth's striking out in the opposite direction, towards the eastern coast of the continent. If he had taken this route, and completed it safely, his name would be better known today; but he does not seem to have considered the proposition as more than an attractive idea. Anyway, he was charged with the task of opening relations with the states of the western Sudan, and so far he had gained the signatures of only Kano and Bornu (he later added Sokoto).

He left Kukawa on the longest part of his travels in November 1852. He was accompanied by Muhammad El-Gatroni, who had recently returned from a visit to his family in the Fezzan (Barth had persuaded him to make the visit and had promoted him to be his chief servant). In his party also were four other young men and two young freed slaves, who later accompanied Barth to England. Barth and his two chief servants rode on horseback. The explorer felt 'as strong as a giant'.

He was feeling a great deal weaker by the time he reached Timbuktu ten months later.

The first part of the journey had been described by Clapperton, though in fact Barth diverged from Clapperton's route. From Sokoto, where he was well-received, he was in unknown territory. He crossed the Niger at Say and followed the direct overland route to Kabara, cutting across the bend of the river. Though ill and tired, he continued his careful studies: 'Having rested awhile, for I felt greatly exhausted after my sickly state in Say, I roved a little about the place . . . and collected several specimens of minerals, which, in the course of my journey, were thrown away by my people.'

In Timbuktu, Barth's position was perilous. Like the citizens themselves, he became a pawn in the struggle for power between Fulani and Tuareg, and he depended utterly on the protection of the honourable if somewhat idle Sheikh El-Backay, a son of the man who had sheltered Major Laing after the Tuareg attack. Although Barth might not have survived his six-month stay in Timbuktu without the protection of this Sheikh, he naturally attracted the hostility of El-Backay's Fulani opponents. However, El-Backay resisted attempts to throw the foreigner out of the city, and when things got too hot inside the town, he set up camp beyond the walls. Barth entered the place only at carefully chosen times.

In spite of these difficulties, the assiduous Barth managed to compile an excellent account of the history and society of Timbuktu (perhaps Barth's greatest discoveries were not rivers or mountain ranges but two documents, the *Tarikh es-Sudan*, a history of Songhai which he found at Gwandu, and the *Diwan*, a chronicle of Bornu).

Another advantage that Barth enjoyed over his predecessors was his ability to tackle learned Muslims on their own terms. Hugh Clapperton had been confounded in theological argument by the better-educated Muhammad Bello, but when Barth was urged in Timbuktu to become a Muslim, 'I challenged him to demonstrate to me the superiority of his creed, telling him in that case I should not fail to adopt it, but not till then. Upon this, he and his people began with alacrity a spirited discussion, in the firm hope that they would soon be able to overcome my arguments; but after a while they found them rather too strong, and were obliged to give in . . . This incident improved my situation in an extraordinary degree, by basing my safety on the sincere esteem which several of the most intelligent of the inhabitants contracted for me.' (It ought perhaps to be noted that Barth's opinion of his intellectual – or other – abilities was by no means modest, and a different account of this argument might have been obtained from the other participants.)

Unlike most 19th-century explorers, Barth was not a man of particularly deep religious convictions; he carried a prayer book around his neck in imitation of a Muslim custom, not because he frequently consulted it, and one sometimes gets the feeling that, after several years contact with the Muslims, he would not have objected very strongly to becoming a convert.

Barth sometimes appeared to maintain that he was a better Muslim than the Muslims because his religion started with Adam rather than Muhammad – a curious argument reminiscent of Disraeli's view of Christianity as merely the natural corollary of Judaism.

Sometimes, even Barth must have been driven to distraction by religious arguments, which may stand as an excuse for some of his more startling remarks: '. . . fresh attempts were made to convert me, even by my friends, who from sheer friendship could not bear to see me adhere to a creed which they thought erroneous. But I withstood all their attacks, and at times even ventured to ridicule some of their superstitious notions. I was far from laughing at the chief principles of their doctrine; but, as they always recurred in their arguments to their belief in sorcery and demons, I declared one day that, as for us, we had made all the demons our "Khodeman". This is an expression with which these people are wont to denote the degraded and servile tribes; and I represented the Europeans as having obtained a victory over the spirits, by ascending in ballons into the higher regions, and from thence firing at them with rifles . . .'

But one cannot live five years in a strange country and preserve complete immunity to its ways of thought. In this connection, Barth's journals contain some revealing remarks. In Masena, for example, he greatly admired the appearance of a young woman who had applied to him for medical aid,

A Tuareg on his maherry, a long-legged, fast camel on which, according to Lyon (the artist also in this case) 'they perform extraordinary journeys. The saddle is placed on the withers, and confined by a band under the belly. It is very small and difficult to sit, which is done by balancing with the feet against the neck of the animal'. According to Lyon, long journeys could be accomplished at an average speed of nine miles an hour, perhaps a slight exaggeration.

A raid witnessed by Barth, ostensibly to punish a refractory vassal; 'the chief motive of the enterprise, however, consisted in the circumstance of the coffers and slave-rooms of the great men [of Bornu] being empty'.

Ougana the witch doctor exorcising a sorcerer, an incident witnessed by Paul du Chaillu. 'When all was ready for the trial, I went down to look at the doctor, who looked literally like the devil. I never saw a more ghastly object. His eyelids were painted red, and a red stripe, from the nose upward, divided his forehead in two parts. Another red stripe passed round his head. The face was painted white, and on each side of the mouth were two round spots . . . From each shoulder down to his hands was a white stripe, and one hand was painted quite white.'

Du Chaillu encamped for the night. 'The negroes have a particular delight in lying around a comfortable fire at night and telling stories, and I have often found them thus engaged late at night when entering a village.'

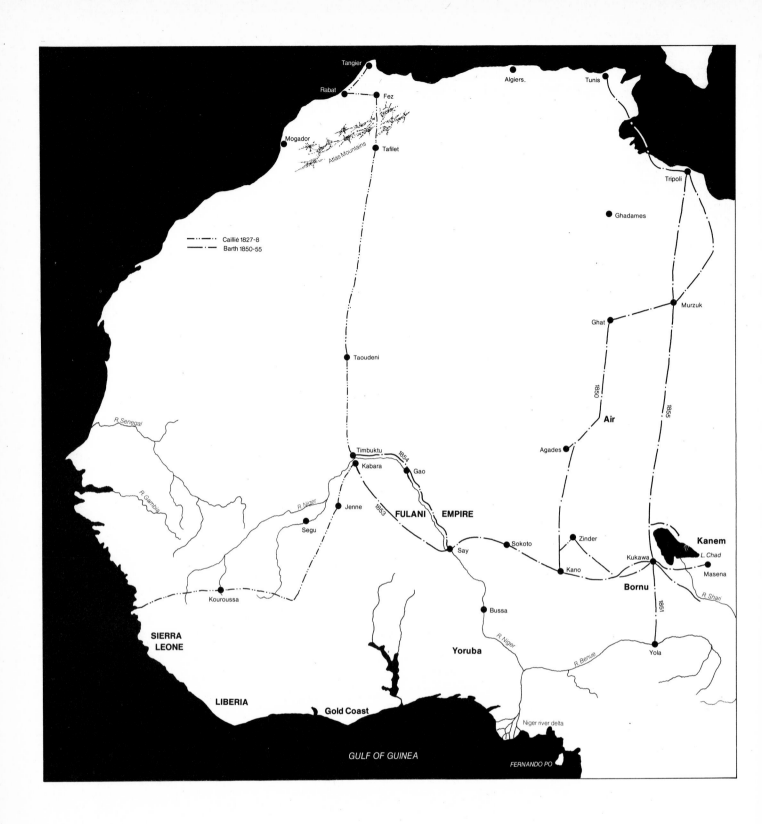

saying that she would have been taken for a great beauty in Europe, except for 'her skin, the glossy black of which I thought very becoming *at the time*, and almost essential to female beauty' (italics added). Attitudes to skin colour are certainly very strange and hard to explain. At a tournament held at the court of James IV of Scotland in 1507, the presiding lady was a Negro. No one appears to have thought this particularly outlandish, yet a late 19th-century historian, reviewing the episode, was half-inclined to dismiss it altogether as unbelievable – not because James IV's court was primitive but because it was so strikingly cultured.

Still under the protection of Sheikh El-Backay, Barth finally escaped from Timbuktu in May 1854. He was now, not surprisingly, anxious to bring his travels to an end. But he had a long way to go.

On his return eastward, he followed the Niger from Timbuktu. The Sheikh accompanied him as far as Gao, the old Songhai capital on the bend of the river, where Barth crossed over before continuing to Say. South of this point, the river had not been described by Europeans but Barth was prevented from going farther by reports of warfare and by his increasingly impedient lack of funds. Unfortunately, he was to find that the supplies he had left behind at Kukawa had been dissipated, either because he was believed to be dead (an

A caravan in the Sahara. A desert journey was, and is, a carefully calculated exercise. 'The Arab sets out on his journey,' Frederick Horneman reported at the end of the 18th century, 'with a provision of flour, Kuskasa, onions, mutton suet, and oil or butter; and some of the richer class add to this store a proportion of biscuit, and of dried flesh. The water . . . is carried in bags made of goat-skins, unripped in the middle, and stripped from the animal as entire as possible; those made at Soudan are the strongest and best; water may be preserved in them for five days, without acquiring any bad taste.'

The red sand of the Kalahari Desert. One of Livingstone's first journeys took him – and his pregnant wife and small children – across the Kalahari to the discovery of Lake Ngami in 1849.

97

'The [Victoria] falls are singularly formed', Dr Livingstone observed. 'They are simply the whole mass of the Zambesi waters rushing into a fissure or rent made right across the bed of the river and adjacent country, and after the leap the river is not much different from what it was above the falls . . .' In his later, published account, he was more enthusiastic, though he seriously underestimated the dimensions of the falls. (Rather a common mistake among explorers: waterfalls seem to be peculiarly difficult to judge with the naked eye).

'Above the Kebrabasa Rapids' by Thomas Baines, 1859.

*Confrontation between Livingstone's steam launch and an elephant on
the Shire River, 1859. This is the most famous painting of Thomas
Baines (1820–75), the recent centenary of whose death was celebrated
with an exhibition of his work in King's Lynn (his birthplace) and
elsewhere. Baines' large oil paintings were usually completed later,
after sketches made on the spot. He did not, in fact, witness this
incident, and the picture, which is now in the Royal Geographical
Society's headquarters, is based on a description by George Rae, the
engineer on the Zambezi expedition.*

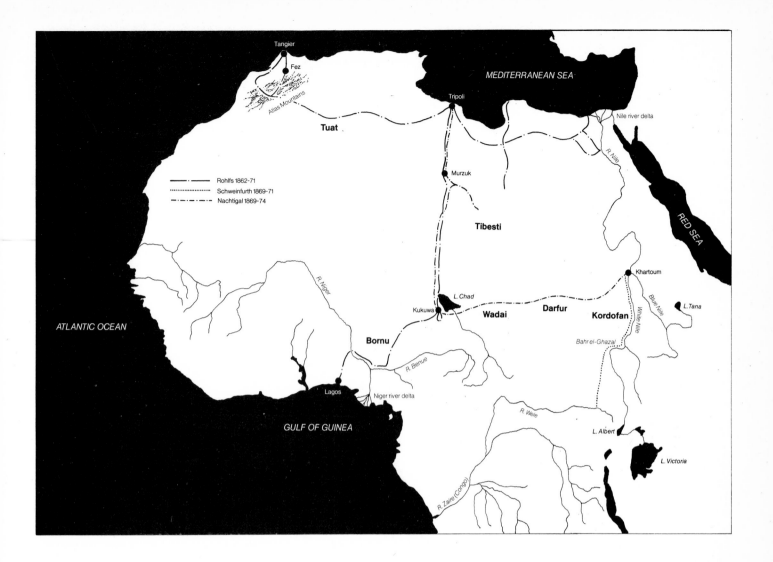

obituary actually appeared in Germany), or in the chaos caused by civil war, which broke out in Bornu during Barth's westward journey.

But Barth was no longer out of touch with Europe. Despatches awaited him at Sokoto, along with one very old copy of the *Athenaeum* and a message advising him of the despatch of Edward Vogel, a young German astronomer and naturalist, as a replacement. Some weeks later, the two men met west of Kukawa. Vogel was the first European Barth had seen since the death of Overweg two years earlier.

Vogel had been accompanied across the desert by two British sappers, Corporal Church and Private Maguire, but had quarrelled violently with them on the journey. Maguire was subsequently soothed by Barth into accompanying Vogel on a journey to the south-east (from which neither man returned). Corporal Church remained mutinous, and eventually went back with Barth, who was so cross with him by the time they reached Murzuk that he refused to sit at the same table.

In Kukawa, Barth was much troubled by rheumatism, lack of funds, and the unwillingness of the Sheikh (or of some of his circle) to let him go. He remained there four months, and except for the brief period before Vogel left, it was a very tiresome wait, making great demands on Barth's normally considerable resources of patience. His favourite horse, 'Blast of the Desert', which had carried him for three years, had recently died, and though the Sheikh gave him some camels,

they were inferior specimens. (Many explorers in Northern Africa became fond – and with reason – of their horses. Major Denham's splendid beast would stand still for long periods in the desert sun while he took a nap in the shade of its body.)

'I endeavoured to pass my time as well as I could, studying the history of the empire of Bornu, and entering occasionally into a longer conversation with some of the better instructed of my acquaintances, or making a short excursion; but altogether my usual energy was gone, and my health totally undermined, and the sole object which occupied my thoughts was, to convey my feeble body in safety home.'

Barth left Kukawa for the last time on 9 May 1855, though he did not cross the border of Bornu until ten days later. In spite of this delay and subsequent diversions, he was in Tripoli on 24 August. Two weeks after that, he was clasping the palsied palm of the prime minister in Downing Street.

The remainder of Barth's life (like many African explorers, he died young – in 1865 at the age of forty-four) was a disappointing anticlimax. Always a difficult character, he proved highly sensitive to the slights and insults – some imagined, some accidental, a few deliberate – that he encountered in England. He had many friends, or at least warm acquaintances, in the Royal Geographical Society, the Anti-Slavery Society, and even in the government, but he quarrelled with all those organizations. He rightly resented the failure of the British to exploit his hard diplomatic work in the Sudan, and at last fell out with his chief supporter,

August Petermann, over the failure to send a relief expedition in search of Vogel. The two Africans whom Barth brought back to Europe became the subject of a silly attack on him by people who seemed to imagine the young men were his slaves.

The reception of his great book, *Travels and Discoveries in North and Central Africa* (vols I–III 1857, vols IV–V 1858) was a sad disappointment. Reviews were mediocre, and little more than two thousand copies were sold. This was a poor sale for a work that E.W. Bovill described as 'one of the principal authorities on the Western Sudan', and of which Anthony Kirk-Green has written, 'For those of us who have trekked through the Barth country, the journal of that "indefatigable African traveller" remains a delightful companion, a source of priceless knowledge, and a humbling testament to his wondrous fortitude and resolution.'

A number of distinguished French and German travellers followed up the work of Caillié and Barth. Henri Duveyrier, who became Europe's greatest expert on the Tuareg, made his first journey to the northern Sahara when he was only nineteen years old (1859). In the same year another Frenchman (though he was a citizen of the United States) returned from three years in Gabon. He had lived there for a time in his youth, his father being a trader, and his expedition was sponsored by the Philadelphia Academy of Natural Sciences. Paul du Chaillu's work belongs to the 'exotica' of African exploration: his Africa is a place of lush jungles, weird native rites and, above all, dangerous beasts. He was largely responsible for the long-lived myth that the gorilla (which he was perhaps the first European to see in its natural state) was a ferocious creature. Many of Du Chaillu's stories seemed to his contemporaries much too good to be true (some still do), though on the whole he was a more reliable observer than he was given credit for. On a second expedition in the 1860s he encountered forest-dwelling pygmies, whose existence was then still uncertain. Later in life, his interests turned towards the Arctic (a not uncommon development in African travellers; Barth once contemplated a polar expedition). Du Chaillu died in Russia, aged sixty-eight, in 1903.

Among distinguished German travellers in Africa north of the equator in the second half of the 19th century, three must be briefly mentioned.

The most energetic was Gerhard Rohlfs (1831–96). Indeed, if it were possible to compute the total mileage of the major African travellers, Rohlfs would come high if not top of the list. A man of immense courage and resource, he lacked Barth's intellectual equipment but shared a certain remoteness in personal relations. Rohlfs appears to be a good example of the explorer in search primarily of himself. However, there is little evidence of this in his published writings which, standing at the opposite pole from Du Chaillu's, are steadily non-sensational. This, plus his habit of using European titles for African officials ('mayors', 'councillors', etc.), sometimes conveys the impression (as Wolfe Schmokel says) of 'a rather pleasant walking trip – sometimes one feels Rohlfs might as well be writing of a hike through the North German countryside'.

Popular fame as an explorer came to Rohlfs as a result of his journey across the continent, from Tripoli to Lagos, in 1865–67. He went via Bornu and the Niger and, with some small exceptions, the whole route had been traversed by earlier explorers. Nevertheless, if Caillié is discounted (and he started from halfway round the bulge), Rohlfs was the first European in modern times to travel overland from the Mediterranean to the Gulf of Guinea.

With Barth dead, Rohlfs became the premier German Africanist until Gustav Nachtigal (1834–85) became suddenly famous in 1875. The son of a Prussian clergyman, Nachtigal studied medicine as a young man but went to North Africa for the sake of his own health. A more approachable figure than Rohlfs, he made a number of journeys into the interior, and in 1869 he was sent on a government mission to Bornu. Diverging eastward from the (by then) well-travelled route, he penetrated deeply into what is now the Republic of Chad, visiting Tibesti and other parts of the central Sahara that had not been seen by Europeans. From Bornu he turned towards the east, to Wadai. Rohlfs had hoped to take this route on his trans-continental journey but had been refused permission to enter Wadai. Nachtigal, who by this time had been given up for dead in Germany, passed through Darfur and Kordofan and finally struck the Nile a few miles south of Khartoum in 1874 – a truly remarkable journey, nearly half of it through unexplored territory.

Of this famous trio of German explorers, the man who came nearest to Barth in scholarly attainments was Georg Schweinfurth (1836–1925), whose niece, quite coincidentally, became Rohlfs's wife. A scientist of wide interests, his early journeys in the region of the Red Sea earned him a reputation as a capable and observant traveller, and resulted in his appointment to lead an expedition towards Central Africa. From Khartoum, he set out in 1869 towards the south, following the Nile into the Bahr el-Ghazal (the route followed seven years earlier by Samuel Baker) and, turning west and then south again, eventually reached the banks of the Wele. The direction of the river's flow told him that he had left the Nile basin but, as the course of the Zaire in the interior was still unknown, Schweinfurth made the natural error of concluding that the river was linked with the Chad system. He travelled some of the journey with a party of ivory traders, and among the less attractive people he encountered were a cannibalistic tribe, one of whose raids he was compelled to attend. His encounter with the Akka pygmies finally settled the much-argued pygmy question, and he also brought back (in 1871) important information on the flora and fauna of the regions he visited. He made many more journeys in north and east Africa, accompanying Gerhard Rohlfs on an expedition into the Libyan Desert in 1873. His last visit to Africa took place when he was nearly sixty, and he lived to the age of ninety – probably a record for a 19th-century explorer of Africa.

The careers of Rohlfs, Nachtigal, and Schweinfurth spanned the 'colonial-adventure' period, when African exploration took on a political colouring. Together with the geologist, Baron von Richtofen, the three men – an impressive team – represented Germany at the international conference on Africa at Brussels in 1876, when the smooth imperialist, King Leopold II of the Belgians, by a remarkable coup made himself the patron of African exploration and so took the first step towards obtaining his vast colony of the Congo. Schweinfurth remained a scholar first and foremost, but the scarred and battered figure of Rohlfs ended up as German consul in the political hot spot of Zanzibar, where he encountered stiff competition from his British counterpart, Sir John Kirk, and was soon relieved of his post. Nachtigal was instrumental in securing Togo and Cameroun for Germany's colonial empire in 1884.

Missionary Journeys

In the early years of the African Association, the predominant motive for journeys of exploration in Africa was geographical; commercial, political, and other motives were muted. During the first half of the 19th century, rising public awareness and opposition to the slave trade gave, increasingly, a humanitarian cast to African expeditions – to officially sponsored ones anyway. Mungo Park, though his remarks on the slave trade were sensible and his general attitude not inhumane, was no Abolitionist. But by Clapperton's time, antipathy to the slave trade was a standard ingredient in the mixture of motives for exploration; in Sokoto, Clapperton had more or less formally requested Sultan Muhammad Bello to stop the trade.

Together with the growing opposition to slavery, the activity of Christian – especially Protestant – missions was expanding.

Most of the first explorers of Africa, as of Asia and the Americas, were Roman Catholic missionaries, mainly Portuguese and Spanish. Protestant churches, less securely established, at first showed no corresponding zeal. But in the 18th century, Roman Catholic missions declined and, as far as Africa was concerned, they did not recover until the mid 19th century with the foundation of the Congregation of the Holy Ghost (1848) and Cardinal Lavigerie's White Fathers (1868).

The Protestants stepped into the gap. The rapid growth of Protestant missions, roughly coinciding with the Roman Catholic decline, was associated with the rise of movements for reform such as the Pietist movement and the Moravian revival in Germany and the Wesleyan movement in Britain. In 1792, following the publication of William Carey's influential *Enquiry into the Obligations of Christians to Use Means for the Conversion of the Heathen*, the Baptist Missionary Society was founded. The non-denominational (but Protestant) London Missionary Society, which was to employ David Livingstone, was formed three years later. The Church Missionary Society, a product of the evangelical movement in the Church of England, was established in 1799, and more societies soon followed.

Missionaries were not, of course, sent to Africa to make geographical discoveries. But, inevitably, some of them did.

'In the course of time it became ever more evident to us, impressing itself upon us with all the force of a positive command, that it was our duty not to limit our missionary labours to the coast tribes . . . but to keep in mind as well the spiritual darkness of the tribes and nations of Inner Africa. This consideration induced us to take important journeys into the interior.' Thus wrote Dr Ludwig Krapf, a missionary sent to East Africa in 1843 by the Church Missionary Society;

Livingstone was to evolve similar motives. Krapf, like his colleague Johann Rebmann, was a German. The British missionary societies were not at first able to find enough volunteers within the British Isles, and it was not uncommon for German candidates to be appointed.

Although the geographical mysteries of central Africa were to be largely unravelled by explorers starting from the east coast, East Africa was the last major region of the continent to attract European travellers. When the Portuguese were driven from their settlements north of Mozambique in the late 17th and 18th centuries, they were replaced as the dominant power in the area by the sultanate of Oman, which had been involved in East Africa long before the Portuguese first arrived. Omani authority, however, was slight, and for some time the coast remained the preserve of numerous quarrelling local rulers. The assertion of Omani control was foreshadowed by the accession to the sultanate in 1804 of the impressive figure of Seyyid Said. In his efforts to control the prevailing anarchy, Said sought the assistance of Britain and, after initial reluctance, the British signed an agreement with him in hope of thus restricting the long-established East African slave trade. By so doing, Britain appeared to recognise Said's authority over the East African coast from Cape Delgado to the Gulf of Aden.

Some years passed before Britain decided to give Said full support, and a much longer period before it became virtually 'protecting' power on the east coast. The position was complicated in the 1820s by the activities of Captain W. F. Owen, a strong-minded opponent of the slave trade who carried out extensive charting of the east coast, including the lower reaches of important rivers. At Mombasa, the local ruler asked Owen for assistance in his struggle against Said, and Owen signed a treaty promising protection for Mombasa in return for suppression of the slave trade. The British government, however, was not yet willing to become territorially involved in East Africa, and Owen's treaty was repudiated. Subsequently, Said gained control of Mombasa. Gradually he extended his influence further, opening diplomatic relations with the United States among other countries, and growing rich through the export of cloves. In about 1840, he transferred his court and government to Zanzibar. Thus he became an African rather than an Arabian ruler (after his death, the thrones of Zanzibar and Oman were occupied by two of Said's sons, and the separation proved permanent). The British maintained a resident in Zanzibar who was, in effect, the Sultan's prime minister, although success in restricting the slave trade was rather slight until some years after Said's death in 1856.

Under British influence, Said opened his dominions to

Christian missionaries. Krapf was an early arrival. He landed at Zanzibar in 1843, but subsequently moved his headquarters to Mombasa, where Rebmann joined him in 1846. The two missionaries made a number of short journeys into the interior and heard several stories that reminded them of Ptolemy's description of East Africa.

Rebmann was the first European in modern times to see Mount Kilimanjaro, in May 1848. 'This morning we discerned the mountains of Jagga [Chagga] more distinctly than ever; and about ten o'clock, I fancied I saw the summit of one of them covered with a dazzlingly white cloud. My guide called the white which I saw merely *Beredi*, cold; it was perfectly clear to me, however, that it could be nothing else but snow ... The whole country between Teita and Jagga has a sublime character. To the west was the lofty Mount Kilimanjaro with its perpetual snow; to the southwest was the massive and monotonous Ugano; to the north-west, the extended mountain-chain of Kikumbulia; and to the east, the chains of the Teita mountains ...

In 1849–51 Krapf made several journeys to Kamba, where he hoped to establish a mission, and to Kitui. His hopes were frustrated, partly by an attack on his caravan in which his protector in the area was killed and himself deserted, so that he spent a night on his own in the bush. The discovery of Mount Kenya, hitherto unknown to Europeans, was some compensation for these disasters.

The well-meaning missionaries often had a rough time on their expeditions. Their beliefs were too remote from African society to have much effect, and they could only console themselves with the thought that Christ's name was being uttered in regions where it had never been uttered before. They suffered the usual difficulties with rulers eager to make the most of their presence and prevent them moving on: 'When by order of the King I was obliged to part with piece after piece of the calico which I had reserved [as presents] for my further journey, I could not suppress my tears,' confessed Rebmann. More sophisticated presents were not always welcomed for the right reasons: '[the King] visited me again on the 19th for a few minutes, having a fork (which along with a knife I had presented to him), in his hair as an ornament! I explained to him the use of it; he laughed, but did not seem to understand'. Exposition of the Gospel often had a similar effect. One can hardly feel surprised: the distance between the two cultures was immense.

On a journey south-west to Usambara, Krapf was told of a great inland sea, on which his informant had sailed for eight days. This early report of Lake Tanganyika (?Lake Victoria), like the accounts of snow-covered mountains, were widely scoffed at in England, where Krapf's *Researches and Missionary Labours* was published in 1860.

David Livingstone.

The London Missionary Society concentrated its efforts on southern Africa. Its servants were a mixed bunch, but included some sterling characters, notably a great black-bearded Scot named Robert Moffat (1795–1883). Moffat arrived at Cape Town in 1816, spent some time in Namaqualand, returned to the Cape to get married, and eventually settled down (and remained for fifty years) at Kuruman, then the farthest north of South African missions. During a long visit to Britain in 1839 he met a number of young missionary trainees whose zeal he encouraged with emotive talk about the country to the north of Kuruman, where he 'had sometimes seen, in the morning sun, the smoke of a thousand villages, where no missionary had ever been'. Among those whose hearts were lifted by this vision was an earnest, harsh-voiced, rather uncouth young man – a fellow Scot from Blantyre near Glasgow. Two years later, en route for Kuruman, David Livingstone landed at Cape Town.

Reaching Africa at the age of twenty-eight as a qualified doctor and ordained Congregationalist minister was not the least of Livingstone's achievements. The story of his deprived childhood is well known: the seven-member family living in a one-room apartment; the work as a ten-year-old 'piecer' tying frayed threads in the cotton factory for twelve hours a day excluding meals; the determined striving for an education (but what prompted this urge?) at night-school and through reading, in spite of workmates' jeers; the stern though loving father; the fears of eternal damnation, ultimately resolved by the books and sermons of liberal theologians; the early belief in self-reliance, and the evidence of a spirit of independence bordering on obstinacy.

At the age of twenty-three, he had saved enough money to study medicine in Glasgow, working in the Blantyre mill during vacations. His father had opposed any kind of scientific training without a religious purpose, but the conflict had been solved by a call for medical missionaries to go to China, which seemed the answer to the young Livingstone's vague but powerful desire to do some good in the world. The outbreak of the Opium War put China off limits for missionaries, and Livingstone's thoughts turned to Africa. The London Missionary Society, having accepted him on probation, sent him to study with a minister near London, while he continued his medical studies in the capital. Though handicapped by a serious illness, by a lack of confidence in the pulpit which aborted his first sermon, and by a contradictory tendency to argue with his superiors, Livingstone passed his exams, was ordained as a missionary priest, and set sail for South Africa in December 1840.

At that age, Livingstone was not a particularly attractive young man. Smooth Londoners had found him an uncouth provincial, neither handsome nor elegant, opinionated but inarticulate. The humour that bubbles through his account of his *Missionary Travels* (1857) seems to have been largely absent from his conversation. The qualities that Livingstone possessed, which were to make him the most famous explorer of his own and perhaps any other time, were a determination to succeed in any task that he set himself (or, as he looked at it, that God set for him), a determination that was to grow into something almost superhuman; and with this indomitable will, a strength of body to match.

Livingstone swiftly formed a poor opinion of missionaries in South Africa; he regarded them as lacking in initiative and too fond of comfort. Even Kuruman was too soft for him. He soon began (without waiting for permission) to explore the surrounding country, venturing into the territory of the Bakwena and learning to speak Sechuana. His criticisms of current missionary activity, though usually accurate, did not make him popular with his fellows. Shocked by the relative lack of progress at Kuruman and elsewhere in making Christian converts, Livingstone decided that Africa would never be Christianized by whites. Better results could be achieved by a smaller number of white missionaries working with African assistants.

The London Missionary Society eventually gave permission for Livingstone and another man, Rogers Edwards, to set up a new mission station at Mabotsa, some two hundred miles north-east of Kuruman. It was here that Livingstone had his famous encounter with a lion which, having survived shots from both barrels of Livingstone's gun, seized him by the upper arm and shook him like a dog shaking a rat. His life was saved by the intervention of an African convert, Mebalwe, and another man whom Livingstone had once treated for buffalo wounds. Livingstone's upper arm was badly smashed and he was extremely ill for some time.

A lady in a London drawing room is said to have once asked Livingstone what he was thinking when the lion had hold of him. 'I was thinking what part of me he would eat first,' he replied with great seriousness.

Recuperating at Kuruman, Livingstone became engaged to Robert Moffat's daughter, Mary. She was, he wrote in a letter, 'a plain common sense woman . . . a little thick black haired girl, sturdy and all I want'. No one could pretend it was a romantic match. Livingstone had felt handicapped by bachelorhood: Edwards was married; and Africans thought celibacy a distinctly odd custom. Mary, who knew no other home but Kuruman, was probably glad to get out of the parental household. It cannot be said that the marriage was a great success, for Mary Livingstone was to have a rather miserable life; but there was certainly affection and comradeship in the early years, if not much intellectual compatibility.

Livingstone had given early signs of the difficulty he experienced in attempting to co-operate with almost anyone on a footing of equality, and it is not surprising that he eventually fell out with his partner at Mabotsa, Rogers Edwards. The documentary evidence for their dispute does not make edifying reading, but rather too much has been made of it, as of other quarrels in which the prickly Livingstone became involved. Historians and biographers sometimes fail to make sufficient allowance for the influence of physical conditions on human behaviour. Isolation and hardship can have profound effects. A group of young people recently made the experiment of living entirely off the land on Dartmoor using no (or almost no) artefacts of modern society. In less than two weeks, these nice and gentle people, craving red meat, were setting snares for deer, a practice that is cruel as well as illegal. They admitted that normally they would have been horrified at such an act. It is not to be expected that two or three people, living in the bush 200 miles from the nearest European settlement, building their own house, providing their own food, for a period of months or years, would maintain the easy relationship of two accountants working in the same office.

From Mabotsa, with the permission of the London Missionary Society, the Livingstones moved first to Chonuane, then to Kolobeng (Livingstone building each house with his own hands), under the protection of an attractive chief of the Bakwena, Sechele. They remained with the Bakwena, except when travelling, for nearly seven years. Five children were born, though one died as a baby.

Livingstone's critics point derisively to the fact that during his long communication with the Bakwena he made only one firm convert to Christianity. Others may find it surprising that, in the circumstances, he made even one, especially as that one was the most powerful and most intelligent man among them – none other than Sechele himself.

A considerable act of sacrifice was required from Sechele, as his baptism entailed dismissing his wives and making himself unpopular with his people; his acceptance of Christian dogma should probably be seen more as a magnificent act of personal friendship than a true religious conversion.

Although Livingstone was obviously disappointed that the Bakwena refused to take Christianity seriously ('We like you as well if you had been born among us . . . but we wish you to give up that everlasting preaching and praying'), he had the sense to realize that knowing how to dig an irrigation channel was just as important as knowing the Lord's Prayer. Moreover, he was able to interpret the situation as supporting his belief that more might be accomplished by broadcasting the Gospel far and wide than by sitting down in one place and plugging away hopefully year after year. Others, of course, not least his employers, found such reasoning hard to justify.

Livingstone's early journeys from Kolobeng could not have been accomplished on his £100-a-year salary without the help of friends, in particular a rich hunter named William Cotton Oswell. The motives for his northward treks were two: to make contact with the Makololo king, Sebituane, of whom he had heard impressive accounts, and to discover the unknown lake which was said to exist in the north. The way led across part of the Kalahari Desert, a forbidding place but not entirely barren. Water could sometimes be obtained even in arid parts by digging six to eight feet down; and Bushmen driven from more fertile areas by the Bantu expansion managed to live there.

The usual means of travel was a covered wagon, larger and heavier than the prairie schooners of North America, and drawn by a team of ten or more oxen. When all this was going well, it could be a delightful experience: 'Waggon-travelling . . . is a prolonged system of picknicking, excellent for the health, and agreeable to those who are not over fastidious about trifles, and who delight in being in the open air.' But there were times when even Livingstone realized that travelling through unexplored desert with a pregnant wife and young children was hardly the ideal family life. Once they ran out of water and, as their guide had disappeared, did not know where they would find more. 'The idea of [the children] perishing before our eyes was terrible.' Fortunately they reached a river next day and tragedy was averted.

Livingstone was fiercely criticized for gambling with the lives of his wife and young children. Robert Moffat had profound misgivings and Mrs Moffat protested vigorously. The attitude of Mary Livingstone herself is not known, but she presumably consented to take the risk. If she had been dragged around Africa against her will, there would indeed be reason to accuse Livingstone of callousness. Livingstone cannot be exonerated from the charge of grossly neglecting his family; neglect is usually the fate of the families of great men of action, and perhaps too much has been made of this sad side effect of Livingstone's career. One thinks of the wife

Missionaries, black and white, as imagined in the 19th century expounding the Gospel. The efforts of Christian missionaries in Africa were a great deal less successful than the propaganda of the mission societies made people believe; many missionaries lacked the qualities of self-sacrifice and perseverance that distinguished the best of them. Nor were Africans accurately characterised in hymns and sermons that described a band of unfortunate heathens waiting to be set free from the shackles of paganism by the True Light of the Gospel. Nevertheless, the missionaries altogether had an impact on African society perhaps greater than that of any other group – explorers, traders or government officials.

of Robert E. Peary, similarly criticized for taking his family on his early travels, writing plaintively of time slipping away while her husband struggled with Arctic ice.

The discovery of Lake Ngami by Livingstone and Oswell in 1849 brought the name of Livingstone to the notice of the general public for the first time. At least two attempts had been made to reach the lake (which, nowadays anyway, is unfortunately not so much a lake as a particularly damp swamp), and it had become an important goal for explorers. Otherwise, the lake had little importance, as Livingstone soon realized. It was very shallow and it did not, as Livingstone had hoped, form part of any really useful river system.

Livingstone's work in south-west Africa was continued by the Swedish naturalist, K. J. Andersson, in the 1850s. From the western coast he reached Lake Ngami and the Okovanggo River – 'a cry of joy and satisfaction escaped me at this glorious sight' – and slew the odd rhinoceros on the way.

The next objective of Livingstone and Oswell was Sebituane and the land of the Makololo, 200 miles farther north. The first attempts failed, partly through the unwelcome appearance of the tsetse fly, deadly to most domestic animals, and a menace that Livingstone had not encountered before. At the third try, Livingstone and Oswell reached the Chobe River, and found that Sebituane had sent men to meet them – news travelled fast in Africa without the aid of modern media, and Sebituane knew about Livingstone probably sooner than Livingstone knew about him. At this time Sebituane was about forty-five years old; he was, said Oswell, a 'really great Chief and man . . . and treated us right royally; he was far and away the finest Kafir I ever saw'. He was particularly glad to welcome Livingstone and his family because he knew of their connection with Robert Moffat, and that Moffat had considerable influence over Mosilikatze (Mzilikazi) King of Matabele (Ndebele), the most dangerous enemy of the Makololo, who had driven them from their pleasant homeland on the Batoka plateau to their current, not very healthy, place of settlement. Through Livingstone's influence, the aggression of the Matabele might be checked. Soon, the Livingstone family had taken up residence in their new home at Linyanti.

Livingstone's relations with Europeans in Africa were usually bad and sometimes awful, though he remained lifelong friends with the modest and generous Oswell, whose refusal to fall out with Livingstone over the latter's alleged attempts to deprive him of his due credit as an explorer has received ample compensation in the works of recent writers. With Africans his relations were almost universally good. His attitude to African society was more enlightened than that of most men of his time. For instance, he made himself unpopular with fellow-missionaries by suggesting that certain tribal rituals should be regarded as necessary social conventions, not as un-Christian barbarism. He was not blinded by the strangeness of the African way of life, nor by the colour of the African's skin. He was, in short, realistic. He did not expect Africans to behave like Europeans, and when he encountered hostility he was slow to take offence, seeking and often finding a good reason why hostility should exist. On the other hand, he did not make the mistake of excusing the evil behaviour of Africans because they were Africans. Some men that he encountered during his travels were murderous villains, and Livingstone said so.

Livingstone lived a long time in Africa and covered a great deal of ground; he was also a prolific writer. But he was not a profound or systematic thinker. It is therefore not very difficult to find inconsistencies and contradictions in his attitudes and behaviour. He can be found, for example, extolling the benefits of tribal society and comparing it favourably with the society of capitalist Europe. He can also be found, in his moods of deep depression, condemning it for its superstitions and violence in phrases worthy of an Isaiah; and it is true that his work pointed towards the destruction of traditional society (though it is perhaps doubtful that the undermining of tribal society was so conscious and deliberate an aim as Tim Jeal implies in his thorough, well-written, but basically unsympathetic biography).

The great snow-capped summit of Africa's highest mountain, Kilimanjaro (19,340 feet), the existence of which was first reported to a doubting European public by the German missionaries, Krapf and Rebmann in 1848.

Livingstone's cry was for 'Christianity and Commerce'. If that sounds rather similar to Cecil Rhodes's 'Philanthropy plus 5 per cent', his motives were very different. Livingstone believed, and believed the more fervently as he uncovered more and more evidence of the extent of the slave trade in Central Africa, that trade as well as the Bible was necessary for African enlightenment. It is rather pointless to suggest that the Africans would have been better off if Europeans had left them alone and 'unenlightened'. Europe had not left Africa alone, was not leaving Africa alone, and increasingly would not leave Africa alone. Not that Livingstone would have approved of such a course anyway. The Victorians believed in the benefits of material progress and the perfectability of human nature. Livingstone himself was an excellent example of what a man might achieve in capitalist society in spite of serious disadvantages. Those people in Victorian England who, like Charles Dickens, opposed missionary activities, certainly did not base their opposition on the welfare of 'untutored natives'. They believed, like those who oppose space flights, that there was more important work to do at home.

It was an important moment for Livingstone when he and Oswell, travelling to the Makololo town of Sesheke, found themselves in June 1851 standing on the banks of the Zambezi. If Central Africa was to be opened up to legitimate European trade, it was necessary to find a 'highway' from the coast to the interior. The Zambezi, here in the middle of the continent still a mighty river, held promise of just such a highway. From this point, Livingstone's strange and formidable career as missionary-explorer really began.

*   *   *

The following spring Livingstone was in Cape Town preparing for his first great expedition. He could not take his family with him, and, sadly, he watched them sail for England on the *Trafalgar*. He was not to see them again for over four years.

In June he set out northward. At Kolobeng, he found ruin and devastation. The Boers had attacked Sechele on flimsy grounds and plundered the town, killing sixty people. They had destroyed Livingstone's house and possessions because he had, they said, given the Bakwena 200 rifles and a cannon (in reality, five muskets and a stewpot). The protests of Livingstone and Sechele brought no compensation. The British government had recently agreed to the independence of the Boers in the Transvaal; and Sechele was turned back on his way to Cape Town to lodge a complaint. It was largely the hostility of the Boers that ruled out the road from Cape Town as a highway to the interior.

Livingstone reached Linyanti in May 1853. Sebituane was dead and in his stead ruled his young son, Sekeletu, not quite the leader his father had been but equally friendly towards Livingstone and almost as keen as Livingstone to establish a trade route to the coast. He provided twenty-seven men (only two of them true Makololo) to accompany Livingstone to the coast. He also provided ivory to be sold there (most of it had to be sold on the journey, to buy food).

Livingstone had decided to try the westward route (to Angola) first, partly because it was, he estimated, somewhat shorter than the more obvious route down the Zambezi to the east coast. He left Linyanti in November 1853.

It is not easy to comprehend the difficulties of travelling in Africa over a century ago. The regions that Livingstone passed through were, for all practical purposes, unexplored, and very little was known of the inhabitants or the nature of the country. Although part of the journey could be accomplished by canoe, and part on the back of an ox (neither very comfortable), long distances had to be covered on foot. Rivers had to be crossed and paths had to be cut. Travelling across a grassy plain may sound straightforward, but it is not so simple when the grass grows higher than your head. Hostile people, dangerous animals and, above all, tropical diseases presented a fearful multiformity of hazards.

In his published account, Livingstone deliberately made

Livingstone reading the Bible to his men; a drawing made on the basis of Stanley's description.

light of the physical difficulties: 'as I am getting tired of quoting my fevers . . . I shall henceforth endeavour to say little about them'. His private journals, recently edited by I. Schapera, are more revealing. Throughout his journey to the west coast, Livingstone was continually attacked by malaria. Sometimes he was so weak that he had to be helped along; sometimes the party had to halt while he recovered from a particularly severe bout. He tried the remedies of African doctors without success, but his life was saved by quinine. Eventually he evolved his own remedy which, besides that all-important ingredient, contained others less useful, including the popular Victorian cure-all, rhubarb. This medicine was sold in pill form in England under the name of 'Livingstone's Rousers'. The cause of malaria was not known until after the period covered in this book, although Livingstone came near it when he observed that mosquitoes were always present in fever-ridden areas.

At first they followed the Zambezi towards the north-west. Against the current, the canoes went slowly, but kept pace with the oxen plodding along the bank. When they came to rapids, the canoes were landed and carried around the obstacle; Livingstone told himself that trade goods could be handled similarly.

The valley seemed fertile and well-populated. Livingstone, between attacks of fever, was in high spirits and, as he usually did when feeling brisk, admired the scenery: 'The trees have put on their gayest dress, and many flowers adorn the landscape.'

He gave an account of a typical day's progress. They rose as dawn was breaking and made coffee – a novelty to Sekeletu's people and one they greatly appreciated. The canoes were loaded, and they paddled for about two hours in the early morning light. This, said Livingstone, was the best part of the day. At about eleven they stopped for a meal – meat if they had any, or a biscuit with honey – and a drink of water. After resting for an hour, they set out again, now cowering under umbrellas from the fierce rays of the sun. Sweat poured from the men paddling, and towards late afternoon their efforts began to slacken. An hour or two before sunset, they began to look for a place to spend the night. Coffee was brewed again and drunk with coarse bread, or the thin and tasteless manioc porridge that was the staple diet of Central Africa. If they had killed some animal during the day, they enjoyed the luxury of meat. The method of cooking was simple. The meat was cut into long strips, tossed into a pot, and covered with water. When the water had boiled away, the meat was 'cooked'.

Livingstone slept in a small tent, just big enough to lie down in, and Sekeletu's men rolled themselves in blankets in the shelter of a swiftly erected shed made of grass laid on branches. They could build this kind of temporary shelter in less than an hour. Fires kept wild animals away and reassured the oxen.

Sometimes they stayed a night or two at a village where they were given food and lodging. Livingstone paid tribute to the generosity of their hosts, and the graceful way in which they made their gifts. An owner presenting an ox would say modestly, 'Here is a little piece of bread for you.' This, said Livingstone, was a pleasant change from some people farther south who used to say, 'Here is a great ox for you,' and present an ancient and half-starved goat.

About three hundred miles north of Linyanti they came to a fork in the river. Livingstone decided to take the left-hand branch, towards the north-west, which he believed was a tributary of the Zambezi; in fact, it was still the main stream. The valley soon became narrow. They had to leave the canoes behind and continue on foot or on oxback.

No scenery could have been more different from the Kalahari desert, the region of Livingstone's early explorations. Instead of a dry and treeless plain, they were travelling through dense, rainy forest. Day after day the rain poured down, bringing new attacks of fever. But Livingstone looked on the bright side; he noted in his diary that the scenery made a pleasant change after the brilliant sun and waterless ground of the Kalahari.

Another change, which not even Livingstone could pretend was pleasant, was in the welcome they received from the people they encountered. In this part of Africa (now Angola) there were no kings as powerful as Sekeletu, only a collection of minor chiefs who ruled a few square miles each. Although most of these people had never seen a European, their way of life had been disturbed by the European slave trade, for which Angola had been one of the chief suppliers. The pleasant African custom of hospitality to travellers, a great benefit to explorers, had almost disappeared in this part of the country. Livingstone was greeted with suspicion, and instead of free food, everything had to be paid for. The slave traders who passed through these villages needed the chiefs' co-operation and offered them large bribes in guns, or cloth, or slaves. Livingstone grew sick of the eternal demand for 'a man, an ox, or a gun'. In vain he explained that they were all free men, that he could no more sell one of his comrades than they could sell him. As they had no guns and few oxen to spare either, they often went to sleep hungry.

At a place called Shinte's village they saw some young female slaves in chains, the property of a group of traders who were passing through. (The slave-traders in this region were usually Afro-Portuguese.) According to Livingstone, his men were horrified by this sight. 'These are not men who treat their children so!' they exclaimed. As the Makololo were acquainted with slavery, their reported reaction may owe more to Livingstone's disgust than their own.

Shinte offered Livingstone himself a slave-girl of about ten, and when he refused, replaced her with a bigger girl. He could not understand Livingstone's explanation that it would make him happier to see the girls working for their mothers.

Shinte himself was a kind old man, who knew no other system. After some difficulties to start with, he treated Livingstone well and provided him with porters to help carry his supplies on the next stage of the journey. Just before they left, Shinte visited Livingstone's tiny tent. He removed the valuable shell that he wore on a string and placed it around Livingstone's neck.

Livingstone remained in Shinte's village for almost a week. He was glad to rest as he was suffering from a particularly bad attack of fever and the rain was still pouring down. But such delays could be very irritating. It was considered bad manners, if nothing worse, to pass through a district without visiting the local chief and, of course, giving him a present, and as there were so many chiefs, Livingstone's party often made slow progress. All the diplomatic courtesies had to be observed. A messenger would be sent ahead to explain the purpose of the travellers, and they might have to wait a day or more until summoned to the chief's presence. Nor was their reception always friendly. As they advanced, the people became more hostile, food became more scarce, higher prices were demanded, and guides could not be trusted. All this Livingstone put down to the evil effects of the slave trade.

Not long after leaving Shinte's village, they crossed the plain of Lake Dilolo, but did not visit the lake itself because Livingstone was ill again and wanted to hurry onward. They found that the rivers they crossed as they moved farther west flowed in the opposite direction from the Zambezi; they were crossing the central watershed of southern Africa. Despite his fever, Livingstone took careful note of their surroundings. He had spent many hours in Cape Town with an astronomer, learning how to measure latitude and longitude, and added new details to the map of Africa each day. He gathered specimens of the strange plants they found, and in his diary wrote long descriptions of the behaviour of animals.

At the end of February 1854, they reached the Kasai river, the largest of the Zaire's many tributaries. It was a beautiful sight and reminded Livingstone of the Clyde. High praise! But the people who controlled the ford were not so pleasant, and they caught Livingstone's party in a crafty swindle. They dropped a knife secretly on the bank and, when half Livingstone's party was across the river, raised the cry of thief. One of Livingstone's young men had picked up the knife, quite innocently, but the keepers of the ford demanded a heavy fine for this 'theft'.

Livingstone's next objective was the town of Cassange, a Portuguese outpost nearly 300 miles distant. This proved to be the worst part of the journey. It was a poor country: Livingstone knew they must give up hope of eating meat when he saw the local people digging moles out of their burrows and setting traps in the forest for mice. The effects of the slave trade were plain everywhere, and the demands made by chiefs whose territory they passed through grew higher and higher.

Early in March, they entered the territory of the Chiboque and came to the village of a chief called Njambi. Desperate for meat, they killed one of their oxen and sent choice parts of the carcase to Njambi.

He returned thanks and a promise of food. But next morning his manner changed, and he demanded a more expensive present, preferably a man, an ox, or a gun. Livingstone replied that he had no such articles to spare, and about midday the chief appeared with all his men, who surrounded the camp. The Chiboque warriors, who looked very ferocious with their menacing frowns and teeth filed into points, muttered among themselves: 'See, they have only five guns.' The situation looked desperate.

Livingstone seated himself on a stool, his gun resting on his knees, while Njambi and his chief counsellors sat on the ground before him. A long parley began. Livingstone explained that they were all ready to die before giving one of their comrades into slavery. 'Then give us your gun,' was the reply. 'But,' said Livingstone, 'you obviously mean to rob us, and if I give you one of our guns, that will merely make it easier for you.' The Chiboque denied that plunder was their aim. They only wanted 'the customary tribute'. Livingstone then shifted his argument. By what right did they demand a tribute? The ground belonged to God, not to the Chiboque. If they walked on Chiboque farmland they would pay, but they would not pay to walk on God's ground.

At one point one of the young Chiboque rushed at Livingstone brandishing a spear, but a quick movement of Livingstone's gun in his direction made him fall back. Meanwhile, Livingstone's men had very quietly surrounded Njambi and his counsellors. If a fight started, the Chiboque leaders would not escape the spears of the Makololo. However, it was also obvious that the first casualty on either side would be Livingstone himself. He knew that the Chiboque would fire at the white man first which, as he said with characteristic understatement, 'was rather trying for me'.

Although they were superior in numbers, the Chiboque had probably heard of the Makololo reputation in battle, and they were not eager to test it. Gradually, the tension relaxed, although Livingstone had to give up one of his precious oxen.

This was the most dangerous experience that Livingstone had survived so far in his contacts with the Africans. When he came to describe the incident in his book, he was careful to explain to his English readers why the Chiboque were so aggressive: 'We were taken for interlopers trying to cheat the revenue of the tribe. They had been accustomed to get a slave or two from every slave trader who passed them, and now that we disputed the right, they viewed the infringement on what they considered lawfully due with most virtuous indignation.' Livingstone always drummed into all who would listen that, if Africans behaved like savages, it was the slave trade that made them do so.

Encounters with hostile tribes were disappointing as well as dangerous. But Livingstone found some compensation for such disappointments as the Chiboque in the loyalty and affection of his fellow-travellers. One day, Livingstone was crossing a stream on the back of his ox, Sinbad, when he fell off into the water. Without waiting to see if he could swim, his followers immediately leaped into the water and hurried to help him.

Sinbad was not Livingstone's favourite animal. He described their unfriendly relationship amusingly in his book. Sometimes, when too ill to keep a sharp lookout for low branches, Livingstone was knocked off the ox's back. Sinbad 'never allowed an opportunity of the kind to pass without trying to inflict a kick, as if I neither had nor deserved his love'.

Travelling westward through the Chiboque country, they entered dense and dangerous forests, where the light never penetrated through the roof of leaves and creepers. It made riding Sinbad more awkward than usual, but as Livingstone was too weak to walk he had to try and stick on the irritable animal as long as possible. He fell frequently nonetheless, and suffered several kicks from the crafty beast as a result. He was almost too ill to care but, as he remarked, continually falling on one's head is not the best cure for fever.

At the end of March they were in the broad, green valley of the Quango (Kwango). Although he was so weak and ill, Livingstone was still capable of appreciating the beauty of the scenery: 'Emerging from the gloomy forests, the magnificent prospect made us all feel as if a weight had been lifted off our eyelids. A cloud was passing across the middle of the valley, from which rolling thunder pealed, while above all was glorious sunlight.' He also noted down the type of trees, the formation of the rocks, and the character of the soil. Very rarely did he forget his role as a scientific observer.

They were now near the border of Portuguese territory, but the people on the east bank of the Quango insisted that no one should pass unless a slave was given as tribute. There was

Above: Livingstone attacked by a lion: 'I saw the lion just in the act of springing on me . . . Growling horribly close to my ear, he shook me as a terrier dog does a rat. The shock produced a stupor similar to that which seems to be felt by a mouse after the first shake of the cat. It caused a sort of dreaminess, in which there was no sense of pain nor feeling of terror . . . The shake annihilated fear, and allowed no sense of horror . . . This peculiar state is probably produced in all animals killed by the carnivora; and if so, is a merciful provision by our benevolent Creator for lessening the pain of death.'
Below: Discovery of Lake Ngami. From a sketch by Alfred Ryder, '. . . an enterprising young artist,' says Livingstone, 'who had come to make sketches of this country and of the lake immediately after its discovery', but died of fever soon afterwards. The garb, and even gesture, of the parent are amusingly echoed in the child.

William Cornwallis Harris hunting. Harris was one of many Indian army officers who, having acquired a taste for big-game hunting in India and being accustomed to call at the Cape on their voyages to and from India, found in South Africa a new playground.

A Matabele warrior, from a 19th-century lithograph.

nothing to do except ignore these demands and proceed. At the ford they were fired on, but none of the bullets went near. An African sergeant in the Portuguese militia helped them to cross, and on the other side they were safe. Next morning they had their first real meal for several days: peanuts and roasted maize, boiled manioc roots, guavas and honey. 'Delicious!', said Livingstone. A few days later they reached Cassange, where a number of Portuguese traders lived. Livingstone and his men were hospitably received, and Livingstone was glad to note that in Cassange there was none of 'the stupid prejudice against colour' that he had seen in South Africa.

Three weeks more and they arrived at Luanda. The date was 31 May 1854: the journey had taken six months.

* * *

Livingstone probably arrived at Luanda just in time. He was a living skeleton, so feeble that he could hardly stand, and he suffered from daily attacks of malaria and dysentery. He had not intended to remain long in the Portuguese town, but he stayed for four months. It took that long for him to recover his health. He was well cared for by the British commissioner for the suppression of the slave trade, and the Portuguese authorities were helpful too. Although Livingstone was to have some hard things to say about the Portuguese administration in Africa, he did not forget the personal kindness with which he was treated. The Makololo, who had been naturally fearful at entering the white man's town (some of them had heard stories that they would be eaten), were fascinated by the strange sights. They were shown over a British frigate in the harbour, and delivered their verdict. 'This is not a canoe [the only kind of ship they knew], it is a town.'

Having regained his health and completed his journals of the expedition, Livingstone was faced with what, to any other man, would have been a difficult decision. News of his achievement had reached England, where it caused an immense sensation. Universities wanted him to accept honorary degrees; public bodies wanted him to make speeches; the Royal Geographical Society awarded him its prestigious gold medal. Last but not least, his family longed to see him. A British ship was in the harbour. But his mission was unfulfilled. Although he could not admit it in so many words, his long and dangerous journey had proved that the route from the west coast to the interior was not a practicable highway for trade. On 20 September 1854, he began the long journey back.

Angola showed Livingstone that the presence of Europeans did not necessarily lead to an improvement in the living conditions of Africans. He was shocked to find that those who lived under Portuguese authority were no better off – in some ways worse – than those who lived in the remote parts of Central Africa. Livingstone put this down to the inefficiency and corruption of the Portuguese, towards whom he became increasingly hostile. The British, he believed, would do much better.

From the vileness of man, Livingstone took refuge in contemplating the beauty of nature. Here was a land, he wrote early on the return journey, 'that angels might enjoy . . . Green grassy meadows, the cattle feeding, the goats browsing, the kids skipping, the groups of herd boys with miniature bows, arrows, and spears; the women wending their way to

African river contrasts. Rapids on the Zambezi: the Devil's Cataract below Victoria Falls, and the Pongola River. Swaziland.

the river with watering-pots poised jauntily on their heads; men sewing under the shady banians; and old grey bearded fathers, with staff in hand, listening to the morning gossip, while others carry trees or branches to repair their hedges; all this, flooded with the bright African sunshine, and the birds singing among the branches before the heat of the day has become intense, form pictures that can never be forgotten'.

Soon, though, this attractive scene faded. Malaria returned with the rains, hostile villagers hazarded progress, and at one place Livingstone ferociously brandished a six-barrel 'pepper-box' pistol to discourage an attack. At Lake Dilolo, from which two rivers flowed in opposite directions, Livingstone was able to confirm current theories about the Central African watershed.

Once, Livingstone was caught in the open by an angry buffalo. His single shot diverted it from its course and it charged past him into a swamp. Back on the river, his canoe was upset by a hippo, but all on board struggled safely to the bank.

At the end of August 1855, Livingstone and his attendants reached Shesheke. They had been presumed dead, and some wives had acquired new husbands, though the dispossessed husbands did not seem greatly distressed. All Livingstone's possessions had been kept safely.

As the westward route had proved unsatisfactory, Livingstone pinned his hopes on the Zambezi valley. Sekeletu was still enthusiastic, and when Livingstone set out in November on his journey to the east coast he was accompanied by more than one hundred men. Sekeletu himself came part of the way.

Livingstone had often heard the Makololo speak of a place they called *Mosi-oa-tunya*, 'the place of sounding smoke', which he was to name, less attractively, Victoria Falls. When Livingstone first set eyes on this stunning spectacle (the largest waterfall in the world), he did not show much enthusiasm, although he did surrender to an uncharacteristic impulse and carved his initials on a tree growing on an island near the falls (he also planted a small 'garden' there, but the hippos made short work of it). His mind was still dominated by the idea of the Zambezi as a commercial route, and a greater obstacle to transport than the Victoria Falls could hardly be imagined. However, the falls were a long way upstream – beyond the Batoka Plateau. If boats could sail so far, it would be enough.

Livingstone was more favourably impressed by the Batoka highlands north of the river below the Falls: 'scenes so lovely must have been gazed upon by angels in their flight', he thought. This had been the Makololo homeland, before they were driven out by the Matabele, and it struck Livingstone as a place where European missionaries and merchants might exist in comfort, secure from the deadly fevers of the lowlands.

Livingstone and his party did not follow the Zambezi all the way to the delta. They left the winding river twice for a long distance in order to shorten their journey, and as a result missed seeing the rapids of Kebrabasa (Cabora Bassa). This omission was to have dire effects. By the time he reached Tete, at this time the farthest place upstream directly controlled by the Portuguese, Livingstone was confident he had found his highway.

In spite of Livingstone's abuse of the Portuguese régime, individual Portuguese often showed him remarkably generous hospitality. One such was Major Sicard, the commandant at Tete. He provided food and lodging for the whole party (still about one hundred strong) and promised to look after the Makololo men until Livingstone should return, which he promised to do in a year's time (in fact, it was two years).

In a Portuguese boat, accompanied by a Portuguese officer, Livingstone arrived at the port of Quelimane (north of the Zambezi delta) on 20 May 1856. His first and greatest expedition was over. Almost four years had passed since he had left Cape Town, and twenty months since he had left Luanda on the other side of Africa. By canoe, oxback, and on foot, he had travelled over four thousand miles, most of it through unknown country. Only a man of iron will and strong constitution could have done it. He had no outside support and insignificant financial backing. He had no money to buy equipment and no companions other than Africans (when he arrived home he found it difficult to speak English, he was so out of practice).

Most explorers like to be first, and Livingstone is a prime example. He hated to admit that others might have made his discoveries before him, and he sometimes used rather disreputable means to ensure that no one else shared the credit that he (in spite of his occasional denials) craved for himself. Strictly speaking, Livingstone was not the first man to cross Africa, although he was the first that most of Europe had heard of, and he was indisputably the first European. However, two Portuguese *pombeiros* (possibly more than two) had travelled from Angola to Mozambique, and two Arabs from Zanzibar, a few years before Livingstone, had crossed to Angola and back again.

Livingstone was not the only European moving about in Central Africa in the 1840s and 1850s. He met two Portuguese, Caetano José Ferreira and the better-known Silva Porto, in Linyanti in 1853. Livingstone later tended to write these men off as half-caste slave traders, although when he met them he clearly knew them to be pure Portuguese. Since Lacerda's journey from Mozambique, on which he reached Lake Mweru, the Portuguese had penetrated to Katanga, and Silva Porto himself had been on the upper Zambezi three or four years before Livingstone. According to Porto's own account of one of his meetings with the British explorer, Livingstone was somewhat annoyed by the inaccuracy of Portuguese maps and by Porto's inability to answer some of his questions. Nevertheless, he was wrong in insisting that he and Oswell were the first Europeans to discover the upper Zambezi in Central Africa.

Another traveller, a Hungarian adventurer named Ladislaus Magyar, recently rescued from undeserved obscurity by Judith Listowel (*The Other Livingstone*, 1974) was in the neighbourhood of Linyanti in 1853. It is, however, hard to believe that the reason for his not meeting Livingstone was that Livingstone simply refused to see him. Livingstone could act very badly when his reputation was at stake, but could he have been so incurious? And would the mettlesome Magyar, who was then not much more than one hundred miles away and knew the road to Linyanti, have been content with this reported answer? There must be more to this story.

The importance of priority in geographical discovery is sometimes over-emphasised. Magyar wrote only in Hungarian; Portuguese accounts were known to few outside Portugal, so their activities were not of great significance. None of these men approached Livingstone's stature in any respect, even as explorers.

The Great Lakes

When Livingstone landed in England in November 1856 he found himself a national hero; fêted by the Royal Geographical Society and presented with its gold medal by Sir Roderick Murchison; embraced by the London Missionary Society, whose chilly response to Livingstone's path-finding did not prevent its cashing-in on his fame; invited to fashionable houses, and summoned to an audience with the Queen. Livingstone set himself the task of 'selling' Africa to an eager public, and his popularity made that task none too difficult. But, taking no chances, Livingstone painted a very rosy picture of Central Africa and its peoples. He told Manchester mill-owners that cotton could be grown on the highlands of Zambezia more cheaply than in America; he told Dublin businessmen that steamers could sail up the Zambezi to the Batoka Plateau. Disease, hostile tribes, warfare – these little problems were lightly brushed over. Livingstone's published account of his adventures, though it remains one of the most delightful of African explorers' tales, gave a very misleading view of the prospects for 'Commerce and Christianity'.

The government listened sympathetically to Livingstone's proposals for the Zambezi and put up £5,000 for an expedition, the objects of which Livingstone later summarized thus: 'to improve our acquaintance with the inhabitants, and to endeavour to engage them to apply themselves to industrial pursuits and to the cultivation of their lands, with a view to the production of raw material to be exported to England in return for British manufactures; and it was hoped that, by encouraging the natives to occupy themselves in the development of the resources of the country, a considerable advance might be made towards the extinction of the slave trade'. When Livingstone suggested British colonists, the government hastily stamped on the idea. Apart from the fact that Portugal claimed authority over the area, territorial involvements in East Africa were out of the question.

The Zambezi expedition, 1858–63, was to appear an almost total flop. It took a month for the *Pearl*, carrying the personnel and equipment (including a paddle-steamer for navigating the Zambezi), to find a way through the delta, and the river was too shallow for the swift voyage up to Tete that Livingstone had banked on. From that time on, the expedition was dogged by bad luck as one setback followed another. That the aims of the expedition proved impossible to fulfill was due not only to ill fortune but also to Livingstone's over-optimistic view of the situation and to his unsuitability as leader of a government-sponsored project.

In rare times, with his family or among his admirers, Livingstone could appear charming, gentle, and affectionate. But on the whole, he found it extremely difficult to relate to people on a more or less equal level, especially when his personal mission was involved. He was arbitrary, demanding, and ungrateful. His endless tolerance towards Africans was balanced by his irritable impatience with Europeans. He expected the British members of his expedition to work as hard as he did, which is perhaps too much for a leader to ask and was certainly too much for the almost superhuman Livingstone to expect. Moreover Livingstone had little judgment of people: his character in that respect was dangerously simple and this, combined with his thorny pride, led him to dismiss a man as incompetent or dishonest or both on no better grounds than a piece of malicious gossip from his unlikeable brother Charles, who accompanied the expedition in the curious office (invented by Livingstone) of 'moral agent'. Of the six Europeans, only the phlegmatic Scots engineer, George Rae, and the immensely capable botanist, Dr John Kirk, managed to avoid a disastrous quarrel with Livingstone. Even the patient Kirk eventually formed the opinion that Livingstone was more than half crazy.

After endless troubles with their steamer, the *Ma-Robert* (feelingly renamed the *Asthmatic*), and weeks of miserable discomfort amid the mudbanks and mosquitoes of the lower Zambezi, the party reached Tete, where Livingstone was ecstatically welcomed by the Makololo whom he had left there in 1856.

Some of them began to feel less amiable when they accompanied Livingstone and Kirk as porters to view the Kebrabasa rapids. They had to clamber over slippery black rocks, suffering blistered feet in temperatures over 100°F. They wanted to turn back. Livingstone urged them on and, for him, they went; but they told him they no longer believed he had a heart.

The rapids destroyed the whole purpose of the expedition. Through a sheer-sided gorge over twenty miles long, the foaming water pounded over upthrust rocks. At one place the angle of the cataract was as much as 30°. No steamer could pass here. Livingstone clung to a belief that a more powerful steamer than the *Ma-Robert* might force her way through at high water, but the more realistic Kirk saw at once that the obstacle was insuperable. Even Livingstone admitted there was no point in exploring the river farther.

The Batoka Plateau might be inaccessible, but Livingstone was not beaten. He decided that an equally favourable site might be found in the highlands flanking the River Shire, which flows into the Zambezi about one hundred miles from the coast. Accompanied again by Kirk he piloted the battered and rusty *Ma-Robert* (an experience worse, he said, than driving a cab in a London fog) up the Shire.

The political situation in the Shire valley was, to say the

least, complicated, and Livingstone did not realize what he was running into. A number of Maravi chiefs were contending for supremacy, while the more violent Ajawa (Yao), acting as agents of Zanzibar slave merchants, preyed on relatively peaceful villages. Others waited in the wings, including the warlike Ngoni and slave-trading Portuguese from the Zambezi; Livingstone was later to express the fear that by forcing his way up the Shire – the *Ma-Robert* was attacked at least once – he had opened a way for slave traders.

On their second trip up the Shire, Livingstone and Kirk reached Lake Shirwa, the first substantial geographical discovery of the Zambezi expedition. In 1859, having left the steamer below the Murchison Cataracts (named by Livingstone for his friend and patron, the influential president of the Royal Geographical Society), Livingstone reached Lake Nyasa (Malawi). His journal merely noted grimly, 'we are in the centre of the slave market'. One party of Arab slavers, with their yoked and chained captives, tried to sell him some young girls. 'It is against this gigantic evil that my mission is directed.'

The beautiful lake, stretching far beyond the horizon to the north, inspired no lyrical description. Livingstone sensed the menace that hovered over the lake, a sinister atmosphere so well evoked by a later traveller, Dr Oliver Ransford: '. . . we saw the lake turn blank under a leaden sky, like a mirror left with nothing but the past to reflect . . . A great lethargy had settled over Nyasa. The majestic fish eagles perched motionless in their trees, all thought of flight forgotten in the breathless heat, and even the flies moved slowly. It was as though a mask had been pulled away from the lake that morning and suddenly we saw her as an ugly woman scarred from all the cruelties of the past and grimacing with satisfaction at her curious ability not only to captivate men but to set them quarrelling together'. (*Livingstone's Lake*, 1966.)

It should be said that Livingstone was not strictly the first discoverer of Lake Nyasa. It had certainly been visited, for instance, by Candido Cardoso, whose friendliness to him at Tete Livingstone had acknowledged in *Missionary Travels*. But Cardoso's description of the lake differed so drastically from what Livingstone saw with his own eyes that he was able to convince himself that Cardoso must have been describing some other lake: Livingstone was, of course, only too willing to be convinced. Livingstone did not call Cardoso a half-caste – a device which helped him to dispose of Silva Porto and other Portuguese predecessors – although,

ironically, the Tete-born Cardoso actually was one.

Livingstone evolved a bold plan for action against the slave trade. A British steamer on the Shire and Lake Nyasa would, he wrote to the foreign secretary, 'through the influence of the English name, prevent slave parties from passing the fords'. One small problem: the steamer would have to be built in pieces to be carried past Murchison Cataracts. Rae was sent back to England with instructions that if the government would not provide such a steamer (it would not), then Rae should pay for it with the £6,000 that Livingstone had earned from his book.

Two years passed before Livingstone again visited Lake Nyasa. First, he made a belated journey to Sesheke in fulfilment of his promise to lead the Makololo home. Not many of them wanted to go, however, and the twenty-odd that did return were massacred with their fellows a few years later.

From Sekeletu, Livingstone heard of the fate that had befallen the party of missionaries whom the London Missionary Society had sent to take Livingstone's place among the Makololo. Of four adults and five children, only three had survived. There seems to be little doubt that they were badly treated by the Makololo. Livingstone, however, took the side of Sekeletu and harshly criticized the missionaries' conduct. This wretched episode has brought much posthumous opprobrium upon Livingstone, although he can hardly be blamed for the tragedy.

Worse was to come. Inspired by Livingstone's memorable address at Cambridge in 1857, the Universities Mission to Central Africa had been set up, and a party of missionaries sent out to the Shire highlands under the leadership of a bishop, no less. This was a 'muscular Christian' of the better sort, Charles Mackenzie, who had some experience serving in Natal. Livingstone met the new arrivals at the mouth of the Zambezi early in 1861. There was some disagreement over his obligation to the mission. Bishop Mackenzie expected to be conducted at once to the scene of his future labours but Livingstone, having travelled all the way to the coast, was anxious to take the opportunity of exploring the River Rovuma, which on slender grounds he hoped might furnish a northern route to Lake Nyasa in the event of the Portuguese shutting off the Zambezi. The missionaries had to wait; they

A kudu drinking at a water hole. The havoc wreaked on the fauna of Africa by the white man's introduction of firearms and their subsequent widespread use led to the near-extinction of several species, and desperate efforts at conservation – such as game reserves – are now being made. From the Mzuki Game Reserve, Zululand.

A fishing village on Lake Victoria, first seen by Speke on 3 August 1858. The view, he wrote, was one 'which, even a well-known and explored country, would have arrested the traveller by its peaceful beauty'.

Kilimanjaro in the morning light. The highest mountain in Africa (19,340 feet), it lies near the north-eastern border of Tanzania. It was discovered by Joahnnes Rebmann in 1848.

East African scenery: 'How splendid the whole landscape, with its rich variety of mountain, hill, and dale, covered by the most luxurious vegetation!' (Johann Rebmann, 1848).

did not arrive at Chibisa's village, on the Shire, until July. Shortly afterwards, they had an unfortunate encounter with a Yao caravan returning from a successful raid. They were attacked and fired back, inflicting several casualties. It was the first time, Livingstone lamented, that he had fired on Africans.

Leaving the Bishop to establish his mission near Lake Shirwa, Livingstone made his second visit to Lake Nyasa. The scene was desolate; death, disease, and starvation stalked the landscape. 'The shores,' wrote Kirk, 'are covered with skulls.' Lack of food compelled Livingstone to cut short his exploration of the lake, and on the way south, he heard startling news from Bishop Mackenzie. The missionaries had decided to take the initiative against the slavers and, crozier in one hand and rifle in the other, the Bishop had led an attack on a Yao camp. Livingstone knew the perils of involvement in African feuds but, in the circumstances, it was difficult for Mackenzie to take any other course.

Livingstone was on his way to the coast again, to meet more visitors. One of them was the Bishop's sister, a frail lady advanced in years, bringing trunks full of bric-a-brac. Another was the young wife of one of the Bishop's assistants. Grim news awaited them. Arriving late at the rendezvous, they found no sign of brother or husband. Waiting for weeks at this unhealthy spot after losing their medicine chest, the Bishop and the young missionary had sickened and died. Their grieving relatives returned to England.

There was a third lady who arrived from England on the *Hetty Ellen*, and she was not to return. Mary Livingstone, fat and middle-aged, unhappy and worried about her children, finding no comfort in God and seeking it in liquor, was reunited with her husband. The *Pioneer* (the steamer sent to replace the *Ma-Robert*) faltered in the Zambezi mud and Mary Livingstone, under the assault of malarial mosquitoes, went down with fever. Her condition soon became serious, and it was obvious that she would not recover. Livingstone, distraught, clasped her in his arms: 'My dearie, my dearie, you are going to leave me . . . Are you resting on Jesus?' She died on 27 April 1862. Her remains still lie beneath the great baobab tree where they buried her.

Livingstone was hit hard by Mary's death and his biographers have detected in this event a turning point in his life. It was borne upon him what a sad life his family had led as a result of his long absences, and remorse made him more tender towards his children. He seemed gentler even to his British comrades on the expedition. But at the same time his determination stiffened: 'I shall not swerve a hairbreadth from my work while life is spared.' Livingstone had often shown a will to press onward that verged on the fanatical. From this time his search – for a way into Africa, for the sources of the Nile, for a solution to the slave trade, for his own soul – became something like an obsession.

The Zambezi expedition was folding up. Those who were left of Bishop Mackenzie's mission had retired to a safer spot; later they withdrew altogether, earning Livingstone's undying scorn. The explorer's strong and ugly face, tanned and pockmarked by the sun, was still turned towards the interior. The Portuguese were corrupt and wicked. The slave trade was the greatest shame upon God's earth. He would fight on.

He made a second visit to the Rovuma, battling upstream, dragging the canoes over rocks and shingle, far beyond the point of practical navigation. Then the portable steamer had to be taken up the Shire. Against all expectations, Livingstone got it as far as Murchison Cataracts, where it had to be taken to pieces. There it remained. Charles Livingstone and John Kirk, the last survivors of the original party, left for England in May 1863. Two months later, Livingstone received the government's order terminating the expedition. While waiting for the Zambezi to rise, Livingstone made a final trip to Lake Nyasa. He took with him the steward of the *Pioneer*, 'to improve his health'. They covered 700 miles on foot, eating only poor African meal and plagued by illness and exhaustion. On their return, Livingstone reported the sickly steward 'stronger than he had ever been before'. In January 1864 he sailed down the Zambezi for the last time.

The Zambezi at Tete in 1859, a painting by Thomas Baines, the King's Lynn-born artist who had served as official war artist in South Africa and on an Australian expedition, but was less capable as a store-keeper – or so Livingstone thought.

Speke escaping from the Somali raiders.

An island in Lake Victoria. Islands like this were often thickly inhabited in the time of Speke and Stanley, but the spread of the tsetse fly caused depopulation a generation or two later.

There is a footnote: the *Lady Nyasa*, built at Livingstone's expense to sail on the lake, had to be sold. There were no likely buyers on the east coast, so he decided to sail her to Bombay – 2,500 miles across the Indian Ocean, in a boat built for an inland lake, captained by a man with no experience of navigation, and the monsoon about to break! Needless to say, he made it. No one noticed his arrival, and for a day he wandered happily about Bombay unrecognized.

* * *

Livingstone had been anxious to reach Lake Nyasa before he was forestalled. He knew nothing of the young German missionary, Albrecht Roscher, who discovered the northern end of the lake some two months after Livingstone's first arrival at the southern end (Roscher was murdered soon afterwards and his journals were lost), but he was apprehensive that Burton or Speke might get there first. Their successful journey to Lakes Tanganyika and Victoria had been concluded in the same year (1858) that the Zambezi expedition began.

Superficially, Richard Francis Burton (1821–90) and John Hanning Speke (1827–64) had much in common: both came from middle-class English backgrounds; both were officers in the Indian army. In fact, two men more different could hardly be imagined. In a word, Speke was conventional; Burton was emphatically not. Speke could stand as almost the archetypical Victorian explorer – brave, vigorous, determined, rather insensitive (except where his own status was concerned), a poor linguist, but otherwise well-equipped as an explorer, possessing an indefinable geographical sixth sense that led him to correct conclusions on the barest evidence. In addition there was something reserved and aloof about Speke; it is apparent in his portraits – an air of rigid self-containment that is something more than the consciousness of being an officer and a gentleman.

Unlike Speke, Burton was a perfectly extraordinary man, an ill-integrated mixture of brilliant talents – a first-rate swordsman and one of the outstanding oriental scholars of the age, an inveterate traveller who was equally (perhaps more) happy in the study, a man suspected of unspeakable vices and thoroughly content with this sinister reputation (which, indeed, was largely his own creation: Burton's promise to one of his kinkier friends to bring him the flayed skin of a Negress is not to be taken seriously). Burton did not underrate his own abilities, and there was truth in Speke's complaint that he was 'one of those men who never *can* be wrong'.

The sexual make-up of both men is a puzzle, though for different reasons. Speke is not known to have had sexual relations with anyone in his life; Burton was allegedly a great experimenter in this area, though Fawn Brodie suspects him of impotence – in later life anyway.

The idea behind the expedition was Burton's; its primary purpose, he said, was to investigate reports of the 'Sea of Ujiji', known to Arab travellers from Zanzibar, and its secondary purpose to explore the society and commerce of the East African interior. The Royal Geographical Society approved the plan (though in somewhat different terms, mentioning Lake Nyasa and the sources of the Nile as the objectives), and succeeded in attracting the support of the Foreign Office – to the extent of £1,000. Burton was anxious to enlist Rebmann, but the German missionaries had offended the Sultan of Zanzibar by some scathing remarks regarding the lack of authority of his government on the mainland, and if the Sultan's approval was to be obtained, Rebmann had to be excluded.

Burton's decision to invite Speke to join him was surprising. One must assume that his reason for doing so was just what he said it was: 'As he had suffered with me in purse and person at Berberah, in 1855, I thought it but just to offer him the opportunity of renewing an attempt to penetrate into Africa.' The incident to which he referred so casually had very nearly resulted in the deaths of both men when their camp was attacked by Somalis. Speke was actually speared several times while lying, with hands tied, on the ground. Miraculously, he still managed to escape. Burton was stabbed through the face, thus acquiring a romantic scar for life.

That brief expedition, during which Burton had visited the 'forbidden city' of Harar in disguise, had at least proved Speke's physical resilience. In other ways, though, his performance had not been impressive. Burton, who had no notion of tact, had said things that Speke had deeply resented – more deeply than Burton realized until Speke blurted out his grievances while delirious with fever on the way to Lake Tanganyika two years later. Speke knew no languages bar some Hindustani, and he was no scholar. Burton's remarkable abilities he treated with indifference born of a feeling of inferiority. Speke, like many another Indian army officer, had come to Africa to hunt; Burton treated his shooting with open derision and suggested that Speke was not so good a shot as he considered himself. It remains, therefore, rather odd that two men with such contrary interest, should have agreed to go together on the expedition to discover Lake Tanganyika.

In his book on their expedition, Burton spoke frankly about his companion: 'I could not expect much from his assistance; he was not a linguist – French and Arabic being equally unknown to him – nor a man of science, nor an accurate astronomical observer ... During the expedition he acted in a subordinate capacity; and ... was unfit for any other but a subordinate capacity.' This of course was written

Richard Burton, the well-known portrait by Lord Leighton, 1876, displaying the scar made by a Somali spear thrust.

after they had fallen out. When the expedition began, they were amiable enough together; and ironically each man was probably responsible for saving the life of the other in the course of the expedition, by careful nursing during severe illness.

For the journey, though it mostly followed a route known to Arab traders for thirty years, and to Africans before that, turned out to be tougher than might have been expected.

It took some time to get under way. After one false start, it was not until June 1857, nine months after leaving England, that Burton and Speke set out from Zanzibar, and what Burton calls 'a vista of unexpected difficulties' opened up before they started inland from the coast. These mostly concerned the alleged savagery of the people they would meet, the likely scarcity of food, and the ferocity of wild animals. The experienced Burton was aware that these were the customary preliminaries of African expeditions – the shop stewards making the worst of the job in order to strengthen imminent demands for higher wages. The total number of porters at the start was 132 (fewer than Burton wanted), and there were thirty mules, none of which reached Lake Tanganyika. Progress was slow; both Burton and Speke suffered severe attacks of fever. By the time they reached Tabora (Kazeh) about six hundred miles from the coast, after nearly twenty weeks travelling, they were feeble and exhausted. Several stragglers among the porters had been robbed or killed; desertions continued fairly regularly. Still, they entered the town in some style: 'when the line of porters becoming compact began to wriggle, snake-like, its long length over the plain, with floating flags, booming horns, muskets ringing like saluting mortars, and an uproar of voice

John Hanning Speke, in his much-favoured Englishman's tweed sporting waistcoat, pictured against the background of Lake Victoria.

which nearly drowned the other noises, we made a truly splendid and majestic first appearance' (Burton). Tabora was an Arab colony, and 'contrary to the predictions of others, nothing could be more encouraging than the reception experienced from the Omani Arabs; striking, indeed, was the contrast between the open-handed hospitality and the hearty goodwill of this truly noble race, and the niggardness of the savage and selfish African' (like other British Arabophiles Burton, for all his sensitivity and anthropological knowledge, never quite overcame his dislike of Negroes).

They spent over a month in Tabora, regaining their health, replacing their supplies, and hiring new porters. Neither Burton nor Speke could communicate directly with the Africans of the interior, but Burton's Arabic was fluent, and had allowed him to make his famous visit to Mecca in dis-

guise. Speke, dependent on the interpreting of the capable Sidi Bombay ('for all his faults', even Burton admitted, 'truly valuable') must have felt left out of things in Tabora.

From Tabora, Speke wished to turn north to investigate the reported 'Ukerewe lake', but Burton insisted on pursuing a westward line. Within a month, both men were suffering again, Burton from a severe attack of malaria which left him too weak to walk for months afterwards, and Speke from trachoma, a disease of the eye still prevalent in the tropics, which made him, for a time, almost blind. There were rivers to cross – the Ruguvu, with its 'foul swamp of black mire', the Uvungwe, 'girt in as usual by dense vegetation' – then came 'the weary toil of fighting through tiger and spear-grass', along paths 'broken, slippery, and pitted with deep holes' until, on 13 February, a streak of light appeared beyond them. 'What is that?' Burton inquired of Sidi Bombay. '"I am of opinion," quoth Bombay, "that that is *the* water."' It looked insignificant at first, but as they advanced the whole breadth of the lake came into view. 'Nothing, in sooth, could be more picturesque than this view of the Tanganyika Lake, as it lay in the lap of the mountains, basking in the gorgeous tropical sunshine. Below and beyond a short foreground of rugged and precipitous hill-fold, down which the foot-path zigzags painfully, a narrow strip of emerald green, never sere and marvellously fertile, shelves towards a ribbon of glistening yellow sand, here bordered by sedgy rushes, there cleanly and clearly cut by the breaking wavelets. Further in front stretch the waters, an expanse of the lightest and softest blue, in breadth varying from thirty to thirty-five miles, and sprinkled by the crisp east-wind with tiny crescents of snowy foam.' Poor Speke could see little except a 'mist and glare before his eyes'.

After some days rest at Ujiji, on the shore of the lake, Speke volunteered to go by canoe to an island near the farther shore in hopes of hiring a decent boat to explore the lake. After five stormy days the party of thirty-two reached a small island where Speke took refuge in his tent. The light of a candle attracted a hoard of small black beetles, which swarmed over everything. Having tried in vain to get rid of them, Speke put out the candle and lay down to sleep, 'trying to overcome the ticklish annoyance occasioned by these intruders crawling up my sleeves and into my hair, or down my back and legs'. At length he fell asleep, but was awoken by one of the insects crawling into his ear. 'He went his course, struggling up the narrow channel, until he got arrested for want of passage-room. This impediment evidently enraged him, for he began with exceeding vigour, like a rabbit at a hole, to dig violently away at my tympanum. The queer sensation this amusing *measure* excited in me is past description.' He felt like galloping madly around, as he had seen donkeys do when attacked by bees. 'What to do I knew not. Neither tobacco, oil, nor salt could be found: I therefore tried melted butter; but that failing, I applied the point of a penknife to his back, which did more harm than good; for though a few thrusts quieted him, the point also wounded my ear so badly, that inflammation set in, severe suppuration took place, and all the facial glands extending from that point down to the point of the shoulder became contorted and drawn aside, and a string of boils decorated the whole length of that region. It was the most painful thing I ever remember to have endured; but more annoying still, I could not masticate for several days, and had to feed on broth alone. *For many months the tumour made me almost deaf* [in fact his hearing never recovered completely], and ate a hole between the ear and the nose, so that when I blew it, my ear whistled so audibly that those who heard it laughed. Six or seven months after this accident happened, bits of the beetle – a leg, a wing, or parts of its body – came away in the wax.'

Speke returned after a month to find the still prostrate Burton in equally poor condition – and with no boat. He had some information, however, including interesting news of a river in the north, which suggested a possible source of the Nile. On further inquiry, it appeared that the Ruzizi unfortunately flowed into, not out of, the lake. (Nevertheless, Burton later came to believe that the original report was correct and that Lake Tanganyika – *his* lake – was the source of the Nile.) By canoe, they went only as far north as Uvira, just short of the river, and further exploration had to be abandoned through failing supplies, a lack of boats, and Burton's poor health. Burton had seen enough, and was looking forward to a renewal of his learned discourse with the sheikhs of Tabora. Speke, on the other hand, perhaps smarting from his failure to get the necessary boat, was anxious to investigate the Ukerewe lake, which was said to be not many days distant. They agreed that Burton should return to Tabora and endeavour to discover as much as he could about the whole region through conversation, while Speke made his northward dash.

'Dash' is not quite the right word, as Speke and his thirty men took nearly four weeks over the journey, though the direct distance was not much more than one hundred miles. Dependent on Bombay, who happened to be feeling less than usually co-operative, Speke had difficulty controlling the porters. The going through Nyamwezi was not difficult, with much of the ground cultivated and the people reasonably amiable, and on 30 July they reached a stretch of water which proved to be a southerly arm of the great lake that Speke was to name after the Queen (though his most recent biographer, Alexander Maitland, suggests this was a subconscious tribute to his mother). A few days later, he climbed a hill from which he could see the lake – the second largest fresh water lake in the world – stretched out before him, receding mistily into apparently limitless distance. Local inhabitants told him they assumed that it went on to the end of the world.

Speke leaped to the conclusion that he had discovered the source of the Nile. It is often said that he had no reason to do so – 'He had not a shred of practical evidence to back up this assertion' (Alan Moorehead) – but he did have what criminal lawyers might describe as strong circumstantial evidence – the apparent size of the lake and its high altitude. (Although his thermometers were faulty, Speke's estimate of the altitude was nearly correct. And, of course, Speke's interpretation, if based on slight evidence, was right.)

But Burton scoffed at the idea: Speke had merely glimpsed the lake, he had not explored it in any way. Of course, Burton must have felt a powerful disinclination to believe that his somewhat despised inferior should make so important a discovery on *his* expedition, but he was nevertheless entirely justified in doubting the significance of Speke's discovery. He might have been more restrained in expressing his doubts. In the event, the two men quarrelled so fiercely that they eventually agreed not to mention the matter until they reached the coast. The return journey took place in a strained atmosphere.

Nevertheless, they parted at Aden on superficially amiable terms. Burton remained there to recover his health. Speke hastened back to England. 'Good-bye, old fellow; you may be quite sure I shall not go up to the Royal Geographical Society until you come to the fore and we appear together. Make your mind quite easy about that.'

When Speke arrived in England he did exactly what he had promised Burton he would not do; he went straight to the Society and laid his views before Sir Roderick Murchison. The president was enthusiastic: 'Speke,' he said, 'we must send you there again.'

Speke's action is hard to condone, although it is possible to feel some sympathy for the predicament he believed himself to be in. If he waited quietly in the wings while Burton stepped forward into the limelight, Burton would steal the credit that was due to him, as had happened (Speke believed) after their adventures in Somalia. If an expedition were sent, as it surely would be, to explore Lake Victoria farther, Burton and not himself would get command of it. The sight of Lake Victoria and the ensuing flash of conviction that here was the original source of the Nile had been momentous for Speke. He felt passionately that the discovery belonged to him. Alexander Maitland writes of Speke 'dedicating himself to exploration and travel as a priest or monk dedicates his life to the service of God'. But the trouble with travel as a religion is that the final object, the ultimate desire, the godhead, is often uncertain; an image or a symbol is necessary, whether it be the city of Timbuktu or, as it was for Speke after 1858, the source of the Nile.

It is also likely that Speke would not have behaved as he did if he had not been encouraged by his ship-board companion, Laurence Oliphant, who, apparently from sheer malice, played a large part in keeping the whole 'unmanly dispute' (as Burton called it) on the boil.

When he arrived in England two weeks after Speke, Burton found himself thoroughly upstaged. Admittedly he, and not Speke, was the man who got the Royal Geographical Society's gold medal, but to Sir Roderick Murchison and his supporters, it was Speke who was the man of the hour. 'Let us hope,' said Sir Roderick, that 'the undaunted Speke may receive every encouragement to proceed from Zanzibar to his old station and there to carry out to demonstration the view that he now maintains, that the Lake [Victoria] Nyanza is the main source of the Nile.' Speke did not help his case by swiftly publishing his journal in the popular *Blackwood's*

Speke presents the heads of three white rhinoceros to Rumanika, the tall and smiling monarch of Karagwe. 'In utter astonishment he said, "Well, this must have been done with something more potent than powder, for neither the Arabs nor the Nnanaji, although they talk of their shooting powers, could have accomplished such a feat as this. It is no wonder the English are the greatest men in the world".' From a drawing by Zwecker, based on sketches by Speke and Grant.

Ripon Falls, source of the Nile. Speke spent a day 'watching the fish flying at the falls, and [I] felt as if I only wanted a wife and family, garden and yacht, rifle and rod, to make me happy here for life, so charming was the place'. This engraving, usually described as based on a drawing by Grant, is actually from a sketch by Speke. Grant did not visit the Falls, which have since been submerged by the Owen Dam.

Forest country in Uganda, at the foothills of Mt. Elgon. The gorge of the Suan River in the distance.

A peaceful scene at sunset – bathing time – on the Nile near Khartoum.

magazine, thus cocking a snook at the Royal Geographical Society's more sedate journal, as well as at Burton. Moreover, his articles were 'somewhat incautiously composed' (Maitland), and Burton was able to criticize them on the grounds of inaccuracy.

Sir Roderick Murchison remained constant and persuaded the long-suffering Treasury to fork out £2,500, though only after pulling some highly placed strings ('I must say,' said the under-secretary, who had recently paid out £5,000 for the Zambezi expedition, 'the Geographical Society draws largely on us.') Speke planned a two-pronged assault on the sources of the Nile – himself from East Africa to go north, around Lake Victoria, and up the Nile; and the Welsh trader-explorer-emissary, John Petherick, to approach up the Nile from the North, leaving boats and supplies for Speke at Gondokoro, where an Austrian mission had been established some years earlier.

It was out of the question for Speke to invite Burton to go with him. The man he chose was a friend from Indian army days, a steady, self-effacing Scot, James Augustus Grant, whose modesty and lack of fuss make him one of the most likeable of Victorian explorers. Speke may have been, as Burton said, fit only for a subordinate position on the Tanganyika expedition; but Speke was a man (like Burton in this respect) who made a very poor subordinate. Grant, on the contrary, had not a jot of Speke's desire to dominate, and he possessed that estimable quality not very common among African explorers, complete loyalty to his leader.

*　　*　　*

By courtesy of the Royal Navy, Speke and Grant sailed via Rio de Janeiro and Cape Town to Zanzibar, where they arrived in August 1860. Bombay and some other old acquaintances of Speke were waiting for them. Speke decided to follow the old track via Tabora, avoiding the more direct route through the land of the Masai (later explored by Joseph Thomson). They set off from the mainland on 2 October (an inventory of their personal equipment is printed in Appendix I, and a list of their attendants in Appendix II).

The march to Tabora was fairly straightforward, marred only by the rapid draining away of porters, and with them a substantial portion of the supplies. Food became scarce as there was famine in the area which led to exorbitant demands from the chiefs through whose territory they passed. Their plight would have been worse but for the skill of both Speke and Grant with their guns. Conservationists would find it hard to approve of Speke, and so would those who dislike cruelty to animals (he wounded as many as he killed). On 8 November they saw 'a rich variety of small birds [which] as often happened, made me wish I had come on a shooting rather than a long exploring expedition'. Without making anachronistic moral judgments, a certain crudeness is apparent in Speke. On the same day one of the Hottentot soldiers hired at Cape Town died. Speke wrote '. . . he died because he had determined to die – an instance of that obstinate fatalism in their mulish temperament which no kind words or threats can cure'. (To be fair to Speke, he goes on to describe the death as a 'terrible catastrophe'.)

In his published *Journal* . . . Speke described his own activities on the march: 'My first occupation was to map the country. This is done by timing the rate of march with a watch, taking compass-bearings along the road, or on any conspicuous marks – as, for instance, hills off it – and by noting the watershed – in short, all topographical objects. On arrival in camp every day came the ascertaining, by boiling a thermometer, of the altitude of the station above the sea-level; of the latitude of the station by the meridian altitude of a star taken with a sextant; and of the compass variation by azimuth. Occasionally there was the fixing of certain crucial stations, at intervals of sixty miles or so, by lunar observations, or distances of the moon either from the sun or from certain given stars, for determining the longitude, by which the original-timed course can be drawn out with certainty on the map by proportion . . . The rest of my work, besides sketching and keeping a diary, which was the most troublesome of all, consisted in making geological and zoological collections. With Captain Grant rested the botanical collections and thermometrical registers. He also boiled one of the thermometers, kept the rain-gauge, and undertook the photography; but after a time I sent the [photographic]

instruments back, considering the work too severe for the climate . . . The rest of our day went in breakfasting after the march was over – a pipe, to prepare us for rummaging the fields and villages to discover their contents for scientific purposes – dinner close to sunset, and tea and pipe before turning in at night.'

Amid stories of exotic rulers, dangerous animals, and extraordinary scenes, the tiresome, difficult, sheer hard work that real exploration demanded is apt to be forgotten. It is for their competence and persistence in these tasks that men like Livingstone and Speke deserve their fame, regardless of how many Portuguese agents, Hungarian adventurers, or Arab traders may have preceded them.

At Tabora, Speke became involved in an attempt to mediate on behalf of a young African chief, Manua Sera, who had been deposed by the Arabs. Although he remained in Tabora for nearly two months, his mediation was not successful.

If the accounts of 19th-century explorers tend to suggest that the East African interior was a place of constant warfare, ambush and siege, it should be remembered that some of these tribal wars produced a remarkably low head-count – as modern military strategists would put it. At one village where Speke and Grant stayed, the chief had just concluded a two-year war with a neighbour in which the total casualties were three. Nevertheless, the explorers were to witness some bloody scenes.

In this environment, the large and well-armed party led by Speke amounted to a considerable military force, and it was undoubtedly their fire-power that got him through places where the people were not disposed to be friendly.

Speke advanced northward, leaving Grant at a friendly village to recuperate from a severe bout of fever. They were short of porters, though the exigent demands of the chiefs (one of them succeeded in reducing Speke, of all people, to tears) considerably lightened the load to be carried. Speke too was suffering from ill-health, and in an effort to relieve the intense discomfort of what sounds like some kind of 'flu, he tried to bleed himself; but the needle was too blunt. Meanwhile, Grant was attacked and robbed, though most of his goods were restored and the attack explained as a 'mistake'.

Reunited again, the two explorers moved on through country that reminded Grant of a Highland moor, though dotted with patches of plantains. Stories were circulating that they had supernatural powers, that they killed all the people in the places they passed through, that they 'took possession of all countries', stories no doubt exaggerated in order to prise larger payments out of them. Endless delays were caused by negotiations over 'presents'.

Prospects brightened when they reached the interlacustrine kingdoms. Karagwe was green and hilly, more like the English Lake District Grant thought, and the king, Rumanika, and subordinate chiefs, were more hospitable than most of their recent hosts. 'Having shaken hands in true English style,' Rumanika inquired with the confidence of a favourable reply, what the travellers thought of his country, 'for it had struck him his mountains were the finest in the world; and the lake, too, did we not admire it?' This gentle (there was no capital punishment in Karagwe – rather a contrast with 19th-century England) and always smiling monarch, with his remarkable appreciation of the beauty of landscape, was a surprise, and a very welcome one, to Speke. The explorer maintained that the King was descended from

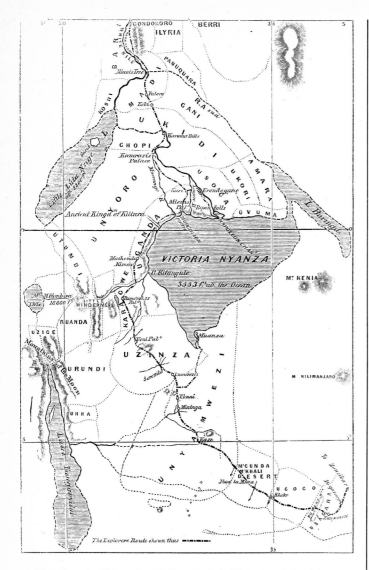

Speke's map of his route with Grant to Lake Victoria and Gondokoro.

state. It was only feather weight in reality but, being loaded with charms, became so heavy to those who were not entitled to the crown, that no one could lift it but the one person whom the spirits were inclined towards as the rightful successor. Now, of all the three brothers, he, Rumanika, alone could raise it from the ground; and whilst his brothers laboured hard, in vain attempting to move it, he with his little finger held it up without exertion.'

Serenaded by the King's musicians (woodwinds, drums, dulcimer, and harp), attended by the King's sons, soothed by the King's 'excellent beer', entertained by the King's archers ('I must say I never witnessed better feats in my life'), it was a pleasant existence. But Speke was anxious to press on to the north, to the kingdom of Buganda (so called to distinguish it from the much larger modern state of Uganda), which lay at the northern end of Lake Victoria. However, he made no serious effort to depart from the pleasant environment of Karagwe until the arrival of messengers from Buganda, sent to escort him thither, virtually compelled him to move.

Grant was suffering from horrible abscesses in the leg, and remained behind. Not for five months could he stand on his feet. In his book, *A Walk Across Africa* (the title was suggested by Lord Palmerston's famous greeting, 'You have had a long walk, Captain Grant') it is just possible to detect between the lines a faint sorrow – nothing more – at Speke's desertion.

* * *

Speke's visit to Mtesa, the Kabaka of Buganda, was the most memorable part of the whole Nile journey, and his account captured the imagination of his British readers as nothing like it had done since James Bruce's description of Ethiopia. As a raconteur, Speke was not in Bruce's class, but otherwise the two episodes had much in common. In both places, violence of a truly savage kind twisted and ruined what in other respects might have been an attractive society. Mtesa's acts of arbitrary cruelty have passed almost into legend – how he tested a new rifle by telling a page to go outside and shoot someone with it; how a woman who had irritated him merely by proferring fruit would have been clubbed to death had not Speke, with an act of genuine courage, stayed the King's arm. Such incidents are easily remembered, while the circumstances and underlying reasons for this behaviour are ill-comprehended. Mtesa had but recently established his power; his ritual sacrifices of literally hundreds of people were not merely the whims of a crazy tyrant, they had a political purpose also. Nevertheless, Buganda was a rather frightening country, and it is not surprising that the Ganda court existed, as Timothy Severin puts it, 'in a state of semi-hysteria'.

Mtesa, when Speke met him, was 'a good-looking, well-figured, tall young man of twenty-five . . . The hair on his head was cut short, excepting on the top, where it was combed into a high ridge, running from stem to stern like a cockscomb. On his neck was a very neat ornament – a large ring, of beautifully-worked small beads, forming elegant patterns by their various colours. On one arm was another bead ornament, prettily devised; and on the other a wooden charm, tied by a string covered with snakeskin. On every finger and toe he had alternate brass and copper rings: and above the ankles, half-way up to the calf, a stocking of very

Ethiopian stock (this was Burton's theory), and his people would be Christians, had they not lost their knowledge of God. 'A long theological and historical discussion ensued . . .' Like other Victorian explorers, Speke felt confident of racial superiority in the presence of Africans and, perhaps understandably, gave himself an importance hardly merited by facts (in Buganda, he claimed to be a prince of royal blood). His appreciation of the culture and intelligence of Rumanika is a point in his favour.

Rumanika was astonished that the white men should spend so much of their property simply travelling about: 'when men had such means they would surely sit down and enjoy it'. It is doubtful if he were convinced by Speke's explanation that they had had enough of 'the luxuries of life'. What had brought them to Karagwe, he said, 'was to see your majesty in particular, and the great kings of Africa – and at the same time to open another road to the north, whereby the best manufactures of Europe would find their way to Karagwe . . .'

From Rumanika, Speke heard the story of how he had gained his throne, a story which has countless variants throughout the world; 'When Dagara died, and he [Rumanika], Nuanaji, and Rogero were the only three sons left in line of succession to the throne, a small mystic drum of diminutive size was placed before them by the officers of pretty beads. Everything was light, neat, and elegant in its way; not a fault could be found with the taste of his "getting up". For a handkerchief he held a well-folded piece of bark-cloth [like corduroy, according to Samuel Baker], and a piece of gold-embroidered silk, which he constantly employed to hide his large mouth when laughing, or to wipe it after a drink of plantain-wine, of which he took constant and copious draughts from neat little gourd-cups, administered by his ladies-in-waiting, who were at once his sisters and his wives. A white dog, spear, shield, and woman – the Uganda cognisance – were by his side . . .' When he walked it was with what Speke called 'a very ludicrous kind of waddle', intended to represent the gait of the lion.

Mtesa had never seen a white man before, and the news of Speke's approach had filled him with neurotic excitement. He had sworn not to eat until Speke arrived in order to hasten his progress, and he showed considerable tolerance of the airs that Speke gave himself – refusing to wait outside in the sun, insisting that he should sit on a chair (a mark of status reserved for the king), and generally displaying an unattractive, though possibly not ill-advised, determination to stand no nonsense from a lot of blacks. He could put on a performance of outraged righteousness worthy of James Bruce.

The King was apparently well-informed of Speke's ambitions, for one of his first questions was 'What would you say if I showed you a road by which you might reach your home in one month?' However, owing to the difficulty of communication – everything had to pass through two interpreters – this interesting remark was not followed up. The next question, more predictable, was 'What guns have you got? Let me see the one you shoot with'. Speke was asked to demonstrate his prowess by shooting four cows, assembled for the purpose. He had only a revolver with him, but 'shot all four in a second of time'. He did not think much of this sport, and when asked to shoot a bird in a tree he tried, in the best traditions of British sportsmanship, first to make it take wing by throwing stones.

Breaking through the court ceremonial proved difficult, and Mtesa's unpredictable behaviour did not make Speke's task easier. He was compelled to enter the game of court politics: by paying court to the Queen Mother, who still retained some influence in Buganda, he managed to draw out the King. He was becoming quite adept at what he called 'a figurative kind of speech to please Waganda ears'. Explaining that more white men would follow him, he compared his visit to one coffee seed which brings forth fruit in plenty. 'All appreciated this oratory, saying, "The white man, he even speaks beautifully! beautifully! beautifully! beautifully!" and, putting their hands to their mouths, they looked askance at me, nodding their admiring approval.' Perhaps his interpreters did him more than justice; nevertheless, Speke's 'African diplomacy' was on the whole very skilful. It was a sign of how he had matured since his first arrival in Zanzibar eight years before. Indeed, the growth of understanding and tolerance in Speke resulting from his experience of Africa is a noticeable feature of his comparatively brief career.

Speke stayed six months in Buganda, but it cannot be said that he and Mtesa came to know each other well in that time. The enormous gulf between the societies of Equatorial Africa and Victorian Britain could not be bridged so easily. It was British conventions, though on the whole preferable, that were the more rigid, and Speke's irritation at misunder-

standings or ignorance was sometimes no better than block-headedness. The King said one day, 'Now, Bana, I wish you would instruct me, as you have so often proposed doing, for I wish to learn everything, though I have little opportunity for doing so.' Exhilarated by this receptiveness, Speke told the King to ask any questions he liked, and he would answer them. He hoped to find Mtesa 'inquisitive on foreign matters; but nothing was more foreign to his mind: none of his countrymen ever seemed to think beyond the sphere of Uganda'. Speke seems to have been surprised by the King's lack of interest in a purse full of coins, and annoyed by his belief that the attachment of a wooden charm improved the accuracy of a Whitworth rifle.

Speke was often exasperated by what he considered the absurd pretensions of Buganda. Mtesa's chief general had heard that Speke's country was governed by a woman; 'what would I say if he made the Waganda dethrone her, and create me king instead?' By way of reply, Speke opened a map and indicated the territories of the British empire compared with those of Buganda. This 'shut him up'.

Equally irritating was the lackadaisical manner of doing business. Decision-making in Africa had nothing in common with the ostensibly more efficient method familiar to a European soldier or bureaucrat; conversation always seemed to end in the middle. The royal family of Buganda 'give orders without knowing how they are to be carried out, and treat all practical arrangements as trifling details not worth attending to', Speke wrote after one trying interview.

To be fair to Speke, he had ample cause for exasperation, and while he occasionally made his irritation plain (especially when he felt insufficient respect was being shown) he also showed considerable patience, waiting for hours on end in the hope of an audience with the King or his almost equally unpredictable mother, being stranded on the shore because Mtesa had blithely gone off with all the boats and forgotten about him, deprived of food for his men (whose hunger was perhaps aggravated by the fact that most of them suffered from tapeworms) because the King had forgotten, or could not be bothered, to make a regular arrangement for feeding them.

And yet just as, one feels, James Bruce had half-consciously felt a certain sympathy with the Ethiopian warlord, Ras Michael, so Speke was drawn to some aspect of the character of the Kabaka of Buganda. As he told him on one occasion, temporizing in reply to the tricky question whether he loved Rumanika or Mtesa better, he and Mtesa shared a love of hunting (the King went into ecstasy over the effects of Speke's guns on the local fauna, though their hunting expeditions, accompanied by Mtesa's wives and the court band, warned off all game long before they came within range). But as well, and in spite of the horror he felt at the almost daily execution of the King's numerous women, Speke's desire to dominate perhaps found some vicarious satisfaction in the imperious authority of the Kabaka.

Grant arrived, still barely able to walk, in May, and in the first week of July the two explorers took fond leave of Mtesa and his extraordinary entourage. After a week they separated again, Grant making for Nyoro, where King Kamrasi was expecting him, and Speke turning eastward, north of Lake Victoria, to confirm his belief in the origins of the Nile. He has sometimes been accused of deliberately depriving Grant of the chance to partake in this great geographical discovery,

James Augustus Grant, the modest, unassuming Scot who was Speke's companion on the expedition of 1860.

Baker pursued by a wounded elephant. 'It was exceedingly difficult to escape, owing to the bushes which impeded the horse, while the elephant crushed them like cobwebs: however, by turning my horse sharp round a tree, I managed to evade him after a chase of about a hundred and fifty yards.'

but as Grant himself would give no countenance to such suggestions, perhaps Speke should be exonerated.

Having struck the river some miles below its outlet, he turned to follow it back to the lake, naming the falls where it emerged after Lord Ripon, a former president of the Royal Geographical Society. They were, he wrote, 'by far the most interesting sight I had seen in Africa'. The view was not spectacular, 'for the broad surface of the lake was shut out from view by a spur of hill, and the falls, about 12 feet deep, and 400 to 500 feet broad, were broken by rocks. Still it was a sight that attracted one to it for hours . . .'

'The expedition,' Speke roundly proclaimed, 'had now performed its functions. I saw that old father Nile without any doubt rises in the Victoria Nyanza.' So it does, though that is not the only source and, more important, Speke was still relying on inspiration as much as indisputable evidence. He says he had seen 'fully half' the lake, but that was an exaggeration and, in any case, hardly enough. Moreover, on the final stage of the expedition to Gondokoro, he did not follow the whole course of the river and thus could not know for certain that it was the Nile and not a tributary. He felt sure of it, but others, as he was to discover, remained unconvinced.

Rejoining Grant in Nyoro, Speke was received by Kamrasi, who proved to be a 'morose autocrat' (in Grant's description) and far less flamboyant (and less cruel) than Mtesa. 'Our presents of beads, boxes, guns, cloth, etc., were received by Kamrasi very coolly, with no sign of pleasure, only an occasional remark. He sat, as Bombay said, "like a cow", showing neither astonishment nor delight.' Nevertheless, his appetite for presents was large, and he was reluctant to let his visitors depart. He did allow Bombay to take a scouting party north to Faloro, where it was hoped he might find Petherick, of whose presence occasional rumours had been heard.

Bombay returned at the beginning of November with the news that Petherick was absent on a trading trip in the west. From this time, Speke appears to have begun to feel suspicious of Petherick. As Speke and Grant were almost exactly a year behind schedule (they had planned to meet Petherick at Gondokoro on December 1861), Petherick could hardly have been expected to be sitting on his haunches waiting for them. But Speke felt he had been let down, and on the basis of nothing more than a malicious rumour, he began to suspect that Petherick, who held the post of British consul, was involved in the slave trade. He was later unwise – and unkind – enough to make his suspicion public, with deleterious effects on Petherick's career. This was another example of Speke's unfortunate tendency to turn friends into enemies.

Having given Kamrasi everything they could afford to give away, Speke and Grant reached Faloro, having travelled mainly overland, in the first week of December. They were effusively welcomed by an Egyptian officer who, after some delay, escorted them (in a slave and ivory cafila 1,000-strong) to Gondokoro, where they arrived on 13 February.

There was no news of Petherick. Yet they were not to be deprived of a welcome in Gondokoro, for suddenly they saw, said Grant, 'a sturdy English figure approaching. With a hearty cheer, we waved our hats and rushed into the arms, not of Petherick, but of Baker, the elephant-hunter of Ceylon'.

* * *

Murchison Falls, on the Victoria Nile, where the river drops sharply to the altitude of Lake Albert. Unable to resist the temptation to bag a specimen among the crocodiles that lay in lines like tree trunks on the rocks, Baker startled his boatmen and nearly caused a nasty accident.

Samuel White Baker (1821–93) was a large, bushy-bearded, ebullient character, slightly larger than life. In 1863 he was in the middle of his adventurous career which included not only elephant-hunting in Ceylon, but hunting slave traders in the Sudan (where he was governor of the province of Equatoria in 1869–73) and hunting various kinds of game in India, Japan, and North America. His expedition to North Africa in 1861–65 was self-financed and designed to lead him to the sources of the Nile, with a possible meeting with Speke and Grant somewhere about Lake Victoria (Egyptian opposition to his movements had set him back even farther than Speke). Baker, moreover, was accompanied into Central Africa by the woman who became his second wife. She was a beautiful blonde whom, according to a persistent rumour, he had purchased in a Hungarian slave market.

Baker was able to supply Speke and Grant with boats, and to replenish their supplies. When Petherick arrived, also accompanied by his wife, he was cold-shouldered. Speke and Grant set off downstream to Khartoum, Cairo (where Speke's nineteen 'Faithfuls' who had accompanied him from Zanzibar,

were paid off), and home, while Mr and Mrs Baker prepared to plunge into Central Africa. Speke's discoveries had apparently made their main object redundant. 'Does not one leaf of the laurel remain for me?' asked Baker. One did: he planned to investigate the report, heard at several places by Speke, of another large lake lying to the north-west of Lake Victoria, which also contributed to the waters of the Nile.

The Bakers travelled at first with suspicious slave-traders, some of whom eventually deserted them and encouraged mutiny among their porters – a mutiny put down by Baker 'with an iron hand'. In spite of intense heat and anxiety over the behaviour of both their own men and the allegedly hostile tribes through whose country they had to pass, Baker found time to contemplate the differences between black men and white, or at least he inserted his – well-meant though dubious

– thoughts on this subject into the splendid book in which he described his expedition (*The Albert Nyanza*, 1866). 'It is unfortunately the fashion for one party to uphold the negro as a superior being, while the other denies him the common powers of reason. So great a difference of opinion has ever existed upon the intrinsic value of the negro, that the very perplexity of the question is a proof that he is altogether a distinct variety. So long as it is generally considered that the negro and the white man are to be governed by the same laws and guided by the same management, so long will the former remain a thorn in the side of any community to which he may unhappily belong. When the horse and the ass shall be found to match in double harness, the white man and the African black will pull together under the same *régime*. It is the grand error of equalizing that which is unequal, that has lowered the negro character, and made the black man a reproach ... The negro may be an important and most useful being; but if treated as an Englishman, he will affect the vices but none of the virtues of civilization, and his natural good qualities will be lost in his attempts to become a "white man".'

The Bakers made rather slow progress. 'For months we dragged on a miserable existence at Obbo, wracked by fever; the quinine exhausted; thus the disease worried me almost to death, returning at intervals of a few days. Fortunately my wife did not suffer as much as I did.'

Baker nevertheless painted an amusing picture of Katchiba, the old chief of the Obbo who was much respected although

Punch's comment on Speke's achievement.
Britannia: 'Aha, Mr Nilus! So I've found you at last!'

he 'behaved more like a clown than a king'. He held his authority by his reputation as a powerful rain-maker and sorcerer. 'There are no specific taxes, but he occasionally makes a call upon the country for a certain number of goats and supplies. These are generally given, as Katchiba is a knowing old diplomatist, and he times his demands with great judgment. Thus, should there be a lack of rain, or too much, at the season for sowing the crops, he takes the opportunity of calling his subjects together and explaining to them how much he regrets that their conduct has compelled him to afflict them with unfavourable weather, but that it is their own fault. If they are so greedy and so stingy that they will not supply him properly, how can they expect him to think of

their interests? He must have goats and corn: "No goats, no rain; that's our contract, my friends," says Katchiba. "Do as you like. I can wait; I hope you can."'

Not until the New Year (1864) did the Bakers resume their progress. Making for Nyoro, after a week or two they joined Speke's river, the Victoria Nile. The scenery was splendid: 'Our course through the noble forest was parallel with the river, that roared beneath us on our right in a succession of rapids and falls between high cliffs covered with groves of bananas and varieties of palms, including the graceful wild date – the certain sign of either marsh or river.' They crossed the river near the Karuma Falls and entered Nyoro. '*Speke's brother* has arrived from his country to pay Kamrasi a visit, and has brought valuable presents.' 'Why has he brought so many men with him?' Baker, having changed into a tweed suit, 'something similar to that worn by Speke', climbed to a high point on the cliffs so the people could see him ('I looked almost as imposing as Nelson in Trafalgar Square'). The resemblance to Speke being obvious enough (both favoured very large beards), they were welcomed in the usual intimidating fashion, the men dashing up as though to attack and thrusting the points of their spears close to the visitors' faces.

Baker was relieved to be in the 'comparative civilization' of Nyoro, although Kamrasi had not become any less grasping since he had entertained Speke and Grant. His suggestion that Mrs Baker should be handed over among other presents was received with high indignation, much to Kamrasi's puzzlement, no doubt. Since Speke's departure, Nyoro had been raided by slavers from the north, and Kamrasi was understandably suspicious. In order to discourage Baker from advancing farther, the King declared that the lake was six months' journey away, news which drove Baker's porters to desert in droves. But by this time Baker had heard many reports of the lake, and though they were not all reliable (it was said, perhaps to please him, that the lake was far bigger than the Victoria Nyanza of Speke, and Baker himself subsequently exaggerated the size of his most famous discovery), he knew that it lay nearby.

After leaving Kamrasi, Mrs Baker was struck down with a severe attack of fever, and for seven days she tossed and turned in a litter, hopelessly delirious. Soon after her recovery, they reached their destination. 'The 14th March [1864]. The day broke beautifully clear, and having crossed a deep valley between the hills, we toiled up the opposite slope. I hurried to the summit. The glory of our prize burst suddenly upon me! There, like a sea of quicksilver, lay far beneath the grand expanse of water – a boundless sea horizon on the south and south-west, glittering in the noon-day sun ... As an imperishable memorial to one loved and mourned by our gracious Queen and deplored [sic] by every Englishman, I called this great lake "the Albert Nyanza". The Victoria and Albert lakes are the two sources of the Nile.' (Not exclusively, however; an important contribution is made by the rivers that drain into Lake Kioga from the Mount Elgon region.)

They tottered down to the shore, Mrs Baker 'in extreme weakness, supporting herself upon my shoulder, and stopping to rest every twenty paces'. Having reached the water, Baker emulated Bruce at Gish and 'drank deeply from the Sources of the Nile'.

In large African canoes, they paddled northwards on the lake, severely discomfited by rain and mosquitoes ('no acclimatization can render the European body mosquito-

The Nile below Murchison Falls.

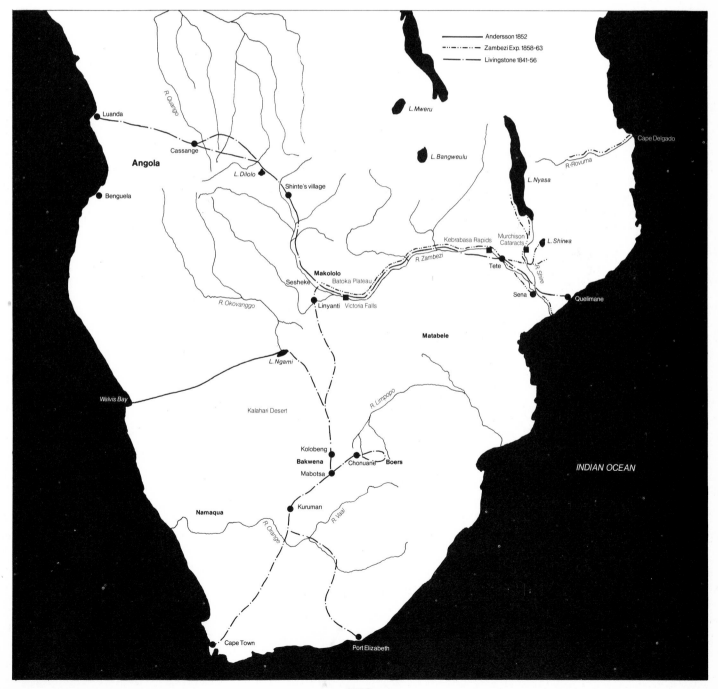

proof'), but consoled by the sight of a herd of elephants bathing. The people, though, were poor and unfriendly, and progress was vastly hindered by the refusal of hired boatmen to proceed out of their own district, so that at one stage they had to change crews four times in half a mile.

Baker was in some ways a more thorough explorer than Speke. He could not be certain that the river flowing into Lake Tanganyika was the same river that Speke had followed from Ripon Falls, so in spite of the weakness of himself and his wife, he set off to trace it upstream to a point where he could confirm that it was the Victoria Nile. In the course of the journey he passed the point where the river hurtled through a narrow gorge and leaped down a 100-feet drop, which he named the Murchison Falls.

Having accomplished his object, Baker realized that it was too late to catch the downstream boats on the Nile from Gondokoro. They went only once a year. After a long and rather dreary wait in Nyoro, the amazing partnership set off, homeward bound, towards the end of the year. They arrived at Gondokoro in February, and were given a noisy and dangerous salute from the guns of the traders.

Waiting for the boats to start, Baker sat looking at the Nile flowing past his feet, and pondered the value of his toil, as he put it. 'Had I overrated the importance of the discovery? and had I wasted some of the best years of my life to obtain a shadow? I recalled the practical suggestion of Commoro, the chief of Latooka – "Suppose you get to the great lake, what will you do with it? What will be the good of it all? If you find that the large river does flow from it, what then?"'

Nearly all explorers suffered such reactions. Stanley explained it thus: 'When a man returns home and finds for a moment nothing to struggle against, the vast resolve, which has sustained him through a long and difficult enterprise, dies away, burning as it sinks in the heart; and thus the greatest successes are often accompanied by a peculiar melancholy.' Different men found different answers to explain the purpose of their travels, but none of their answers are entirely convincing. Everyone travels; no one really arrives.

* * *

While the Bakers were still slogging south towards Lake Albert, John Hanning Speke and James Grant arrived in England. Grant, no lover of controversy, subsequently took himself off to France, while Speke remained to fight for his conviction that he had discovered the source of the Nile. For amid the public acclaim, the enthusiastic toasts, the welcoming speeches, Speke's opponents, notably Burton, who returned from a residence in West Africa in 1864, remained sceptical. Speke made his own position more difficult by withholding his report on the expedition from the Royal Geographical Society, whose officers felt themselves slighted, and by certain careless errors in his account, which was published by his friend Blackwood. The book contained a map which scholars like Burton and Desborough Cooley knew to be a forgery. There was an unfortunate error in altitude which had the effect of making the Nile run for nearly one hundred miles up a steep gradient! Then, in addition to the rather cursory nature of Speke's exploration of Lake Victoria and his failure to follow the river from Ripon Falls, he gave the lake no less than four major outlets in the north. On a different level, less justifiable criticisms were levelled at Speke's style and at his supposed associations with African women.

The great Burton–Speke controversy came to a dramatic climax in September 1864. The British Association and the Royal Geographical Society arranged a meeting in the elegant city of Bath, where Burton and Speke would debate the question of the sources of the Nile. All the great men of the geographical world in Britain who could be there (Baker was of course still in Africa and the discovery of Lake Albert was not yet known) were present. Dr Livingstone was among the distinguished audience; Sir Roderick Murchison presided.

The dice were loaded in Burton's favour; he was an excellent speaker and his rival was not. His theoretical knowledge was far more extensive. And, though nervous, he enjoyed conflict. Speke viewed the whole thing with disgust. He would have preferred a fist fight.

The day before the debate was to take place, both Burton and Speke attended a preliminary meeting at the Mineral Water Hospital. They were seated not far apart, but ignored each other. Isabel Burton, the explorer's wife, thought Speke looked strained. He seemed restless and after a while got up, murmuring, 'Oh I cannot stand this any longer.' A man standing next to him asked if he would be returning to his seat. 'I hope not,' said Speke, and left the building.

The following day, as Burton was on the platform taking a last look at the notes for his speech (which was to put forward a sensational – and wholly erroneous – new theory of the sources of the Nile), a note was handed in. It informed the company of the death of Speke.

After leaving the meeting on the previous day, Speke had ridden to his uncle's estate a few miles away where he was staying, and had gone out with his cousin to shoot partridges. While he was clambering over a low wall, his gun, which had no safety catch, went off and wounded him mortally. A long-lived rumour maintained that Speke's death was suicide. It seems very unlikely (and is effectively demolished in Alexander Maitland's biography). Speke was not frightened of Burton; but it is possible that his state of mind made him uncharacteristically careless in handling his gun.

Burton was sufficiently composed to read a paper on Dahomey which he had prepared for another occasion, though when he got home, according to his wife, 'he wept long and bitterly'. Nevertheless, he later returned to the attack, and Speke was not vindicated until Stanley returned from his long journey in 1877, in the course of which he explored Lake Victoria more thoroughly.

Speke has never been a popular hero. In spite of his denunciations of the slave trade and earnest appeals for missionaries, he lacked the moral standing of a Livingstone. He had little of the scholarship of Burton, or the popular appeal of Baker. His book describing his great expedition did not sell as well as expected, and it is one of the few classics of 19th-century exploration not available in a modern edition. As Alan Moorehead says of him, 'Where other, lesser explorers are revered, he is neglected; [his] name is not even a name that is instantly and indelibly associated with the Nile as Burton's is with Arabia and Livingstone's with Africa.' When those words were written (in *The White Nile*, 1960) Speke had not even been granted a worthy biography (an omission since rectified by Alexander Maitland). But Speke was the man who solved the greatest single problem of African exploration.

The Zaire-the Last Barrier

When Livingstone arrived in London, after the collapse of the Zambezi expedition, in the summer of 1865, he was not quite the adored national hero he had been on his previous appearance in the capital, after his trans-continental journey. His engagements diary was still impressive – '25th July – went to Foreign Office . . . dined with Lord and Lady Dunmore . . . thence to Duchess of Wellington's reception. Met Lord and Lady Colchester . . .' etc., but many people agreed with the sonorous sentence of the London *Times*: 'Dr Livingstone is unquestionably a traveller of talents, enterprise, and excellent constitution, but it is now plain enough that his zeal and imagination much surpass his judgement.'

Nevertheless, Livingstone still had many devoted admirers, not least his favourite daughter, Agnes, and his old friend and patron, Sir Roderick Murchison. Sir Roderick suggested he should go out to resolve the geographical problems of Central Africa on behalf of the Royal Geographical Society, which would put up £500 towards the cost. But Livingstone would not go as an explorer pure and simple. Although he had grown doubtful about the effectiveness of his campaign against the slave trade, he still believed that God had work for him in Africa. The government was not very encouraging and promised to contribute only £500, one-tenth of the outlay for the Zambezi expedition. Livingstone felt bitter about this slight for the rest of his life.

An old friend, Sir James Young, came to the rescue with a magnificent contribution of £1,000, and this was enough for Livingstone, who always prided himself on his ability to travel cheaply. A more recent friend, Sir Bartle Frere, was also helpful, and commissioned Livingstone to deliver a steamship to Zanzibar, thus saving him the fares from Bombay to Zanzibar of the party of Indian sepoys and boys from the Nassick Mission School whom Livingstone hired to assist him.

He arrived in Zanzibar in January 1866, and waited six weeks for a British ship to give him a lift to the mainland. He disliked the place, with its large slave market, and was thankful when HMS *Penguin* arrived to convey his party to a point some miles north of the Rovuma river. Livingstone's first two expeditions had reasonably precise motives and followed straightforward routes. On his third and last expedition (1866–73), his movements were less exact, due partly to bad health and faulty chronometers, and his priorities were not always entirely obvious.

His organization was almost slapdash. He started from Zanzibar with about sixty attendants, all of them strangers except five who had served on the Zambezi expedition. The sepoys were mutinous from the start, and treated the camels so badly that they died before it was possible to judge whether, as Livingstone hoped, they were immune to the tse-tse fly. (They are not.) 'Sepoys are a mistake,' Livingstone glumly noted in his diary. Most of the porters engaged in Zanzibar deserted as soon as the going got rough, and the Nassick boys were only a little better. In less than five months, Livingstone's party was reduced to ten, including himself.

Perhaps his men might have been more faithful if they had understood their employer's aims. Livingstone's assignment from the Royal Geographical Society was to investigate the structure of the Central African watershed, or in other words, ascertain the source of the Nile. Like many others, Livingstone was not convinced that Speke's Victoria Nyanza was the ultimate source: he suspected connections from farther south and south-west, and he was convinced of a northern outlet from Lake Tanganyika to Lake Albert.

A second great question was raised by the course of the Congo – or Zaire, to give it its earlier and also its present name. Nothing was known about this huge river beyond the two or three hundred miles nearest the sea, but as it was so large it obviously drained a considerable area. Its lower course suggested that it ran in more northerly latitudes than in fact it does, and although Livingstone spoke of perhaps discovering the upper Congo and tracing it to the sea, it was the Nile that dominated his thoughts. When, later, he came to believe that he was on the track of Herodotus' fountains of the Nile, he was worried by the suspicion – correct, as it happened – that he might be pursuing the Zaire.

No less important than geographical motives – and, in a curious way, intimately connected with them in the mind of the explorer – was Livingstone's desire 'to do something' for Africa. He no longer had much hope that the government could be persuaded to force the Sultan of Zanzibar to outlaw the slave trade in his continental dominions. He could only report the evils that he witnessed and point the way towards ending them. In a wild and dangerous country, he was one rather old and often desperately sick man. What could he do against a system that infected half the continent?

Africa had taken possession of Livingstone's soul, and drew him like a magnet. Its mountains and rivers, its sunny plains and foul swamps, its hutted villages and injured people – seemed to beckon him forward on a pilgrimage that could end only with his death. In a brilliantly imaginative work, *Livingstone's Last Journey*, Sir Reginald Coupland described the old explorer in the grip of his obsession and, although Coupland's book will not stand as history (it was effectively demolished in George Seaver's biography of Livingstone), it retains a certain poetic truth.

Livingstone looked forward to the prospect of travelling as eagerly as a child approaching the sea-shore. 'Now that I am on the point of starting on another trip into Africa,' he wrote in his diary, 'I feel quite exhilarated . . . The mere animal pleasure of travelling in a wild unexplored country is very great. When on lands of a couple of thousand feet elevation, brisk exercise imparts elasticity to the muscles, fresh and healthy blood circulates through the brain, the mind works well, the eye is clear, the step is firm, and a day's exertion always makes the evening's repose thoroughly enjoyable.'

Unfortunately, this exhilaration could not last. Although the country through which Livingstone passed on his third expedition was, on the whole, more healthy than the regions he had explored before, his own condition was more frail. At fifty-two he was not a young man, and years of hard toil had made him older than his years. Food was scarce and meat almost unobtainable. Men and animals created endless problems.

Worst of all was the evidence of the slave trade. Livingstone's diary became a record of atrocities: '19th June, 1866. We passed a woman tied by the neck to a tree and dead, the people of the country explained that she had been unable to keep up with the other slaves in a gang . . . We saw others tied up in a similar manner, and one lying in the path shot or stabbed, for she was in a pool of blood.' The traders naturally distrusted him, but some of 'the better sort' were kind and helpful. Indeed, Livingstone's friendship with several Arab slave-traders was to cause some embarrassment to hagiographers. While blaming the system, Livingstone did not sweepingly condemn all those engaged in it, for he was aware that it had been going on for centuries and that it was not illegal. He knew too, that slavery as an institution in Islam was not particularly cruel or unpleasant; it had little in common with slavery as practised in the plantations of the Americas. That did not, of course, make the raids of the slavers any less shocking. In what Tim Jeal calls 'the most haunting of all his indictments against the slave-trade', Livingstone wrote in Manyuema, 'The strangest disease I have seen in this country seems really to be broken-heartedness, and it attacks free men who have been captured and made slaves.'

In August, Livingstone reached the southern end of Lake Nyasa, and enjoyed a bathe in the breakers. His plan was to march north-west from here, looking for the headwaters of the Nile. Food was difficult to obtain, the Ngoni were said to be sending war-parties in this direction, and the people were suspicious of the strangers led by the man with horribly pale skin. One of Livingstone's veterans from the Zambezi deserted at this point, and when he reached the coast he said, no doubt to excuse his desertion, that Livingstone was dead.

This was but the first of many rumours to the same effect, but an expedition was sent out from England to investigate it. Led by a naval officer, Lieutenant E.D. Young, it proceeded to Lake Nyasa by way of the Zambezi and the Shire. On the way Young accomplished a feat that had defeated Livingstone by dismantling his small steamer to carry it past the Murchison cataracts and subsequently embarking upon the lake. By this time Livingstone was 500 miles away, but there were many reports that he had been alive and fit long after his reported 'death', so Young returned to England without making contact with him.

At the beginning of 1867, Livingstone was in poor shape. His medicine chest had been stolen and that, he felt, was equivalent to 'a sentence of death'. It would not have been like Livingstone to return to the coast for more supplies, though that was the sensible course to follow, and he struggled on. When he reached the southern end of Lake Tanganyika in April, he collapsed, apparently with rheumatic fever, and would probably have died without the succour of some Arab traders.

His actions became a little confused. 'I am rather perplexed how to proceed,' he noted – uncharacteristically – at one point in his diary. Again, the sensible course was to make for Ujiji, where he had arranged for supplies to be sent, but he was anxious to visit Lake Mweru in order to see in what direction its rivers flowed. The position was complicated by tribal wars in the vicinity and by Livingstone's reliance on the Arabs.

It was not until September that he set out towards Lake Mweru, with a caravan led by Tippu Tib, later to become a greater potentate in East Africa than the Sultan himself. On 8 November he reached the lake which, though small after Nyasa and Tanganyika, Livingstone expected to have a significant role in the formation of the Central African watershed. His investigation on the spot soon showed that it did. A large river (a tributary of the Lualaba) flowed out of the lake to the north, and another river (the Luapala) flowed into it in the south, presumably from Lake Bangweulu (which Livingstone had missed on his journey north to Lake Tanganyika). Given Livingstone's basic assumptions, there seemed to be little doubt that the Lualaba was the Nile and its source at least as far south as Lake Bangweulu and the Chambesi – a river that Livingstone had crossed the previous year and now correctly identified as the main feeder of Lake Bangweulu.

All this was first-rate field work. The trouble lay not in Livingstone's investigation of Lake Mweru but in his assumption that the system he was exploring was connected – probably via Lake Albert – with the Nile.

After reaching Lake Mweru, Livingstone again dithered, not sure where to move next. He at length decided that his best plan was to make for Ujiji with the Arabs, but being checked by the onset of the seasonal rains, he turned south again and determined to make the difficult journey to Lake Bangweulu. Half-starved, exhausted, and constantly ill, he struck out with the four men who were the only ones willing to make such a foolhardy effort. Rain poured down incessantly, and they had to wade through swamps where the leeches homed in on them as if radar-directed. Had they not fallen in with the kind and generous Muhammad Bogharib, it is hard to imagine that the journey could have been completed.

Livingstone was not able to explore Lake Bangweulu as fully as he hoped, and he greatly exaggerated its size (the rains temporarily turned swamplands into clear water). Nevertheless, he was able to confirm the hypothesis that he had constructed on the basis of the situation of Lake Mweru. This, however, solved only one half of the complete puzzle. The other half was concerned with the destination of the Lualaba: where did it join the Nile?

Returning northward in company with Muhammad Bogharib, Livingstone once more postponed his visit to Ujiji when his companion told him he meant to go to Manyuema – the region west of Lake Tanganyika through which the Lualaba was presumed to flow. Unfortunately, the way was blocked for the Arabs by the resistance of the local people, and as Livingstone was in no condition to travel on his own he was compelled to postpone his visit to Manyuema.

As they neared Lake Tanganyika, Livingstone became very ill with pneumonia. The nursing of Muhammad Bogharib probably saved his life, but he was still being carried in a litter when he arrived at Ujiji in February 1869. There he found that nearly all his supplies – food, medicine, trade-goods and, worst of all, letters from home – had been stolen or dispersed.

*   *   *

The loss of his supplies was a fearsome blow, and Livingstone's diatribes against the Arabs of Ujiji – 'the vilest of the vile' – were no doubt partly the result of his deep resentment and bitterness at the loss of his vital stores. He decided to send a message to Zanzibar, where his old associate Kirk was now stationed, for more supplies. While waiting for them, he planned to cross the lake again into Manyuema – staked by the ever-amiable Muhammad Bogharib – to locate the Lualaba. They left in July, on a journey that Livingstone expected would take two or three months. In fact he was gone for over two years.

The countryside was pleasant and the people, though suspicious, not aggressive. But travelling soon became very hard. In spite of his long convalescence at Ujiji, Livingstone was not as strong as he had once been. He could not keep up his old pace, and the going was sometimes heavy. They had to wade for miles through thick mud. His party was again

Arab slave traders attacking a village in Central Africa, 1888, from a picture by Harry Johnstone, the pioneer of British East Africa, who also exhibited his paintings of African scenes at the Royal Academy.

reduced to a pathetic minimum – Susi and Chuma and one of the Nassick boys.

Throughout the whole of 1870 he made little progress. The last half of that year was spent, motionless, at Bambarre. Apart from the usual complaints of fever and dysentery, often accompanied by bleeding from the bowels, Livingstone had terrible ulcers on his feet. For three months he could hardly take a step.

Stuck in Bambarre, Livingstone began to weave strange fantasies in which geography and theology were weirdly mingled. His mind went back to Herodotus and the ancients, and he dreamed of finding evidence of the early life of Moses in the forests of Central Africa. To throw some historical light on the stories told in the Old Testament now became part of his task – another jewel in that subjective Holy Grail which he never stopped seeking.

Early in 1871, ten porters arrived from the coast, sent up by Kirk. That they arrived at all was surprising, especially as they proved an unco-operative bunch. But at least Livingstone could move again.

As usual, movement was bracing, and the notes in his diary became more cheerful. He painted an attractive picture of some of the villages he passed through – families gathered around a fire in front of their homes, goats playing, cocks crowing, and thrifty wives making clay pots. But many places had been visited by the slave traders now swarming into Manyuema, and there the scene was different – deserted houses and frightened faces. Some gun-toting Arab traders and their men, as they swept through the region in their search for ivory and slaves, terrorized the people to enforce their demands more easily and to ensure that any signs of opposition were swiftly crushed. At least some of the people realized that Livingstone was 'the good one', who had no slaves, and

they called out 'Bolongo, Bolongo!' Friendship, Friendship!
At the end of March he reached his destination – Nyangwe,
which stood on the banks of the Lualaba. The river was about
1,000 yards wide and flowed steadily north: surely, the Nile.

Livingstone wished to cross the river and continue in a
south-westerly direction where, on the basis of information
supplied by Arab traders, he hoped to find the 'fountains' of
the Nile mentioned by Herodotus. According to Herodotus'
rather offhand accounts, there were two fountains, and this
seemed to be confirmed by the report of a river running
parallel to the Lualaba and joining it north of Lake Mweru.
Again, this was correct in detail, the river in question being
the Lomani; but, like the Lualaba, the Lomani feeds the
Zaire, not the Nile.

Like most explorers, Livingstone tended to place too much
emphasis on facts which apparently supported his own hypothesis and to ignore those that were unfavourable. For
example, he discovered that the Lualaba at Nyangwe was at
about the same altitude as Lake Albert, which he had
hitherto assumed to be its destination, and it could therefore
not be expected to flow into the lake. His answer to this was
that the Lualaba must join the Nile at some point far to the
north of Lake Albert. He could not give up his belief that the
Lualaba was the Nile, though he several times mentioned, in
a worried way, the possibility that it might be the Zaire.

Livingstone was unable to obtain boats in Nyangwe, and
the chief Arab trader in the place, Dugumbe, was unhelpful
(Bogharib had gone off seeking ivory in another direction).
But though tired, depressed, and ill, Livingstone found his
spirits rising as he took a morning walk through the market of
Nyangwe, which attracted people from a wide area. It was a
rule of the country that no one interfered with women going
to market; a man who walked into a strange village risked his
life, but women carrying their vegetables or pots for sale
walked freely to and fro, as their mothers and grandmothers
had done before them. Livingstone had run out of ink and
paper, but recorded the scene on old newspapers, writing
with a red dye made from seeds: 'Chitoka, or market, today.
I counted upwards of 700 passing my door. With market

*'I would have run to him, only I was a coward in the presence of such
a mob – would have embraced him, only, he being an Englishman, I
did not know how he would receive me; so I did what cowardice and
false pride suggested was the best thing – walked deliberately to him,
took off my hat, and said: "Dr Livingstone, I presume?"' The
greeting became a popular catchphrase, and Stanley fervently
regretted having uttered it or said he had uttered it.*

women it seems to be a pleasure of life to haggle and joke, and
laugh and cheat; many come eagerly, and retire with care-
worn faces; many are beautiful, and many old: all carry very
heavy loads of dried cassava and earthen pots, which they
dispose of very cheaply for palm-oil, fish, salt, pepper, and
relishes for their food.' He bought some fish with long snouts –
'very good eating'.

A few days later this pleasant scene was suddenly and
horribly shattered.

It was a hot, still day, and across the river smoke was rising
from a burning village where Arab traders had been enforcing
their demands. But the market at Nyangwe was as busy as
usual, and some fifteen hundred people bustled about, shout-
ing and laughing as they bargained for a chicken or a fish.
Livingstone, strolling among the throng, was surprised to see
three of Dugumbe's men carrying guns, and one of his own
party spoke to them about it, explaining that it was against
the custom to carry weapons in the market. Livingstone paid
little attention to the incident and moved on. A few minutes
later shots rang out.

A massacre began. As the women fled in panic, another
group of the traders' men opened fire from the river. A storm
of bullets cut down those who ran for safety. About fifty
people were jammed into a little creek, where canoes were
tied up. Some of the gunmen turned their fire on them, and
those who escaped from the mass of wounded and dying
leaped into the river, where many drowned. A few canoes got
out into the stream, but they had no paddles. One or two
bravely stopped to pick up swimmers, but became overloaded
and sank. The injured and the dead, and the people desperately swimming for safety, were targets for more bullets.
The killers themselves estimated that four hundred people,

including women and children, died.

Half-mad with shock, Livingstone's first impulse was to shoot the murderers, but he was restrained by Dugumbe, whose role in the affair was, at best, ambiguous. Livingstone's horror still vibrates in the pages of his diary: 'As I write I hear the loud wails on the left bank over those who are slain . . . Oh, let Thy kingdom come! No one will ever know the exact loss on this bright sultry morning, it gave me the impression of being in hell.'

He abandoned his plan to cross the river. With the screams of the murdered still ringing in his ears, he turned back to the east. The journey was horrible. Two of his men were killed and twice a spear flashed out of the trees, missing him by inches. At the beginning of November, more dead than alive, he limped into Ujiji.

He found no comfort there. Once again, the supplies sent up by Kirk had been plundered. He could not expect to get more in less than a year, and he was sick and exhausted. War raged in Nyanyembe and he had little hope of getting to the coast himself. What was he to do? He needed a miracle.

The miracle happened within a week of his arrival at Ujiji. There was a commotion in the town, and suddenly Susi

Stanley and Livingstone catching up on the news in Nyanyembe. This print, from a drawing by J. Zwecker, was published in the Graphic *which, justifiably or not, apparently counted Stanley among its readers; to Livingstone was assigned the heavier diet of the* Times, *while Kalulu, the boy given to Stanley by an Arab trader, seems a bit flummoxed by* Punch.

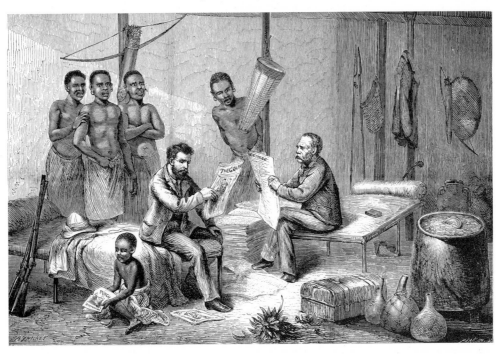

At the mouth of the Ruzizi: Stanley and Livingstone make the disappointing discovery that the river flows into Lake Tanganyika. From a drawing by Zwecker, published in Stanley's How I Found Livingstone.

'Drop that box and . . .' While the others crossed the stream by a fallen tree, 'one young fellow, Rojab – through over-zeal or in sheer madness – took up the Doctor's box which contained his letters and Journal of discoveries on his head, and started into the river . . . Suddenly he fell into a deep hole, and the man and box went almost out of sight, while I was in an agony at the fate which threatened the despatches. Fortunately, he recovered himself and stood up, while I shouted to him, with a loaded revolver pointed at his head, "Look out! Drop that box, and I'll shoot you."'

rushed up to him in great excitement: 'An Englishman is coming!' The crowd parted to reveal an enormous column of porters carrying every type of equipment an explorer could wish for. A short, powerfully built white man in a sun helmet, walked up to him a trifle hesitantly, paused, and raised his hat: 'Dr Livingstone, I presume?'

*   *   *

Henry Morton Stanley was an adventurer. He was born in Denbigh, Wales, in 1841, the illegitimate son of a butcher's teenage daughter and (probably) a farmer's son named Rowlands, who subsequently died of drink. At the age of six he was put into a workhouse where he remained until the age of fifteen. His biographer, Richard Hall, has cast some doubt on the story of his running away after beating a cruel master unconscious. From unpromising beginnings, Stanley was to make himself a great man and a popular hero; it could not be done without some romanticizing of his past.

After half-hearted assistance from various relatives, he signed on as a cabin-boy in Liverpool, bound for New Orleans, where he jumped ship in February 1859. He found a job as a clerk, and was adopted by a kindly British cotton merchant, whose name (Henry Stanley) he took as his own ('Morton' was inserted later after various alternatives had been rejected). The young Stanley was an impetuous, independent youth, and in less than a year quarrelled with his benefactor. He worked for a time in a store in Arkansas and, when the Civil War began, a girl's anonymous gift of a petticoat shamed him into joining the Confederate army. At Shiloh he was captured by the Union and imprisoned in a villainous prison camp in Illinois. There was only one way to get out of the filthy place alive: he accepted an offer to change his allegiance. As he felt no strong commitment to either side, it was not hard to shed Confederate

Stanley with Kalulu, a posed photograph taken in London after Stanley's return from the expedition to find Livingstone.

grey and don the Union blue. But his service was short. He had caught dysentery in the camp, and was discharged as unfit.

During the next few years, this dubious vagabond existence continued. He returned to Wales, was temporarily rejected by his mother (they were later on good terms: Stanley took her to Paris for a holiday) but was apparently helped by his former benefactor, then living in England. He served in various ships, worked for a New York judge for some time, joined the Union Navy only to desert seven months later, and eventually made his way out west. In St Louis he got work as a free-lance reporter for the *Missouri Democrat*. Stanley had, at last, found an occupation that suited him.

Nevertheless, he was soon off on new adventures. With two friends he travelled to Turkey, where they were captured and robbed by brigands. Wearing a naval officer's uniform (to which, of course, he was not entitled) and telling highly embroidered, if not totally false, stories of his exploits, Stanley returned – via Wales – to St Louis, and was sent to report on the Indian wars. He came to feel a good deal of sympathy for the Indians, though his sympathy was more strongly expressed in letters and later writings than in his despatches to the papers. In 1867 he persuaded the *New York Herald* to send him (though at his own expense) to Ethiopia, to cover the invasion of that country by the British military expedition commanded by Sir Robert Napier. He took the precaution of bribing the telegraphist to Suez to give his messages priority, and this, plus a fortuitous cable break, meant that his report of Napier's quick campaign was published in the *Herald* before the official despatches reached Whitehall. It was a brilliant coup, and made Stanley's name as a reporter.

In October 1869 he was summoned to Paris by James Gordon Bennett Jr, the young, vastly rich, and astute proprietor of the *New York Herald*. Stanley's account of this interview, of Bennett's instruction to 'FIND LIVINGSTONE' regardless of cost, is well-known. But he was also instructed to visit various places in the Middle East (he reported the opening of the Suez Canal) and India, and it seems possible that in 1869 the order to find Livingstone was not the central issue that Stanley later made it appear.

Anyway, in January 1871 Stanley arrived at Zanzibar. He found no money from Bennett waiting for him, but having established a good credit rating with the aid of the United States consul, he began his preparations for the largest expedition any European explorer had yet mounted. His supplies included two boats, stripped down and divided into sections, and altogether weighing six tons. To carry them he required two hundred porters.

Stanley told no one except the friendly U.S. consul what his real purpose was in Zanzibar, though Kirk (now acting British consul) must have had a pretty good idea. But Kirk and Stanley did not get on. Kirk struck the brash young reporter as one of those supercilious Englishmen he could not stand, and was jealous of, while Kirk regarded Stanley – at this stage not incorrectly – as a shady adventurer.

Stanley moved fast. He was in Nyanyembe within four months, cutting a month off Burton and Speke's time. But there he was stopped, because war was raging to the west between the Arabs and the guerilla forces of Mirambo – a more formidable successor to Speke's acquaintance Manua Sera, whose death is reported by Stanley in *How I found*

Livingstone. After waiting for three months, with conditions deteriorating, he decided to make a long swing to the south to get round the troubled area. Mud, fever, mutiny, and the deaths of his two European companions hardly held him up. The gun and the whip were rather freely employed to expedite his progress, and in November, having stopped outside the town to change into new clothes and clean boots, he marched into Ujiji with guns firing and the Stars and Stripes waving.

He remained with Livingstone for four months. Together, they explored the north end of Lake Tanganyika looking for the river that was presumed to link it with Lake Albert. They found the river, but it flowed into, not out of, Tanganyika, putting paid to the theory that the lake was part of the Nile sources.

Stanley and Livingstone became deeply attached to each other. On the face of it, their friendship was surprising, for the two men could hardly have been less alike. Kirk had volunteered the belief that if Livingstone knew there was a journalist on the loose looking for him, his reaction would be to put s many miles between them as he could. But Kirk did not know Livingstone's circumstances at Ujiji in 1871. He was in a desperate state, with no food or supplies or money to buy them, lonely and almost at his wits' end. Stanley came like an angel of deliverance, loaded with supplies that he generously shared, and bringing news of a concerned and admiring public. Livingstone was not forgotten outside Africa; on the contrary, no expense had been spared to find news of him and offer assistance – and all this came not from his own country but from foreigners (Stanley suppressed his Welsh origins).

Both men later spoke of their relationship as that of father and son. Stanley had never had a father worth the name and Livingstone became a kind of spiritual father to him. Though their methods and ambitions were hardly similar, their beliefs were not so very far apart. Stanley was later to call for missionary efforts in Uganda with similar results to Livingstone's famous summons in 1857. Stanley, for all his violence, was closer to Livingstone in his attitude towards Africans than many other Victorian explorers; neither man shared the common assumption of racial superiority.

Livingstone made a strong impression on Stanley, who was to be largely responsible for the popular image of the tough old Scottish explorer as a creature of unearthly virtue. It is certainly true, as Tim Jeal has pointed out, that this picture of Livingstone suited Stanley's purpose as a journalist in search of a big story. But the remarks about Livingstone that Stanley made in private were not significantly less enthusiastic than his public laudations, and as Richard Hall says, it is remarkable that Stanley, arriving in Ujiji in search of a quick scoop, remained with Livingstone for four months, every day of which postponed his moment of glory. Moreover Stanley, who was shocked by Livingstone's physical condition, made every effort to persuade him to go back with him to the coast. Had Livingstone agreed, nothing could have more thoroughly ruined Stanley's triumph.

Undoubtedly, Livingstone was much softened since he had given his subordinates such a hard time on the Zambezi expedition, while Stanley, in Livingstone's company, noticeably moderated his behaviour. Once, on Lake Tanganyika, when they were threatened by hostile tribesmen, he reached for his gun; but feeling Livingstone's eye upon him, he quietly laid it down again.

Livingstone returned as far as Tabora with Stanley. The young reporter kept shooting glances at him as they walked side by side, striving to impress on his memory the features of the missionary-explorer who, he perhaps guessed, would never be seen again by Europeans. Livingstone spoke of his past life: 'Loneliness is a terrible thing, especially when I think of my children. I have lost a great deal of happiness, I know, by these wanderings. It is as if I had been born to exile; but it is God's doing, and He will do what seemeth good in His own eyes. But when my children and home are not in my mind, I feel as though appointed to this work and to no other. I am away from the perpetual hurry of civilization, and I think I see far and clear into what is to come; and then I seem to understand why I was led away, here and there, and crossed and baffled over and over again, to wear out my years and strength. Why was it but to be a witness of the full horror of this slave-trade . . .' When Livingstone, at the last moment, poured out the gratitude he felt he had not sufficiently expressed, Stanley was overcome by emotion, and the tears flowed into his beard. Then he marched on. Livingstone's life was almost over. Stanley's great career was just beginning.

Stanley arrived in England to the fame he had sought and earned. But his reception was not so universally warm as he had expected. There were those, especially among the leading men of the Royal Geographical Society, who deeply resented his takeover of their most popular explorer. If Livingstone needed relief, they thought, it should not have been provided by a vulgar little American but by their own expedition, which to their chagrin was still on the coast when Stanley returned from the interior. 'The fellow has done no geography', Clements Markham complained, and even the amiable Grant was antagonized by Stanley's attitude. There were those who said the whole story was a fake: Stanley had never 'found' Livingstone at all. Not even the flat statement of the Foreign Office that the despatches Stanley had brought from Livingstone were genuine entirely stemmed these rumours.

Stanley's behaviour did not help his reputation. He harangued the British Association and stalked out of another meeting when he thought he was being mocked. His literary style was, to say the least, racy; the exclamation mark was his favourite piece of punctuation. That was forgiveable, but his violent assault on the reputation of John Kirk, whom he described as a 'traitor' to Livingstone, was both unpleasant and unjustified. Stanley himself recognized that his language about Kirk had been too strong, but the damage was done, and as in other explorers, pride made it hard for Stanley to retract even a too-hasty remark. His attempts to conceal his humble origins from curious enquirers merely added another shady touch to his dubious public character.

Livingstone himself had been all too willing to agree with, and augment, Stanley's criticisms of Kirk. He was not, however, influenced by Kirk's criticisms of Stanley. When his son Oswell, a member of the English relief expedition, wrote from the coast reporting Kirk's accurate forecast that Stanley would make a fortune out of Livingstone, he replied, 'He is heartily welcome, for it is more than I could ever make out of myself.'

The Royal Geographical Society overcame its repugnance sufficiently to present Stanley with its gold medal, though Stanley's suggestion that the new relief expedition being organized under Verney Lovett Cameron should be merged with one of his own was politely declined. His book, *How I Found Livingstone*, was a best-seller, and his reception in New York, though not unmarred by controversy, was friendlier than London's.

*　　*　　*

After a long and tiresome wait in Nyanyembe, the porters sent up from the coast by Stanley reached Livingstone in August 1872. At once he set out on his last journey.

He still wore his consul's cap and his blue jacket, which gave him the look of a steamboat captain. He carried a walking stick and marched with the heavy, regular tread described by Stanley (years before it had reminded Bishop Mackenzie that this was a man who had walked across Africa). Near him walked Susi and Chuma, faithful servants for nearly a decade, and behind came the long file of porters, carrying their loads on their heads.

Livingstone travelled lighter than most, but his baggage was considerable none the less. Besides clothes, guns, and some food, there were cloth and beads to be traded on the journey. Livingstone had a small tent and the porters had their blankets, but there were bulkier items than these – a folding chair with hinged writing flap, on which the explorer wrote his journal in the evenings, scientific instruments, medicines, brass jugs and basins (for presents), and cases of specimens.

He expected to reach his destination in Katanga within a month or two. He had travelled most of the country before; he was well supplied with medicines, thanks to Stanley; and he told himself that in a few weeks' time he would be sailing down the Nile to Egypt. Fond hopes. Although Livingstone was not yet sixty, he was in reality an old man. He no longer commanded the reserves of strength required to overcome the strains of travelling in Central Africa. He could not keep going indefinitely on a diet of quinine, milk, and self-exhortation. Once he had boasted of his powerful digestion, which had coped with anything except too much elephant's foot. Now he suffered from chronic dysentery, he had lost most of his teeth, and he could eat little except liquids.

He planned to travel south-west via the unmapped south-eastern shore of Lake Tanganyika and around the southern end of Lake Bangweulu, whence he would strike westward into Katanga. Besides his declining health and the loss of all the cows to the tse-tse fly, he was faced with two major obstacles: one of them he intended to ignore; of the other he himself was ignorant. The first was the weather; because of his late start, he would not reach Lake Bangweulu before the rains turned that swampy region into a near-impassable morass. The second obstacle was a mapping error which had resulted from damage to his chronometers on his previous visit to Lake Bangweulu. The rains, descending in unremitting force, compelled him to turn to the west before reaching Lake Bangweulu, and when he reached a point on the north-western shore of the lake, his earlier calculations led him to think he was on the north-east. He therefore turned south, in order to carry out his original plan of rounding the southern shore, and marched straight into hundreds of square miles of sodden, leech-infested swamps.

He remarked that he had never known weather so cold and wet. They advanced only a few miles each day, the powerful young Chuma often carrying Livingstone across streams on

The way to Ilala. David Livingstone nearing the end of his journey.

his shoulders. Not only did Livingstone have little idea of his position, he had lost track of the calendar, and his party were desperately short of food. More miserable conditions could hardly be imagined. Yet Livingstone's observation of wild life was as lively as ever.

By April he could hardly walk and his men had to knock together a litter to carry him. 'It is not all pleasure this exploration,' he observed in what, even for Livingstone, is a memorable understatement. But he still made jokes. At one place a lion roared all night 'as if very much disgusted: we could sympathize with him'.

Soon, his diary became brief, his handwriting spidery. On 27 April he wrote, 'Knocked up quite, we are on the banks of the Molilamo.' After that the pages are blank.

They reached Chitambo's village on 30 April, and laid Livingstone on his litter inside a hut. He was too weak to wind his watch. Late at night, Susi came in to see him. 'How many days is it to the Luapula?' the sick man whispered. 'I think it is three days, Bwana,' Susi replied. In the early hours of the morning, Susi came again to the hut. Livingstone was kneeling as if in prayer, his hands covering his face. He was dead.

Livingstone had made no serious preparation for his death, but his followers, led by Susi and the younger Chuma, acted with extraordinary capability and sense. Supported by the rest of the party, they decided that the body should be carried back to the coast and delivered to the British. The difficulties of the journey were formidable, and the addition of a corpse to their baggage would be bound to arouse hostility. In his biography of Livingstone, George Seaver asserts that the motive of Livingstone's followers for their trek was the fear that they would be blamed for robbing and murdering their master (the murderers of Albrecht Roscher had been executed). No doubt this played a part, but the devotion of men like Susi and Chuma, who had followed

Livingstone through the most appalling hardships for years on end, should not be discounted.

Livingstone's body was cut open, and the heart and innards (which included a blood clot the size of a man's fist) were removed and buried under a tree, on which Jacob Wainwright carved Livingstone's name. The body was filled with salt, smeared with brandy and left to dry for fourteen days before the journey began.

The whole party was struck down by an epidemic soon afterwards; two women died and they made no progress for a month. A friendly chief helped them across the Luapula; a lion took their only donkey; and a fight broke out at an unfriendly village. When they were forbidden passage with their unlucky burden, they pretended to send it back, disguised it to look like a bale of cloth, and moved on. In Nyanyembe they met Cameron, who tried to persuade them to bury Livingstone in Africa as (Cameron felt) he would have wished, but they declined and, accompanied by some of Cameron's men, reached the coast in February 1874. By that time, all but five of the original party had dispersed and, sad to say, they never received even the medal that was struck in their honour.

In the same month, Henry Morton Stanley was on his way back from West Africa, where he had been reporting the Ashanti war for the *New York Herald*. A cable informed him of Livingstone's death. In his diary he wrote, 'Dear Livingstone! Another sacrifice to Africa . . . May I be selected to succeed him in opening up Africa to the shining light of Christianity!' He added, 'My methods, however, will not be Livingstone's.'

* * *

Not for Stanley the calm approval and modest support of the Royal Geographical Society. He went to the *Daily Telegraph* and asked for £6,000. Armed with this promise, it was not difficult to extract an equivalent sum from Bennett and the *New York Herald*. Nor did Stanley want Indian army captains or upper-class sportsmen for company. He hired as his chief assistants the clerk at his London hotel and the sons of a Kent boatbuilder, Frank and Edward Pocock.

There was some smug anticipation of Stanley's likely fate. He had been lucky in 1871–72. This time he might not be so lucky. Moreover, the plans he had announced were ridiculously ambitious: the journey might begin, but Stanley would never live to finish it.

Stanley aimed to complete Livingstone's work and, 'if my life was to be spared, to clear up not only the secrets of the Great River throughout its course, but also all that remained still problematic and incomplete of the discoveries of Burton and Speke, and Speke and Grant'. In short, he meant to solve the outstanding problems of African geography at a stroke. What brash conceit! What vulgar pretension! So many thought, and not a few said. And yet Stanley, between 1874 and 1877, did almost exactly what he promised.

Zanzibar had become the customary starting point for ventures into the interior. Stanley spent two months there assembling his men and supplies. It was a busy time: 'each moment of daylight must be employed in the selection and purchase of the various kinds of cloth, beads and wire, in demand by the different tribes of the mainland'; the merchandise had to be inspected and sorted, accounts settled, messengers interviewed, bargains made, records kept. The hiring of men posed many problems. Stanley, owing (he says) to his good reputation, was inundated by applications. 'Almost all the cripples, the palsied, the consumptive, and the superannuated that Zanzibar could furnish applied to be enrolled [and] hard upon their heels came all the roughs, rowdies, and ruffians of the island.' These were not always easily detected, and Stanley made at least one error in taking

Livingstone's funeral in Westminster Abbey. The pallbearers included Stanley, Kirk and Jacob Wainwright, a former pupil of the Nassick missionary school who had joined Livingstone in 1872. Susi and Chuma did come to England, their passage paid by Livingstone's old friend and benefactor, Sir James Young, but arrived too late for the funeral.

on an alleged murderer who protested his innocence but later proved to have disposed of eight people. At least the leaders were all men of known reputation, and some of them had travelled with Stanley in 1871. When Stanley explained his plans, they were a little alarmed ('But, master, this long journey will take years to travel – six, nine, or ten years'). Stanley allayed their fears, quoting his rapid journey to Ujiji in 1871–72.

Some specific problems arose. When Stanley's portable boat, the *Lady Alice* (named for an attractive seventeen-year-old American girl to whom he had recently become engaged), arrived at Zanzibar, she proved too heavy to be carried. Stanley bribed a carpenter on a mailboat to remain behind for a month to divide the boat into manageable parts. He must have done a splendid job.

Verney Lovett Cameron crossing a tributary of the Kasai. Cameron led the Livingstone Relief Expedition which encountered Susi's party bearing the body, in Nyanyembe, 1873. He decided to continue, and in spite of the deaths of his two European companions (one of them Livingstone's nephew) he eventually reached the coast at Benguela, the first European crossing from east to west. Having turned south at Nyangwe (roughly the direction Livingstone had hoped to take in 1871) he travelled mostly through territory known to Europeans. The much harder, unknown route down the Lualaba thus remained for Stanley to tackle.

On 12 November a fleet of dhows carried the expedition to Bagamoyo on the mainland. Stanley noted its composition in his diary: 224 people, 6 asses, 5 dogs, 72 bales of cloth, 36 bags of beads, 4 man-loads of copper or brass wire, 14 boxes of assorted stores, 23 boxes of ammunition, 2 loads of photographic material, 3 loads of personal baggage belonging to the Europeans, 12 loads of boat (the parts of the *Lady Alice*), 6 loads of pontoons (one was inflatable, but proved inefficient), 1 box of medicines, 1 load of cooking utensils, and 12 miscellaneous loads.

Ammunition is a prominent item, while scientific instruments do not rate special mention. This priority was to be justified by events. Stanley's aim was to get through at all costs, and the most important aspect of his expedition was its military invincibility.

Early progress was rapid though not, to say the least, un-

ruffled. Desertions were frequent, and a conspiracy to abscond was discovered that involved fifty men. The ringleaders were put in chains and their followers disarmed. Stanley was prepared to use harsher methods: on his first expedition he had subdued a hysterical woman with a whip. As Richard Hall says, 'it seemed a matter of course to him that in lawless regions you made your own rules and chose the most direct method to impose your will on malcontents'.

Christmas Day passed without notice. Heavy rains made marching difficult and camps uncomfortable; a harmonium intended for Mtesa was ruined by a flood. Famine stalked the land, and all the Europeans suffered from fever. One group missed the road, and three of them died before they were found. Sickness increased. Edward Pocock went down with typhoid and died in Ugogo; he was twenty-two.

On 3 January two men were killed, perhaps in retaliation for the theft of some milk by the Zanzibaris. 'We were strong disciples of the doctrine of forbearance,' Stanley insists, 'for it seemed to me then as if Livingstone had taught it to me only the day before.' However, an attack followed next day, and twenty-two of Stanley's men were killed. The attackers were driven off, and Stanley 'thought it my duty to seal our victory with a fresh display of force'. A number of villages were burnt, with the incidental advantage that the expedition acquired much-needed provisions.

Engaging some fresh porters some days later, Stanley marched on towards Lake Victoria. On 14 February Gardner, one of Livingstone's faithfuls, died of typhoid. He asked that his wealth (370 dollars) should be given to his friend Chuma, the rest divided among the Zanzibaris.

Moving north, they passed thankfully into the beautiful green plains south of Lake Victoria. 'The delicious smell of cattle and young grass' reminded Stanley of 'home-farm memories'. The people here – being well-fed – were friendly. 'Come yet again . . . Come always, and you will be welcome.' Stanley felt that curious sense of peace, mingled with a kind of unfocussed nostalgia, familiar to many travellers. The only problem was that they were often mistaken for the forces of the guerilla leader, Mirambo, for whom Stanley, being something of a guerilla leader himself, felt great respect.

On 27 February Frank Pocock, who had gone ahead, came running back to announce: 'I have seen the Lake, Sir, and it is grand!' Stanley estimated the journey at 720 miles. It had taken 103 days.

While the main party thankfully prepared for a long rest, Stanley assembled the *Lady Alice* and, having picked a 'volunteer' crew in the traditional sergeant-major manner ('You, you, and you'), embarked upon the circumnavigation of Lake Victoria that was to prove Speke correct.

Stanley's transcontinental expedition, discounting the marches through previously explored territory, falls into two main parts, the first consisting of his exploration of Lake Victoria and its environs, the second of the descent of the Zaire to the west coast. He reached Ujiji, which can be taken as the point dividing the two parts, in May 1876, fifteen months after his arrival at Lake Victoria. He remained at Ujiji three months, reached Nyangwe in October, and arrived at Boma, above the Zaire estuary, in August 1877, one thousand days after his departure from Zanzibar. Of course this was not – could not have been – planned in advance; in fact, at a comparatively late stage Stanley was wondering whether to go north, west, or east! However, it is easier to follow his movements against this brief background.

Stanley's first voyage on Lake Victoria began on 8 March. He followed the unexplored eastern shore, fighting off the odd attack from canoe-borne raiders on the way, though more often the people were friendly. The hippopotami proved to be 'an extremely belligerent species', and the *Lady Alice*, not built to withstand a charge from so substantial a creature, frequently had to make a rapid getaway from their resentful gestures.

Camping, whenever possible, on islands for the night, they finally reached the northern end of the lake (some fishermen had advised them that the circumnavigation of Lake Victoria would take eight years), inspected Ripon Falls and, at the beginning of April, arrived in Buganda.

The Queen Mother had been advised of Stanley's approach in a dream, and no doubt other more conventional means of communication had apprised the Kabaka of the white man's approach. An emissary soon appeared, and showered the party with food and drink in such excess that Stanley, fearing that the ordinary people were being deprived of everything for his benefit, endeavoured to restrain the Kabaka's generosity. It was clear that Stanley and his men were 'about to become acquainted with an extraordinary monarch and an extraordinary people', and indeed their reception, by thousands of people and hundreds of guns, with drums beating and banners flying, took Stanley so much by surprise that he felt 'perplexed, confused, embarrassed'.

As many people (not least Mtesa himself) realized, Buganda occupied a significant position in Africa. It was in contact with the north (Egypt) and the east (Zanzibar) and was subject to commercial and political influence from both directions, especially the former. Indeed, not long after Stanley's arrival, evidence of this appeared in the person of Colonel Linant de Bellefonds, an ambassador from General Gordon, governor of the Egyptian Sudan (the American, Chaillé-Long, also in Egyptian pay, had visited Buganda shortly before; apart from him, Mtesa had seen no white men except Speke and Grant). The Frenchman was a Protestant, and this affiliation was a relief to Stanley, who was endeavouring to wrest the soul of Mtesa from the tightening embrace of Islam and claim it for Christianity. Stanley considered his efforts successful, though it is extremely doubtful that Mtesa felt the slightest commitment to either religion; the missionaries that responded to Stanley's call ultimately met a more grisly fate that those who responded to Livingstone's, though this occurred in the reign of Mtesa's less interesting but equally brutal successor: these events are grippingly described in Moorehead's *The White Nile*.

The Colonel was helpful in other ways. Like most good French explorers, he was well equipped with highly desirable provisions – 'various potted meats of Paris brands, *pâtés de foie gras* and Bologna sausage, sardines and Marseilles biscuits, white sugar, coffee, cocoa, chocolate, and tea'. The two Europeans found each other agreeable, while Stanley was gratified to observe that Linant's more aloof, military behaviour enhanced his own popularity in Buganda.

Stanley's activities as an evangelist, while they were perfectly sincere and cemented his position as Livingstone's heir, were of less immediate importance than the need to gain Mtesa's assistance for his expedition. The King having promised to send canoes to bring the main party up from the south, Stanley re-embarked in the *Lady Alice* and continued

The slave market in Zanzibar in 1872. A year later, one month after the death of Livingstone, a treaty was signed by the Sultan of Zanzibar and John Kirk (representing the British government) which banned the export of slaves from the mainland and closed the Zanzibar market. The sense of outrage aroused by Livingstone's eye-witness reports of the trade during his last expedition was chiefly responsible for pushing the British government into this step.

his thousand-mile circumnavigation of the lake, now sailing down the western shore.

On Musira Island, Stanley wandered away by himself for a time and, in relief at temporarily abandoning his role as the stern commander, indulged in a rather odd display of youthful spirits. 'That impulse to jump, to bound, to spring upward and cling to branches overhead, which is the characteristic of a strong green age [Stanley was thirty-four], I gave free rein to. Unfettered for a time from all conventionalisms, and absolved from that sobriety and steadiness which my position as a leader of half wild men compelled me to assume in their presence, all my natural elasticity of body came back to me. I dived under the obstructing bough or sprang over the prostrate trunk, squeezed into almost impossible places, crawled and writhed like a serpent through the tangled undergrowth, plunged down into formidable depths of dense foliage, and burrowed and struggled with frantic energy among shadowing pyramids of vines and creepers . . .' The thought of Stanley holding in his 'natural elasticity of body' all the way across Africa is arresting.

Participants in the Zaire (Congo) expedition. Left to right: Frank Pocock, Fred Barker, Edward Pocock, Kalulu, with a Zanzibari boy in the centre and Stanley's five dogs. None of them – men or dogs – survived. Engraved from a photograph taken by Stanley.

Two days later, Stanley and his men were surrounded and attacked by a large war party on Bumbiri island. By a clever ruse they escaped, though they lost their paddles and had to tear up boards from the bottom of the boat. Several canoes pursued them, but Stanley blasted holes at water level in the bows of the first two with his elephant gun, and the others withdrew. Stanley's men paddled away, their leader seething with the desire for vengeance, and a week later arrived at the village on the southern shore where the main party was encamped.

Frank Pocock had some bad news. Fred Barker, the eager young hotel clerk, had died not long before, and buried next to him was one of Stanley's favourites among the Zanzibari captains, Mabruki, who was distinguished from several other Mabrukis by the surname Speke, a reminder of his service with the earlier explorer. He had also travelled with Burton and Livingstone and, during Stanley's first expedition, he had seized the gun of a wrathful mutineer, perhaps saving Stanley's life. Now he was dead, along with two of the three Europeans and more than thirty Africans. But the expedition was nowhere near halfway.

*   *   *

Stanley's next objective was Lake Albert; but he was not to attain it. It was almost the only important occasion on which Bula Matari – 'breaker of rocks' – was foiled in his purpose.

Mtesa having been told that Stanley had been killed at Bumbiri, sent no canoes, and Stanley tried to acquire boats locally. A considerable fleet was needed to transport his whole expedition, and in the end he had to make double trips between the south shore and the island he picked as the first stage of the journey to Buganda. Five canoes were lost in this operation, and though all aboard were saved, valuable supplies were lost. Some of Mtesa's men turned up soon afterwards, and with their assistance, Stanley made a punitive attack on Bumbiri island, killing some forty men without a single casualty among his own. His account of this episode aroused strong criticism when it was read in England.

When he reached Mtesa's capital, Stanley discovered that war was being discussed against neighbours to the north. This was awkward, as it was in that direction that Stanley wished to travel. Stanley felt he had no alternative but to lend his aid to Mtesa in this war, which dragged on for a couple of months until peace was arranged in October. Mtesa then promised to provide an armed escort to Lake Albert, and Stanley, collecting the rest of his expedition from its camp farther south, where discipline was beginning to become rather fragile, began the march towards Lake Albert. Some two thousand of Mtesa's soldiers joined him at Christmas, and it was soon evident that even this powerful escort was hardly enough.

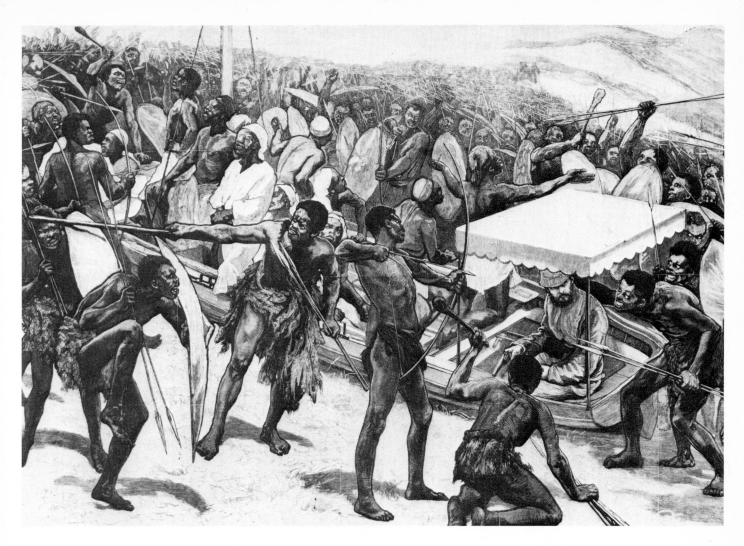

Reception at Bumbiri Island: '. . . a scene which beggars description.
Pandemonium – all its devils armed – raged about us. A forest of
spears was levelled; thirty or forty bows were drawn taut; as many
barbed arrows seemed already on the wing; thick, knotty clubs waved
above our heads . . .' Stanley and his men extricated themselves from
this desperate predicament, and later claimed a bloody revenge for
their ill treatment.

As usual, Buganda and Nyoro were on bad terms, and an atmosphere of heavy menace prevailed. The odd man fell to a flying spear or arrow, and the bodyguard grew increasingly nervous. Even Stanley was forced to recognize that, although he might reach the lake, his chances of carrying out an exploration of it in the face of the inveterate hostility of the whole population were non-existent. With his companions on the point of deserting in masses, and having seen what he took to be the southern end of the lake, Stanley gave the word for a hurried and harassed withdrawal.

On this part of his journey, travelling through territory unknown to Europeans and somewhat misled by Baker's account, Stanley had gone astray. His direction from Buganda was roughly due west; it took him far to the south of Lake Albert and almost into the Ruwenzori range (his true discovery of the Ruwenzori belongs to a later expedition). The lake he glimpsed was not Lake Albert but Lake George – the 'head' on the 'body' of Lake Edward.

Avoiding another meeting with Mtesa, which would have meant inevitable delay, Stanley's expedition, now numbering about 180 people (including a large number hired at various places on the way), made for the third great lake, Tanganyika.

In Karagwe, Stanley met another monarch first introduced to the English-speaking public by Speke, Rumanika, a 'fine old man about 55 or 60 years old'. The King provided a guide to explore the lake (named 'Windermere' by Speke) of which he was so proud and Stanley spent a night in his boat on the Kagera, moored among the papyrus. 'Were it not for the hordes of voracious mosquitoes, we might have passed the night very well.'

In April, Stanley at last met the man he had often – at a distance – been mistaken for, Mirambo, the powerful leader of red-cloaked *ruga-ruga* mercenaries, the scourge of the Arabs and demander of tribute, who sent men a day ahead to advise villagers: 'Mirambo is coming, tomorrow dig potatoes, dig potatoes.' When Stanley met him, he was still approaching his greatest power, but was already such a force in Nyamwezi that the Arabs had given up hope of defeating him and had just concluded peace terms. 'His person,' said Stanley, 'quite captivated me, for he was a thorough African *gentleman* in appearance, very different from my conception of the terrible bandit . . .' Mirambo was the same age as Stanley, nearly six feet tall, with 'not an ounce of superfluous flesh about him'. His manner was quiet and his voice soft; there was no outward sign of what Stanley called his 'Napoleonic genius', except perhaps the steady gaze of his eyes. The two men performed the ceremony of blood brotherhood, mingling the blood from cuts made in their legs (with later chiefs, Stanley usually delegated this ritual to Frank Pocock).

Another interesting person in Nyamwezi at this time was a

*Stanley's Anglo-American expedition (*Daily Telegraph *and* New York Herald*) crossing Lake Tanganyika.*

Swiss trader, Philippe Broyon. Stanley did not meet him, and did not mention him in *Through the Dark Continent*, but they exchanged messages. Stanley forwarded maps to Broyon, and received from him Castile soap, castor oil, and some six-months-old copies of *Figaro*.

Towards the end of May Stanley came, for the second time in his life, to Ujiji. Not much had changed. The mountains looked the same, the surf still pounded on the shore, the sun was as bright and the sky as blue, but, Stanley wrote in his journal, 'from the fact that the imposing central figure of the human group drawn together to meet me in Ujiji in 1871 is absent, Ujiji in spite of the beauty of its Lake and the greenness of its palms, seems strangely forlorn and uninteresting'.

Although the slave trade was still flourishing, Ujiji was a fairly peaceful place, and there was opportunity for rest. Stanley occupied himself writing affectionate letters to his fiancée (who had in fact married a railway heir four months earlier); conducted a meticulous exploration of the entire shoreline of Lake Tanganyika, and wrote long reports on geographical subjects. A bad attack of fever left him very weak, but he made his usual quick recovery before the time – hastened by an epidemic of smallpox – came to leave Ujiji and embark upon the second half of the journey, through country entirely unknown. In October, the expedition reached Nyangwe.

By this time, Stanley had learned that Cameron, who began his trans-continental journey eighteen months ahead of him, had turned south at Nyangwe which, Stanley scornfully observed in a private letter, 'left the question of the Lualaba where Livingstone left it'. This obviously gave Stanley the task of following the Lualaba downstream, but as late as 9 November, four days after leaving Nyangwe, he was still pondering his future course – whether to follow the Lualaba, wherever it led, down to the sea; or to follow it until it turned to the west (as local reports indicated) and then strike out towards the north-east, thus 'joining Livingstone's and Schweinfurth's discoveries'. He was worried that if he went on to the west coast he would not be able to get his men back to their homes in Zanzibar, and that the glory of making a continental crossing would be diminished by Cameron's similar achievement so shortly before.

Meanwhile, Stanley had acquired an important if ambivalent ally in the person of Tippu Tib (Hamed bin Muhammad), a powerful Arab leader who, like many of the Arabs in Central Africa, had African blood. Tippu Tib was in the process of creating a commercial and political empire for himself in Manyuema, and Stanley's advanced weaponry – notably his repeating rifle – impressed him deeply. In exchange for a large fee, he agreed to accompany the expedition for sixty days. Stanley could hardly hope to advance beyond Nyangwe – where both Livingstone and Cameron had been checked – without a very powerful escort of some kind. Ahead lay he knew not what, though cannibals were universally forecast. His men would hardly have followed him to what looked like near-certain death, but if he could get far enough with Tippu Tib's two hundred gunmen, he would, he calculated, reach a point where potential deserters would have no choice but to stick to him.

*   *   *

During the first week or two, the main obstacles were presented by the terrain. 'Woods, woods, woods,' Stanley noted in exasperation: they were travelling through forest as dense as any in Africa. There were not enough boats to take the whole party, even if Tippu Tib and his men had been willing to trust themselves to the river, and Stanley in his boat could make much better speed than the motley army crashing along the overgrown bank. Tippu Tib, moreover, had no reason to hurry. He had agreed to march for sixty days, but the distance to be covered each day was not specified. As the people became more hostile, and arrows began to streak without warning from the trees, Tippu Tib's enthusiasm for the journey dwindled rapidly. The appearance of smallpox among his men did nothing to revive it.

There was still a chance to relax occasionally. Christmas Day, 1876, was spent 'most pleasantly and happily'. Canoe races were held on the river, Tippu Tib won a three-hundred-yards sprint against Frank Pocock, and a race between ten

The Lualaba (the upper reaches of the Zaire) near the point where it crosses the equator above Stanley Falls. A photograph by A.F.M. Woolaston, 1905–06.

young women of the expedition proved the most popular event with the many spectators. On Boxing Day Tippu Tib gave a banquet, but his gratifying success in the foot-race had not persuaded him to remain with Stanley any longer, and two days later the two parties separated. The danger of desertion was averted by Tippu Tib's threat to kill any of Stanley's men who followed him back to Nyangwe, which was still less than 200 miles behind them.

Stanley discussed their chances with Pocock, who had become a close friend as well as a loyal subordinate. 'Before we finally depart, sir, do you really believe, in your inmost soul, that we shall succeed?' Stanley was reassuring. 'Yes, I do believe that we shall all emerge into light again some time.' He admitted that their current position, at an altitude of 1,650 feet above sea level, promised some nasty problems before they reached the sea. 'What conclusions can we arrive at? Either that this river penetrates a great distance north of the Equator, and, taking a mighty sweep round, descends into the Congo . . . or that we shall shortly see it in the neighbourhood of the Equator, take a direct cut towards the Congo . . . or that it is either the Niger or the Nile. I believe it will prove to be the Congo; if the Congo then, there must be many cataracts. Let us only hope that the cataracts are all in a lump, close together.'

'Victory or death,' said Stanley, should be their cry. The latter alternative seemed more likely, and his stirring call had little effect on the Zanzibaris, who seemed apathetic and were smoking more marihuana than usual. Before them lay the strange river, luring them onward for unnumbered hundreds of miles, through jungle, cataracts, and warlike tribes. Their progress was at times a continual running battle, for the people along the banks were almost uniformly hostile. Obviously, Stanley did not want to fight, and he always approached strange people peaceably. But at the first hostile act he opened up. Rifle fire was usually enough to drive the attackers off, and a message was then sent explaining that his purpose was not to make war and that he was willing to conduct peaceful trade. Sometimes this conciliatory approach worked; sometimes it did not. According to Stanley's reckoning, the expedition fought thirty-two battles on the Zaire, and that would seem to exclude one or two minor skirmishes.

Not long after leaving Tippu Tib, Stanley was advised of another obstacle, not unexpected, that lay ahead – a series of cataracts (Stanley Falls). The first cataract was reached on 4 January. As it was clearly too rough to float the canoes down, a roadway had to be built around it. In spite of an attack, quickly repulsed, and the backbreaking labour of the job, it was done in less than three days. The next day the second cataract was reached, with enormous whirlpools whose power was convincingly demonstrated by an experiment with an empty canoe. Before a way round could be found, another attack had to be beaten off and a village was fired in revenge (one advantage of the prevailing hostility was that food, for which the expedition was becoming ill-equipped to pay, could be seized as spoils of war).

By floating the canoes downstream or, where necessary, carrying them along a hacked-out road beside the river, the cataracts were eventually passed. But not without incident. On one 'terribly trying day', a canoe containing three men was upset. Two managed to swim to safety, while the third, Zaidi, was carried down towards the savage falls. Where the

Cutting out the Livingstone *canoe: '. . . we set to work cutting down a teak-tree . . . The tree was 13 feet 3 inches in circumference, and when prostrate we possessed a clear branchless log 55 feet in length'. The finished canoe was 2 feet 4 inches deep and 3 feet 2 inches wide, and held 46 people. Five weeks later it was sucked into a whirlpool at Zinga, drowning the chief carpenter.*

water plunged over the edge, a small rock stuck up out of the water, and Zaidi managed to clamber on to it the instant before he would have been swept to his death. But how to get him back? A canoe was floated towards him at the end of a rope made of creepers, but the current snatched it away and snapped the rope. Stanley called for another canoe to be brought up and tied two thick creepers to it, plus a tent rope an inch thick. Uledi, coxswain of the *Lady Alice*, and another equally courageous volunteer, paddled the canoe out into the stream and, held in check from the bank, attempted to get near enough to throw Zaidi a line. Six attempts failed and at the seventh Zaidi fell over the edge. Thirty long seconds later he reappeared still valiantly clinging to the line. 'Pull away', shouted Stanley, but the increased stress applied by the hauling men on the bank snapped the ropes attached to the canoe. Fortunately, the weight of Zaidi acted as an anchor, and the canoe swung across the falls and came to rest against a larger rocky outcrop. All three men scrambled on to it. They were only a little better off than before – with falls on either side of them and below them 'half a mile of Falls and Rapids and great whirlpools, and waves rising like hills in the middle of the terrible stream'. After many unsuccessful attempts, ropes were flung across. Stanley could see the three men debating who should go first, and at length Uledi grasped the ropes, shouted 'In the name of God', and lowered himself into the water. Almost at once the 'faithless convolvuli' parted, and Uledi was forced to retreat to the rocks. Darkness was falling, and the three unfortunates had to be abandoned for the night. Meanwhile, Stanley was told that another canoe had been wrecked and one of his favourite boatmen drowned.

Next day, stronger ropes were made from cane gathered in the forest, and three lines secured between the bank and the rocks. One by one, Uledi leading, the three men struggled hand-over-hand across the fifty-yards gap. The last, a young fellow named Marzouk, seemed to be tiring as the force of water thundered against him, and two of the ropes slipped from his grip. Perhaps through sheer nervousness, perhaps with good psychological insight, Stanley shouted at him harshly, 'Pull away, you fool. Be a man.' A few more pulls and he was grabbed and hauled ashore. A great cheer went up, heard by the people back at the camp, who 'knew that the three most gallant lads of the Expedition had been saved'.

By the end of January they had passed the last of the cataracts and, significantly, the point where the river turns to the west. But their situation showed no great improvement. In his diary entry for 29 January, Stanley noted that they had three fights that day. The following day they were attacked again, by the bravest people they had met so far. Several casualties were inflicted and a village burned, which 'quelled their courage'.

When they passed by without retaliating against expressions of hostility, they were invariably followed by war canoes. It seemed best to retaliate at once. However, the need for food forced them to seize by force what the owners would not sell. The expedition had only about fifty guns left, and Stanley said he would not attempt the voyage again with less than two hundred.

During February, rapid progress was made. Clashes with the local inhabitants ceased for a while, partly because the expedition was not seeking food, and Stanley even had time to admire the scenery. The Zaire for much of its length is not one single stream flowing evenly between widely distanced banks, but a mass of narrower, interlocking streams, with many islands irregularly shaped. Besides the fearful cataracts and storms, and the ever-present threat of violent death, there were quiet and peaceful stretches where the loudest noise was made by an irritable hippo (provoked, Stanley hazarded, by the sight of the expedition's donkeys which it took to be captured young of its own species).

The most heartening development was the friendly reception of some villagers who, being well-supplied could afford to sell food to the strangers. These people possessed a few old Portuguese muskets, and spoke of white men farther downstream. The river here was definitely turning south, providing the final proof that it would indeed bring the explorers to the estuary of the Zaire. Unfortunately, the friendliness of the people was not a permanent change, and the last battle had not been fought; but at least there were people willing to receive them in peace. A chief called Chumbiri provided guides and advice of more cataracts to come. Though old and amiable, he was, said Stanley, 'a prodigious liar', and his people were 'cunning beyond description'. At the next camp, a man saw, as he thought, a figure approaching him in the gloom and, hailing it, inquired who he was. It was a large boa constrictor, advancing with intent.

*   *   *

By 12 March, Stanley had covered nearly 1,500 miles from Nyangwe, nearly 7,000 from Zanzibar. The river here suddenly widened out into an enormous, almost circular pool, which Stanley named after himself. A row of whiteish cliffs were named Dover cliffs, and the grassy land above was so like the Kent downs that Frank Pocock felt quite homesick. Some local canoers volunteered to show them the cataracts which, they had been warned, lay beyond the pool. The canoers' vivid attempts to describe the noise made by the cataracts (which Stanley named after Livingstone) made the Zanzibaris roar with laughter. Though haggard and half-starved, the members of the expedition were feeling happy. They knew they had not far to go.

It has often been pointed out, and it was indirectly admitted by Stanley himself, that the sensible, almost the obvious, thing to do from the Livingstone Falls was to abandon the river and march the last 160 miles or so overland. The decision to stick to the river is, on the face of it, hard to explain. There is probably some truth in the suggestion that Stanley had become so obsessed with the Zaire that he was simply incapable of seriously considering an alternative. From Tuckey's map he knew there were cataracts, but he did not know how many, as Tuckey had gone no farther upstream than the first series of rapids. Stanley therefore did not realize the extent of the obstacle before him. Moreover, the overland journey may have seemed equally hard – it would have meant a rugged trek up and down over jagged quartz rocks, through thick forest, and across rapid streams. Nevertheless, the decision to stick to the river was disastrous.

The Livingstone Falls mark the place where the mighty Zaire, having reached its full strength (average flow at the sea: 1·5 million cubic feet per second) with the admission of such great tributaries as the Ubangi and the Kasai, forces its way along a narrow gorge through the coastal mountains down to sea level. Stanley found thirty-two cataracts altogether (the number depends on water level), spread out over the whole distance between Stanley Pool and the head of the estuary, in which the river descends about nine hundred feet. There are longish stretches, however, where the flow is fairly even, and the major cataracts occur in two or three relatively short stretches.

In his book, Stanley did full justice to 'the wildest stretch of river that I have ever seen . . . There was first a rush down into the bottom of an immense trough, and then, by sheer force, the enormous volume would lift itself upward steeply until, gathering itself into a ridge, it suddenly hurled itself 20 or 30 feet straight forward, before rolling down into another trough. If I looked up or down along this angry scene, every interval of 50 or 100 yards of it was marked by wave-towers – their collapse into foam and spray, the mad clash of watery hills, bounding mounds and heaving billows, while the base of either bank, consisting of a long line of piled boulders of massive size, was buried in the tempestuous surf. The roar was tremendous and deafening. I can only compare it with the thunder of an express train through a rock tunnel. To speak to my neighbour, I had to bawl in his ear'.

As he had done at the Stanley Falls, Stanley attempted to pass the rapids where possible by carefully floating the canoes down the river, in a current that he reckoned to be thirty miles an hour at the first cataract (a considerable exaggeration; Colonel Blashford Snell's estimate is less than twenty miles an hour). Where the river was too fierce, roads were cut and covered with brushwood and the boats carried overland. The fearful labour was almost too much for men who were at times literally 'fainting for lack of food' and, many of them, 'stiff with wounds' from recent fights. Half a mile a day soon came to seem good progress.

On 25 March two big canoes were lost in 'the cauldron', though one was washed up lower down and recovered. On the wet rocks, men constantly slipped and fell. Stanley himself lost his footing between two great boulders and fell twenty-five feet (expanded to thirty in his published account – a characteristic exaggeration), but suffered nothing worse than bruised ribs. Another big canoe was swept over the falls three days later. Among the dead were three of Stanley's

A motor-boat of the Zaire River Expedition of 1974 disappearing into a 'hole' in the river. One of the nastiest features of the whirlpools of the Zaire is their unpredictability, forming and reforming without warning to snatch at passing tree trunks – or boats.

special favourites, including young Kalulu, whom he had adopted as a child during his first expedition.

Another canoe, swept into midstream, succeeded in shooting the falls, and its two occupants scrambled to safety on the far side of the river. 'As we observed them clamber over the rocks to approach a point opposite us, and finally sit down, regarding us in silence across the river, our pity and love gushed strong towards them.' They could not be reached, nor contacted, for the roar of the falls drowned all other sounds.

Another canoe was lost soon afterwards, with one man in it. '. . . He cried out as he perceived himself to be drifting helplessly towards the falls, "La il Allah, il Allah" – There is but one God – "I am lost! Master!" He was then seen to address himself to what fate had in store for him. We watched him for a few moments, and then saw him drop. Out of the shadow of the fall he presently emerged, dropping from terrace to terrace, precipitated down, then whirled round, caught by great heavy waves, which whisked him to right and left, and struck madly at him, and yet his canoe did not sink, but he and it were swept behind the lower end of the island, and then darkness fell upon the day of horror. Nine men lost in one afternoon!'

The two men stranded on the farther shore and, amazingly enough, the lone canoer (who was not even an experienced boatman) arrived in camp four days later, having skilfully avoided capture and crossed the river in the canoe that had survived the falls.

So many canoes were lost that some of the men had to travel on foot anyway. Yet Stanley still wrestled with the river, making a mile or two a day, and occasionally calling a 'rest day' for repair of boats. Goats and chickens were too

expensive to buy, but there was plenty of fruit (including lemons) and vegetables. When Stanley and Pocock, deciding luxury was permissible for once, purchased a pig on 8 April, it was the first time in a month they had tasted meat. Dysentery, ulcers, and 'the itch disease' weakened half the expedition.

On 12 April, the *Lady Alice* swung out of the grasp of the men cautiously guiding her along the bank and was swept out into the rapids. As she hurtled downstream, Stanley stood in the bow directing Uledi, the coxwain, by hand signals, for his voice would not carry. Narrowly skirting a whirlpool, she eventually reached safety, and Stanley hastily sent a messenger up river to reassure the rest of the expedition that the boat and all in her were safe. The *Lady Alice* had taken fifteen minutes to cover the distance that took the canoes, proceeding by less dangerous methods, four days.

The first thirty-five miles of rapids, according to Stanley's estimate of the distance, were passed in thirty-seven days; but worse cataracts lay ahead, and a gruelling spell of haulage was necessary. The local people regarded these goings-on with understandable astonishment, while Stanley, grimly contemplating the wrathful waters, ruefully remembered the quiet and placid flow of the upper river. He kept hoping that the next set of rapids would be 'Tuckey's Cataracts', the farthest point upstream reached by the unsuccessful expedition of 1816, but as they advanced, Tuckey's Cataracts seemed to recede before them like a mirage. Stanley told himself, 'I must now cling to this river to the end, having followed it so long.'

In the first week of May, while the overland party were

Carrying canoes past rapids, an immense labour, which involved cutting a fifteen-feet road through 'the tangle of rattan, palms, vines, creepers, and brushwood', covering it with cut brushwood, and hauling the great canoes by hand, meanwhile often fighting off the hostile inhabitants.

catching up, Stanley ordered the construction of a new canoe, carved from 'the finest tree in the forest'. A second canoe, made from a great teak log, was made and launched two weeks later – with the help of the people of Nzabi. The new boats were named the *Stanley* and the *Livingstone*. Stanley endeavoured to name the river itself after his hero, and refers to it as the 'Livingstone' throughout his book; the name, however, was never adopted. Stanley's precious *Lady Alice* was holed by a rock when under Frank Pocock's captaincy, and Stanley was quite upset ('my boat, my poor boat'), although the damage was repaired. Some of the local people saw him writing in his notebook, and insisted that this dangerous fetish be burned. He obliged them with a Shakespeare edition (in his diary he says a piece of paper) that roughly resembled the notebook, thus keeping his notes and their goodwill.

The worst disaster of all, the blow that nearly finished

A casuality of the cataracts: 'While delivering my instructions, I observed Kalulu in the Crocodile *... When I asked him what he wanted in the canoe, he replied, with a deprecating smile and an expostulating tone, "I can pull, sir, see!" "Ah, very well," I answered'. The first three canoes came safely to rest in a bay above the falls, but then, 'to my horror I saw the* Crocodile *in mid-river ... gliding with the speed of an arrow towards the falls ... We saw it whirled round three or four times, then plunged down into the depths, out of which the stern presently emerged pointing upwards, and we knew then that Kalulu and his canoemates were no more.'*

Stanley, fell on 3 June. 'A BLACK WOEFUL DAY', Stanley wrote in shaky capitals (his grandson, Richard Stanley, tells us that the rest of the entry is written in a manner quite unlike Stanley's usual firm hand and is scarcely legible in places). Stanley was sitting on the rocks above dangerous rapids watching with fieldglasses for the approach of a canoe he had sent for. The canoe was upset, and he saw eight heads in the water. Some of the men managed to scramble on to the keel and paddle within reach of the shore before the canoe was swept away. Among those who were drowned was Frank Pocock, a strong swimmer but probably stunned in the initial upset. Uledi, himself in the water, had tried to throw a rope to him but he made no response. Pocock had been suffering with ulcerous feet and Stanley had expected him to come up in a hammock overland. His reluctance to be seen as a useless burden had made him insist on a place in the canoe, and in his desire to make haste he insisted, against Uledi's advice, on shooting the falls.

Ironically, on this very day, Stanley was asked whether he were English, French, Portuguese or Dutch – a sign that European habitations were near.

The local people were kind and sympathetic, but Stanley was cast into gloom and despondency, while over the Zanzibaris, whose courage and loyalty Stanley fully acknowledged, there crept an apathy, a dull defeatism, an air of rejection, that warned Stanley they could not stand much

more. 'After this fatal day I could scarcely get a reply to my
questions . . .' Stanley was incapable of asserting his will or
putting spirit into them ('I have publicly expressed a desire
to die by a quick sharp death'). A man arrested for robbery by
local chiefs could not be ransomed, and had to be left in
captivity. Many deserted, though they later wandered back:
Stanley 'did not reprove them'. One man died, his feet and
legs 'eaten away' by ulcers (others died after reaching the
coast – of what seems to have been spiritual exhaustion). A
favoured captain went mad and disappeared into the forest.
The expedition, or what remained of it, was on the point of
disintegration.

Since leaving Nyangwe, Stanley noted, the expedition had
destroyed 28 large towns and 60 or 70 villages, fought 32
battles, overcome 52 cataracts, built 30 miles of track,

hauled boats and canoes up a 1500-foot mountain, and lifted
them over boulders up to 20 feet high; twelve canoes and
thirteen lives had been lost. But by the end of July, Stanley
admitted that the river had beaten him. The *Lady Alice* was
left to rot on a promontory overlooking the falls, and the
march began overland to Boma (only five days away), where
Europeans were resident. 'The delight of the people manifested itself in loud and fervid exclamations of gratitude
to Allah.'

Stanley sent a message ahead addressed to 'any Gentleman
who speaks English' at Boma, appealing for help. Two days
later, Uledi and Kacheche returned at the head of a file of
men carrying 1200 yards of cloth, sacks of rice and sweet
potatoes, bundles of fish and tobacco, a cask of rum, and a few
'little luxuries' for Stanley, including a plum pudding and a
jar of gooseberry jam. Some of his haggard and fainting
people ate the rice and fish raw, and the camp was 'all anima-
tion, where but half an hour previously all had been listless

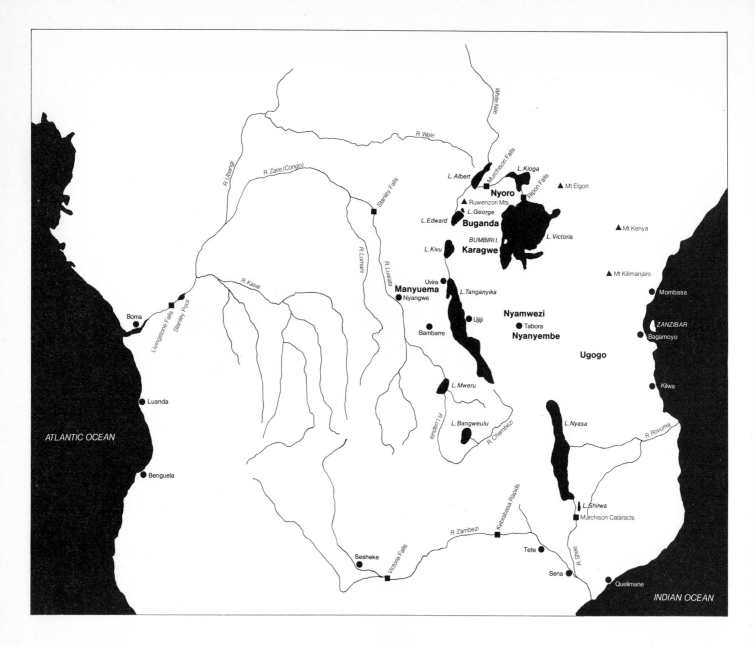

despair'. One of the boat boys struck up an extempore song about 'the great cataracts, cannibals, and pagans, hunger, the wide wastes, great inland seas, and niggardly tribes'. At the end of each verse, all joined in the chorus:

'Then sing, O friends, sing; the journey is ended;
Sing aloud, O friends, sing to this great sea.'

And so, reluctantly conceding to the Portuguese custom of being carried in a litter, the Welsh orphan-boy entered Boma and completed his thousand-days journey across Africa. The first sight of white faces gave him a slight feeling of disgust.

*   *   *

Stanley had confirmed the sources of the Nile and had revealed throughout its length the course of Africa's second-longest river, thus solving the last of the great geographical puzzles of the continent. Much remained to be done, some of it by Stanley himself on later expeditions, and of course the first exploration of the Zaire, as of any other river or region, left many minor points unanswered. For instance, Stanley had failed to observe the junction of the Ubangi (an easier

oversight on the ground than on the map), and one hundred years later, Colonel Blashford Snell found that maps of the Zaire in Central Africa were still far from perfect.

During his Zaire expedition, Stanley committed to a note-book some thoughts on African exploration (printed in his posthumously published autobiography) in which he summed up the attractions of that dangerous activity as they appeared to him. An enduring pleasure, he wrote, is 'derived from exploration of new, unvisited, and undescribed regions . . . Each eminence is eagerly climbed in the hope of viewing new prospects, each forest is traversed with a strong idea prevailing that at the other end some grand feature of nature may be revealed; the morrow's journey is longed for, in the hope that something new may be discovered'. For the traveller who is a true lover of 'wild Nature', where can she be found in such variety as in Africa? 'Where is she so shy, so retired, mysterious, fantastic, and savage as in Africa? Where are her charms so strong, her moods so strange, as in Africa?' Amid the violence and disease, the sorrow and hardship, the sheer romance of pioneer travelling can easily be overlooked. But it is perhaps the romance of exploration, now necessarily much diminished, that above all else explains its attraction today.

154

Appendix I

List of Personal Kit Taken by Speke and Grant
from England in 1859
(From J. A. Grant *A Walk Across Africa*, 1864)

12 blankets (grey Crimean) and 2 pairs scarlet ditto, from Grindlay & Co.'s; 73 lb. weight.
4 leather bags for shooting apparatus, from Grindlay & Co.'s.
1 set of bits in box handle,   ditto.
1 spring balance to 60 lb.,   ditto.
2 iron beds, from Brown & Co.'s, Piccadilly; 28 lb. each.
2 belts for revolvers, from Grindlay.
2 watering bridles,   ditto.
4 packs playing cards, ditto.
2 iron chairs, Brown & Co.'s; each 12½ lb.
1 digester for soup, Grindlay & Co.'s; 15 lb.
4 eye-preservers (glass and wire).
24 flannel shirts, from Grindlay & Co.'s.
12 pairs flannel trousers,   ditto.
1 large housewife,   ditto.
4 hats, wideawake and glazed, from Grindlay & Co.'s.
12 ink-powder packets (black and red),   ditto.
India-rubber and India-rubber rings,   ditto.
6 japanned tin trunks, weights 13, 14 and 17 lb., ditto.
8 table knives, 6 sailors', 24 three-bladed (Rogers') for skinning specimens, from Grindlay & Co.'s.
2 pewter mugs without glass.
1 medicine chest, containing Brown's blistering tissue, plaster, quinine, lunar caustic, citric acid, jalap, calomel, rhubarb, blue pill, colocynth, laudanum, Dover's powders, emetic essence of ginger; 30 lb.
2 mosquito netting.

2 hair pillows.
12 pocket-handkerchiefs.
2 penholders.
6 dozen pencils, Winsor & Newtons, &c.
1 2-feet rule.
2 white serge sheets.
12 pairs shoes, Simnett.
6 dozen socks, half woollen, Grindlay & Co.'s.
2 pairs stirrup-leathers.
4 iron stools, Brown's, and 2 sketching ditto, Winsor & Newton's.
7 saucepans (a nest of block-tin), Grindlay.
16 table spoons, 8 dessert ditto, 8 tea ditto.
12 sail-needles, large and small.
2 lb. mustard and cress seeds.
2 tents (7 by 7, and 7 feet high).
Tools – 2 hammers, 2 saws, pincers, files, chisels, &c.
8 pairs trousers, drill, unbleached.
2 oval tin teapots.
40 lb. tea, from Sterriker.
2 gingham umbrellas, half carriage size, with white covers, Grindlay & Co.'s.
4 waistcoats of Scotch tweed, Grindlay & Co.'s.
2 veils (green),   ditto.
4 waterproof sheets (white), about 10 feet square, Grindlay & Co.'s.
1 photographic instrument for collodion, Bland & Long.

Instruments for Observing; weight 228 lb

3 sextants of 8½ inch radius, Troughton & Simms.
2 stands for ditto.,   ditto.
2 artificial horizons.
1 chronometer (gold), Barraud & Lund.
1   ditto. (silver), Parkinson & Frodsham.
1 lever watch (B. & Lund), with double-detaching second-hand.
1   ditto. (Dent), with split second-hand.
1   ditto. (Jones).
2 magnetic compasses (pocket), Eliot.

3 prismatic compasses, cardless, with platinum rings, T. & Simms.
1 telescope, 1 rain-gauge (Travellers'), and 1 rain-gauge (Livingstone's).
6 boiling thermometers.
1 maximum and 1 minimum thermometer, Casella.
1 Massey's patent log; 10 lb.
2 bull's-eye lanterns, with vessels to fit for boiling thermometers, Casella.

Mapping and Drawing Instruments

2 reams mapping paper. Malby & Sons.
Tracing paper, black and white, Winsor & Newton.
1 circular brass protractor, Eliott; 1 parallel ruler on rollers, Eliott.
1 case mathematical instruments, Eliott.

1 pocket-compass, 1 50-feet measuring tape, one drawing-board.
½ ream open foolscap, graduated in squares.
2 boxes of water-colours, Winsor & Newton.
4 block sketch-books, 2 Clifford's.

Books

1 Raper's 'Navigation'.
1 Coleman's 'Nautical and Lunar Tables.'
4 log-books, 12 field-books, and 5 longitude ditto, F. Galton, Esq.

4 Nautical Almanacks, 1860–61–62–63.
Tables for measuring breadth of rivers, Galton.
Maps of Africa, all the recent, foreign and English.

Rifles – Arms and Ammunition – Revolvers

2 single rifles, Lancaster's elliptical, 40 bore.
1 single   Blisset,   4 ditto.
1 ditto   ditto   16 ditto.
1 double   ditto   20 ditto.
1 ditto smooth ditto   12 ditto.
1 ditto rifle ditto   (?) 10 ditto.
1 six-barrelled revolving Colt rifle.

1 Whitworth sporting rifle.
1 double smooth-bore by –.   12 ditto.
2 Tranter's revolvers; 8 lb. each.
500 rounds for each barrel.
50 carbines, with pouches, sword-bayonets, and belts, Royal Artillery pattern 1860; each 13 lb.
200 rounds to each carbine; caps in complement.

APPENDIX II

LIST OF MEN ENGAGED AT ZANZIBAR

their Pay, their Appointments, and how disposed of
(from J. H. Speke *Journal of the Discovery of the Source of the Nile*, 1863)

Numerical numbers	Pay in dols, one year advanced	Names	What race they belong to	Highest appointments held by each individual	How and where their services terminated	No. of guns stolen by deserters
1	500	Said bin Salem	Arab	Cafila Bashi	Discharged sick at Kazeh	
2	25	Sulimani	Negro			
3	25	Babu	,,	Servants to Sheikh Said	Discharged with Sheikh Said	
4	25	Feraj	,,	,,	at Kazeh	
5	25	Yakut	,.	,,	,,	
6	25	Yusuf	,,	,,	,,	
7	25	Saadi	,,	,,	,,	
8	60	Bombay	,,	Factotum	Paid off, Egypt	
9	60	Baraka	,,	Commander-in-chief	Sent back, Nyoro	
10	60	Rahan	,,	Valet	Sent back, Bogwe	
11	25	Frij	,,	Cook	Paid off, Egypt	
12	25	Mabruki	,,	Valet	,,	
13	25	Uledi, sen.	,,	,,	,,	
14	25	Ilmasi	,,	,,	,,	
15	25	Abedi	,,	Porter	Deserted, Bogwe	
16	25	Rahan	,,	,,	Deserted, Nyoro	1
17	25	Wadimoyo	,,	,,	,,	2
18	25	Wadihamadi	,,	,,	,,	3
19	25	Saad Allah	,,	,,	Deserted, Bogwe	
20	25	Tabibu	,,	,,	Sent back, Usugara	
21	25	Kari	,,	,,	Murdered, Uganda	
22	25	Matiko	,,	,,	Deserted, Nyoro	4
23	25	Nasibu	,,	,,	Left in Uganda	
24	25	Musa	,,	,,	Deserted, Nyoro	5
25	25	Mabruki	,,	,,	,,	6
26	25	Hassani	,,	,,	Died, Kazeh	
27	25	Baraka	,,	,,	Deserted, Nyoro	7
28	25	Johur	,,	,,	Discharged, M'gunda Mkhali	
29	25	Mabruki	,,	,,	Deserted, Nyoro	8
30	25	Mutwane	,,	,,	Left sick, Ukuni	
31	25	Bilal	,,	,,	Deserted, Nyoro	9
32	25	Othman	,,	,,	,,	10
33	25	Muftah	,,	,,	,,	11
34	25	Uledi	,,	,,	,,	12
35	25	Juma	,,	,,	,,	13
36	25	Uledi	,,	,,	Sent back, Nyoro	
37	25	Mabruki	,,	,,	Left sick, Bogwe	
38	25	Sirboko	,,	,,	Deserted, Nyoro	14
39	25	Masibu	,,	,,	,,	15
40	25	Msalima	,,	,,	Sent back, Nyoro	
41	7	Mektub	,,	,,	Paid off, Egypt	
42	7	Baraka	,,	,,	Deserted, Uzaramo	
43	7	Kani	,,	,,	,,	
44	7	Kirambu	,,	,,	,,	
45	7	Kinanda	,,	,,	Died, Miningu	
46	7	Mdara	,,	,,	Deserted, Uzaramo	
47	7	Mdyabuana	,,	,,	,,	
48	7	Uledi	,,	Valet	Paid off, Egypt	
49	7	Mzungu	,,	Porter	Deserted, Uzaramo	16
50	7	Thanun	,,	,,	Deserted, Ugogo	
51	7	Kariombe	,,	,,	Deserted, coast	

Numerical numbers	Pay in dols, one year advanced	Names	What race they belong to	Highest appointments held by each individual	How and where their services terminated	No. of guns stolen by deserters
52	7	Kingunga	Negro	Porter	Deserted, Uzaramo	
53	7	Matona	,,	,,	,,	
54	7	Malini	,,	,,	Deserted, coast	
55	7	Darara	,,	,,	,,	
56	7	Khamisi	,,	,,	Deserted, Uzaramo	
57	7	Yukut	,,	,,	Deserted, Ngoro	17
58	7	Hutibu	,,	,,	Deserted, coast	
59	7	Panamba	,,	,,	,,	
60	7	Pakarua	,,	,,	,,	
61	7	Yaha	,,	,,	,,	
62	7	Namaganga	,,	,,	Deserted, Uzaramo	
63	7	Khamsi	,,	,,	,,	
64	7	Wilyamanga	,,	,,	Deserted, coast	
65	7	Mkate	,,	Pot-boy	Paid off, Egypt	
66	7	Mpuanda	,,	Porter	Deserted, Uzaramo	
67	7	Kirambu	,,	,,	Left sick, Bogwe	
68	7	Msaram	,,	,,	Deserted, Uzaramo	
69	7	Kirumba	,,	,,	Deserted, coast	
70	7	Kamuna	,,	,,	,,	
71	7	Sulamini	,,	,,	Deserted, Ugogo	
72	7	Baruti	,,	Under-valet	Paid off, Egypt	
73	7	Umburi	,,	Porter	,,	
74	7	Makarani	,,	,,	Deserted, Ugogo	18
75	7	Ulimengo	,,	Goatherd	Paid off, Egypt	
76	7	Khamsini	,,	Porter	,,	

HOTTENTOTS, CAPE MOUNTED RIFLEMEN

Numerical numbers	Pay in dols, one year advanced	Names	What race they belong to	Highest appointments held by each individual	How and where their services terminated	No. of guns stolen by deserters
1		Mithalder		Corporal	Sent back, Mininga	
2		Vandermerwe		Trumpeter	Sent back, Usagara	
3		Adams		Private	,,	
4		April		,,	Sent back, Mininga	
5		Jansen		,,	Sent back, Usagara	
6		Lemon		,,	Sent back, Mininga	
7		Middleton		,,	,,	
8		Peters		,,	Died, Usagara	
9		Reyters		,,	Sent back, Usagara	
10		Arries		,,	,,	

MEN ENGAGED IN THE INTERIOR

Numerical numbers	Pay in dols, one year advanced	Names	What race they belong to	Highest appointments held by each individual	How and where their services terminated	No. of guns stolen by deserters
1		Hassani	Negro	Porter	Murdered, Karagwe	
2		Sangoro	,,	,,	Deserted, Nyoro	19
3		Ilmasi	,,	,,	,,	20
4		Khamisi	,,	,,	,,	21
5		Mtamani	,,	,,	Paid off, Egypt	
6		Matagiri	,,	,,	,,	
7		Sadiki	,,	,,	,,	
8		Manua	,,	,,	,,	
9		Mondo	,,	,,	Sent back, Uganda	
10		Sampti	,,	,,	Deserted, Nyamwezi	
11		Farhan	,,	,,	Deserted, Nyoro	
12		Saidi	,,	,,	,,	22
13		Chauri	,,	,,	,,	23
14		Mijaliwa	,,	,,	Deserted, Abu Ahmed	
15		Sangoro	,,	,,		
16		Murzuki	,,	,,	Deserted, Nyoro	24
17		Farhan	,,	,,	Paid off, Egypt	
18		Chongo	,,	,,	Deserted, Nyoro	
19		Mduru	,,	,,	,,	
20		Pulimbofu	,,	,,	,,	
21		Kuduru	,,	,,	,,	
22		Fisi	,,	,,	,,	

A NOTE ON BOOKS

HISTORY OF AFRICA There are a number of one-volume introductions, of which probably the best is the brilliantly organized Roland Oliver and J. D. Fage *A Short History of Africa* (1962) in the Penguin African Library. Basil Davidson *Africa: History of a Continent* (rev. ed. 1972) has a short text and many superb photographs by Werner Forman. The same author has written many useful books on the African background, notably *The African Past* (1964), which contains excerpts from relevant documents. Other recent introductory surveys include Robert W. July *A History of the African People* (1970); Robert I. Rotberg *A Political History of Tropical Africa* (1965), based on a great knowledge, often provocative and witty; and Donald Wiedener *A History of Africa South of the Sahara* (1964), with many maps (and a few mistakes). J. D. Fage *An Atlas of African History* (1958) is limited in scope but invaluable and inexpensive.

HISTORY OF EXPLORATION The subject is so vast that comparatively few authors have attempted comprehensive works. J. N. L. Baker *A History of Geographical Discovery and Exploration* (1931) is useful for reference. Timothy Severin *The African Adventure* (1973) is a brilliant survey of pre-colonial European activities in Africa, covering ground untrodden in this book, and very well illustrated. M. Cary and E. H. Warmington *The Ancient Explorers* (1929) is still the standard work of reference for the early period. Much has been done by French historians, and Charles de la Roncière *La Découverte de l'Afrique au Moyen Age* (3 vols, 1924–27) is an awe-inspiring work of scholarship. Less profound, C. Coquery *La Découverte de l'Afrique* (1965) is worth an English translation. Robin Hallett *The Penetration of Africa* (vol. I, 1964), up to 1815, is based on encyclopaedic knowledge, original, perceptive, and highly influential.

More limited in scope: E. W. Bovill *The Golden Trade of the Moors* (1958), on North Africa and the Sudan before the modern period, is a famous book, gripping in parts, and now available in a paperback edited by Robin Hallett. Bovill's *The Niger Explored* (1968) is also excellent. In the same area, Christopher Lloyd *The Search for the Niger* (1973) is shorter and equally readable. Brian Gardner *The Quest for Timbuctoo* (1968) is an exciting account of Laing, Caillié, Barth, and others.

The exploration of the Nile is brilliantly described in two justly famous books by that marvellous writer Alan Moorehead, *The White Nile* (1960) and *The Blue Nile* (1962). Harry Johnstone *The Nile Quest* (1903) is still worth reading.

On the Portuguese, two general scholarly works are C. R. Boxer *The Portuguese Sea-Borne Empire 1415–1825* (1969) and James Duffy *Portuguese Africa* (1959); a shortened version of the latter, *Portugal in Africa*, is in the Penguin African Library. Edgar Prestage *The Portuguese Pioneers* (1933), a volume in Black's Pioneer Histories, deals with the early voyages. Of several books by Eric Axelson, *The Portuguese in South-East Africa* (1960) is of special interest; *Congo to Cape* (1973) tells all that is known of Diogo Cão and Bartholomeu Dias.

Two books by J. W. Blake, *European Beginnings in West Africa* (1937) and, as editor, *Europeans in West Africa 1460–1560* (1942) describe the early contacts in Guinea. British intrusions are surveyed in the *Cambridge History of the British Empire*, vols I and II (1929, 1940), and V. T. Harlow *The Founding of the Second British Empire* (1952).

R. A. Skelton *Explorers' Maps* (1958) has a chapter on African rivers, with early explorers' maps illustrated.

EXPLORERS' ACCOUNTS The chief books are: Leo Africanus *History and Description of Africa* (ed. 1896).

Samuel Baker *The Albert Nyanza* (2 vols, 1866), jolly. Heinrich Barth *Travels and Discoveries in North and Central Africa* (5 vols, 1857–58), of which an excellent abridgement fortunately exists, A. H. M. Kirk-Greene (ed.) *Barth's Travels in Nigeria* (1962), restricted to the area indicated. Ibn Batuta *Travels in Asia and Africa* (trans. H. A. R. Gibb, 2 vols, 1929), an abridgement. James Bruce *Travels to Discover the Source of the Nile* (5 vols, 1790), skilfully abridged in an attractive edition by C. F. Beckingham (1966). Richard F. Burton *The Lake Regions of Central Africa* (2 vols, 1860), perhaps the best of Burton's numerous books about Africa, recently reissued. René Caillié *Travels through Central Africa to Timbuctoo* (2 vols, 1830), attractive and unpretentious. Verney Lovett Cameron *Across Africa* (2 vols, ed. 1893). Hugh Clapperton *Journal of a Second Expedition into the Interior of Africa* (1829), rather disappointing, partly owing to perfunctory editing. D. Denham, H. Clapperton and W. Oudney *Narrative of Travels and Discoveries in Northern and Central Africa* (1826), mainly Denham's account of the mission to Bornu and somewhat misleading; a beautiful book but of course (like others listed here) scarce. James A. Grant *A Walk Across Africa* (1864), easy to read but perhaps a trifle mundane. W. C. Harris *The Wild Sports of Southern Africa* (1839), a characteristic example of the memoirs of an early big-game hunter. J. L. Krapf *Travels, Researches and Missionary Labours* (1860), recently reissued. A. Gordon Laing *Travels in the Timanee, Kooranko and Soolima Countries* (1825), to be read mainly as an act of respect, remembering the best-seller poor Laing did not live to write. Richard Lander *Records of Captain Clapperton's Last Expedition* (1830) and, with John Lander, *Journal of an Expedition to Explore the Niger* (3 vols, 1830), abridged in one volume with a very useful introduction by Robin Hallett as *The Niger Journal of Richard and John Lander* (1965). David Livingstone *Missionary Travels and Researches in South Africa* (1857), misleading no doubt but one of the best of explorers' stories; with Charles Livingstone, *Narrative of an Expedition to the Zambesi* (1865), slightly less scintillating; and Horace Waller (ed.) *The Last Journals of David Livingstone* (2 vols, 1874); a selection from Livingstone's writings appears in J. I. McNair (ed.) *Livingstone's Travels* (1954), and his private letters and diaries have been recently published in several volumes edited by I. Schapera. Mungo Park *Travels in the Interior of Africa* (1799), superbly written, mercifully brief, consistently popular, and available in paperback. J. H. Speke *Journal of the Discovery of the Sources of the Nile* (2nd ed. 1864) and, perhaps better reading, *What Led to the Discovery of the Source of the Nile* (1864); new editions are planned. H. M. Stanley *How I Found Livingstone in Central Africa* (1872) and *Through the Dark Continent* (2 vols, 1878), racy, ebullient and sometimes exaggerated; his *Autobiography* (1909) was edited by his widow; Richard Stanley and Alan Neame (eds.) *The Exploration Diaries of H. M. Stanley* contains extracts from his diary during the Zaire expedition and provides some revealing comparisons with the published version.

Few people have the time or the desire to ingest the prolix pages of most 19th-century explorers and fortunately there are many excellent general anthologies. Margery Perham and Jack Simmons (eds.) *African Discovery* (1942) is an astute selection from British explorers. Three regional volumes appear in the Oxford World Classics: Eric Axelson (ed.) *South African Explorers* (1954), containing some relatively unfamiliar names; C. Howard (ed.) *West African Explorers* (1951), packed with good things and including an introduction by that ubiquitous historian, J. H. Plumb; and, somewhat shorter;

Charles Richards and James Place (eds) *East African Explorers* (1960).

MODERN BIOGRAPHIES Fawn M. Brodie *The Devil Drives* (1967) is a highly regarded, psychoanalytically oriented life of Burton; S. L. Gwynn *Mungo Park and the Quest of the Niger* (1934) is perhaps the best life of Park; Richard Hall's splendid *Stanley: An Adventurer Explored* (1974) supersedes all earlier biographies, of which A. J. A. Symons *H. M. Stanley* (1933) is one of the most interesting. Tim Jeal *Livingstone* (1973) is the standard work, but the biography by George Seaver (1957) is good on religious matters, and Jack Simmons *Livingstone and Africa* (1955) is an excellent short introduction; Sir Reginald Coupland *Livingstone's Last Journey* is marvellously imaginative if misleading; Judith Listowel *The Other Livingstone* (1974) is mainly about some of Livingstone's little-known contemporaries. Alexander Maitland *Speke* is the only biography, and very good too. J. M. Reid *Traveller Extraordinary* (1968), on Bruce, is shortish, straightforward and attractively written. Robert I. Rotberg (ed.) *Africa and Its Explorers* (1970) is an interesting collection of essays on various 19th-century explorers.

Not much has been written about the African guides and porters who accompanied the European explorers but Donald Simpson's forthcoming *Dark Companions: The African Contribution to the European Exploration of East Africa* will help to fill the gap.

OTHER BOOKS Among the numerous relevant works not mentioned in the foregoing sections, the following should be noted:
Roger T. Ansley *Britain and the Congo in the 19th Century* (1962)
Eric Axelson *South-East Africa 1488–1530* (1940)
C. R. Beazeley and E. Prestage (eds.) *The Chronicle of the Discovery and Conquest of Guinea* (2 vols, 1896–99)
A. A. Boahen *Britain, the Sahara and the Western Sudan* (1964)
E. W. Bovill *Missions to the Niger* (1964)
Reginald Coupland *Kirk on the Zambezi* (1928); *East Africa and Its Invaders* (1938)
G. R. Crone (ed.) *Voyages of Cadamosto and Other Documents in West African History* (1937)
J. J. L. Duyvendak *China's Discovery of Africa* (1949)
C. S. P. Freeman-Grenville *Medieval History of the Coast of Tanganyika* (1961)
Richard Gray *A History of the Southern Sudan 1839–1889* (1961)
C. P. Groves *The Planting of Christianity in Africa* vol. I (1948)
Robin Hallett (ed.) *The Records of the African Association* (1964)
Ibn Hauqal *The Oriental Geography* (trans. W. Ouseley, 1800)
Herodotus *Histories* (trans. A. de Sélincourt, ed. 1972)
John Kirk *Zambezi Journal and Letters* (ed. R. Foskett, 1965)
George Martelli *Livingstone's River* (1970)
Roland Oliver *The Missionary Factor in East Africa* (1952)
Roland and Caroline Oliver *Africa in the Days of Exploration* (1965)
Roland Oliver and Gervase Mathew (eds.) *History of East Africa* vol. I (1962)
J. H. Parry *The Age of Reconnaissance* (1963)
Oliver Ransford *Livingstone's Lake* (1966)
Heinrich Schiffers (ed.) *Heinrich Barth: Ein Forscher in Afrika* (1967)
W. H. Schoff (ed.) *The Periplus of the Erythraean Sea* (1921)
Edward Ullendorf *The Ethiopians* (2nd ed. 1965)
J. P. R. Wallis (ed.) *The Zambesi Expedition of David Livingstone* (2 vols, 1956)